THEORETICAL PERSPECTIVES ON WORD ORDER IN SOUTH ASIAN LANGUAGES

CSLI
Lecture Notes
No. 50

THEORETICAL PERSPECTIVES ON WORD ORDER IN SOUTH ASIAN LANGUAGES

edited by
Miriam Butt, Tracy Holloway King, & Gillian Ramchand

CSLI Publications
CENTER FOR THE STUDY OF
LANGUAGE AND INFORMATION
STANFORD, CALIFORNIA

Printed in the United States
99 98 97 96 95 94   5 4 3 2 1

Library of Congress Cataloging-in-Publication Data

Theoretical perspectives on word order in South Asian languages /
edited by Miriam Butt, Tracy Holloway King & Gillian Ramchand.
p. cm. – (CSLI lecture notes ; no. 50)

Includes bibliographical references and index.
ISBN 1-881526-50-X – ISBN 1-881526-49-6 (pbk.)
1. South Asian languages—Word order. 2. Indo-Aryan languages,
Modern—Grammar, Comparative. 3. Grammar, Comparative—Hindi and
Indo-Aryan. 4. Grammar, Comparative—Indo-Aryan and Hindi.
5. Grammar, Comparative--Dravidian and Hindi. 6. Grammar,
Comparative--Hindi and Dravidian. 7. India—Languages—Word order.
I. Butt, Miriam, 1966- . II. King, Tracy Holloway.
III. Ramchand, Gillian, 1965- . IV. Series.
PK1511.T54 1994
491'.1–dc20   94-28628
CIP

CSLI was founded early in 1983 by researchers from Stanford University, SRI International, and Xerox PARC to further research and development of integrated theories of language, information, and computation. CSLI headquarters and CSLI Publications are located on the campus of Stanford University.

CSLI Lecture Notes report new developments in the study of language, information, and computation. In addition to lecture notes, the series includes monographs, working papers, and conference proceedings. Our aim is to make new results, ideas, and approaches available as quickly as possible.

Contents

Contributors

Tista Bagchi
Department of Linguistics
University of Chicago
Chicago, Illinois

Rakesh Bhatt
Department of English
University of Tennessee
Knoxville, Tennessee

Miriam Butt
Seminar für Sprachwissenschaft
Universität Tübingen
Tübingen, Germany

Veena Dwivedi
Linguistics Department
University of Wisconsin
Madison, Wisconsin

Susan Herring
Program in Linguistics
University of Texas
Arlington, Texas

Tracy Holloway King
Linguistics Department
Indiana University
Bloomington, Indiana

K.P. Mohanan
Linguistics Program
National University of Singapore
Kent Ridge, Singapore

Tara Mohanan
Linguistics Program
National University of Singapore
Kent Ridge, Singapore

Gillian Ramchand
Department of Medieval and Modern Languages and Literatures
Wolfson College, University of Oxford
Oxford, England

Mona Singh
Linguistics Department
University of Texas, Austin
Austin, Texas

Veneeta Srivastav Dayal
Linguistics Department
Rutgers University
New Brunswick, New Jersey

K.G. Vijayakrishnan
Central Institute of English and Foreign Languages
Hyderabad, India

1

Introduction

TRACY HOLLOWAY KING & GILLIAN RAMCHAND

Perhaps one of the most perceptually obvious features of a language one encounters for the first time, whether as a linguist or a traveler, is its word order pattern. The relative order of the sentential elements, the ordering of noun and adjective, the degree of flexibility within the basic pattern, all vary from language to language in a way that is readily accessible to the general observer. Indeed, so salient have these characteristics seemed to linguists in particular, that they form the basis for many systems of traditional typology and descriptions of language universals (Greenberg 1966). The paradox of this situation for modern linguistics is that the issue of word order and word order flexibility remains one of the most difficult and problematic areas for formal theories of grammar. In fact, the modern linguistic goal of arriving at an invariant and regular set of structures for natural language in general (Universal Grammar) is in tension with the palpable variability in surface word order among and within particular languages. Rather than relinquishing its mysteries gracefully to the 'superior' techniques of modern linguistics, the problem of word order variability has become, if anything, more complicated and more intractable.

In terms of the variability between languages, one formal linguistic strategy has been to maintain a universal template which encodes hierarchical relationships between elements in the syntax (phrase structure) while subjecting the particular orderings of Head, Complement, and Specifier positions to parametric variation. Word order variation *within* a particular language has traditionally been captured by various movement processes (topicalization, Wh-movement, heavy NP shift, etc.) from a basic phrase structural position (Chomsky 1981). In theories which do not employ explicit movement from an initial phrase structural configuration, the different base generated orders are often

Theoretical Perspectives on Word Order in South Asian Languages
Miriam Butt, Tracy Holloway King, Gillian Ramchand (Eds.)

related by indexing mechanisms to some presumably basic positioning. The strategy of de-linking the basic representation of predicate argument relations from the ultimate phrase structure or word order of the sentence is easy to implement in non-movement theories (see Bresnan 1982, Alsina 1993 on Lexical-Functional Grammar (LFG) and Gazdar et al. 1985, Pollard and Sag 1987 on Generalized/Head-driven Phrase Structure Grammar (G/HPSG)). Such theories make it easy to represent word order variation, but must always say something extra whenever word order is fixed, or when certain orders are ruled out by a language. However, under both types of theories, a given predicate and its arguments appear in a specific basic configuration, and the variations in word order are derived from this basic configuration, either via movement (e.g., Government and Binding (GB) frameworks), or by relating it to a different level of representation in some systematic way (e.g., LFG).

In the traditional cases of 'movements', the deviation from the basic order goes along with some identifiable semantic or pragmatic function. For example, in many 'discourse configurational' languages (cf. Kiss to appear a), specific structural positions are associated with topic and/or focus interpretation. The occurrence of constituents in these positions can be thought of as licensing: in order to receive a particular discourse function interpretation, an argument must move into a particular position, and any argument which moves into such a position receives the associated discourse function interpretation. These different structures result in the different linear orders. Since these discourse functions are in some sense superimposed on the stable predicate-argument relations of the sentence, we can justify this analytical dependence on the underlying or basic order. There are a number of basic questions which emerge here. At what level of linguistic representation do we represent the basic unity behind all the variants of a particular sentence type? What kinds of semantic, pragmatic or functional differences are concomitant with those variants? Additionally, within any given framework, we need to establish the formal strategies for representing those differences in a way that makes sense for the organization of grammar as a whole.

South Asian languages are particularly challenging because of the general flexibility of their word orders, independent of the discourse and pragmatic strategies that are well known from other languages. Movement to certain positions does appear to be associated with discourse functions (e.g., Dwivedi this volume). However, some of the variations from the default order do not result in such interpretations, although they may have other semantic reflexes (e.g., Singh this volume). Thus, while there do seem to be broad constraints on the allowed word orders in these languages, a wide variety of word orders is possible which often do not seem amenable to any of the 'movement' analyses proposed in the literature, and which have none of the discourse and functional effects traditionally associated with those 'movements'. This kind of 'movement' has been called 'scrambling', and has been the subject of much controversy in the literature (see Mahajan 1990 and Srivastav this volume). The phenomenon of scrambling is problematic because it is not always clear what the semantic/pragmatic/functional consequences are, if any. To put this in terms of 'movement' analyses, it is not clear what the *motivation* for this kind of movement might be, and is thus hard to derive in a principled way.

If scrambling is truly qualitatively different from explicit 'movements' such as topicalization, NP-movement and Wh-movement, then it may prove necessary to allow this type of word order relationship to be stated and parameterized independently of (although possibly constrained by) the hierarchical organization constructed for predicate argument relationships. Alternatively, one can persist in attempting to employ the subtle semantic or functional effects of scrambling to analyze these word orders via the traditional 'movement' approaches. If this second alternative is successful, however, it will still seriously modify our present knowledge of the variability and typology of 'movements' across languages. In view of the current theoretical thrust towards more and more rigid phrase structural templates accompanied by more complex 'movement' strategies, the problems presented by South Asian languages have a greater force and urgency.

The concern is not only to capture to range of permissible word orders and their related interpretations, but also to encode the default word order without prohibiting the alternatives. The languages discussed in this volume all appear to have a default word order. Regardless of whether this default forms a 'base' structure from which constituents can scramble to other phrase structure positions or not, the question remains as to what defines the default order: grammatical functions, thematic roles, argument structure, or some combination thereof? In many theories, these notions are interdependent, making the task of untangling them all the greater. Similarly, how do we characterize and represent the non-default orders and their associated linguistic differences, if any?

The problem of scrambling raises the issue of non-configurationality, and also of the possible independence of word order and hierarchical structure. The issue of whether a theory allows phrase-structure movement or not is independent of the issue of the existence of phrase structure. GB, LFG, and HPSG all assume a phrase structure which encodes both precedence and dominance relations. The word order of a phrase is assumed to be derivative from the phrase structure, modulo certain constrained phonological reorderings, e.g., the placement of certain clitics. However, it is possible to have an analysis of word order which is independent of phrase structure; such an account involves precedence, but no dominance, relations among lexical items. In phrase-structure theories which do not require binary branching trees, this type of analysis can be mimicked by a 'flat S' structure in which all items are sister to one another with their relative orderings generated by independent constraints.

Thus, the question one must ask when approaching these phenomena is to what extent linear precedence relations (word order) are determined/constrained by lexical, discourse, or purely syntactic levels of organization; and to what extent they represent an independent system of organization with its own language-particular constraints and relations. Some specific questions which arise when trying to determine the universal role of phrase structure while accounting for the full range of data are: Are all structures binary branching? If flat structures are permitted, are they all endocentrically headed? What types of roles do specifier positions play and are they always present? At what level of representation are discourse functions encoded? How does scrambling differ from movement of topics and foci? Do languages without subject-object asymmetries have flat structures within the VP? If there are subject-object asymmetries in a language, are these always the result of a difference in structural position between the subject and object?

The papers for this volume emerged from a special parasession on Word Order at the fourteenth meeting of the South Asian Language Analysis Roundtable (SALA) held at Stanford in May of 1992. The purpose of the parasession was to bring together both theoretical and empirical perspectives on word order variability within a wide variety of South Asian languages. These papers have been selected as contributing particularly to a fuller description and understanding of the phenomena. They embody widely differing theoretical perspectives and concerns, and this is in part a reflection of the far reaching effects and problems associated with word order possibilities for many different linguistic domains: morphological, lexical, syntactic, semantic and discourse/pragmatic.

One of the most important aspects of word order differences in South Asian languages is their use as a diagnostic for distinguishing various construction types. In 'Compound Typology in Tamil',

K.G. Vijayakrishnan uses scrambling, adjacency facts, and the possible intrusion of focus phrases to distinguish between different types of compound verbs in the language. Although the two types of compounds are superficially similar in that they involve verb-noun sequences, it is clear that word order possibilities make crucial distinctions between the types of compounds in Tamil, and this is used to motivate phrase structural and morpholexical differences. In particular Vijayakrishnan proposes that Type I compounds are of category V^0, members of which can participate in derivational morphology, while Type II compounds are of the distinct category V' and do not pattern with X^0 categories for lexical processes. Of particular theoretical interest is the claim that non-zero level categories participate in compound formation within the lexicon. The formation of these compounds in the lexicon is supported by their noncompositional semantics and unpredictable subcategorization and selectional properties, while the word order and other morphosyntactic facts support the V' vs. V^0 category distinction.

Although word order has been used profitably as a diagnostic in much work on South Asian languages, the question which naturally arises is what precisely these word order differences should be taken to be diagnostic *of*. In 'Complex Predicate Scrambling in Urdu', M. Butt uses word order variability to demonstrate the ambiguous constituency structure (within an LFG framework) of two complex verbal sentential types in Urdu. Butt argues that while scrambling possibilities reflect constituent structure fairly directly, this in turn does not seem to distinguish predicational structures on the basis of argument structure or functional structure differences. Specifically, she claims that while the two different predicational structures she considers differ with respect to functional and argument structure, both types nevertheless have the same constituent structure as diagnosed by scrambling possibilities. Not only this, *each* type seems to have the option of projecting to either of two different constituent structures. This is an interesting proposal precisely because of the relationship it suggests between functional structure and argument structure on the one hand and constituent (phrase) structure on the other. Many linguistic theories have proposed quite systematic and restrictive mappings between the encoding of argument relations (D-structure plausibly) and syntactic relations (S-structure) (Baker 1988, Speas 1990, and references therein). In fact, the intuition behind the Projection Principle (Chomsky 1981) seems to be that the relations encoded at an argument structure level must be represented identically at every level of linguistic representation (Speas 1990). The data from Urdu argues to the contrary that differences in argument structure between two different verbal constructions are *not* reflected in the constituent structure representation, but that these distinctions are effectively lost at that level. If this is true, then it means that traditional mapping theories need to be revised, or weakened to accommodate the data from this language. If one wishes to deny that word order possibilities are diagnostic of syntactic constituency *per se*, the burden is on the objector to elucidate exactly what level of organization these facts *are* diagnostic of.

V. Srivastav Dayal, in 'Binding Facts in Hindi and the Scrambling Phenomenon' addresses a slightly different theoretical issue, but one which has nevertheless been central to the debate on movement processes in languages which exhibit scrambling. A distinction is made in the recent literature between movement that is to a possible 'argument' (A) position, and movement that is to a non-argument (A′) position (Chomsky 1981, Déprez 1989). Scrambling has posed a problem for the general theory in that it seems to exhibit diagnostic properties of both A-movement and A′-movement. Saito (1985) for Japanese and Gurtu (1985) for Hindi have both argued that scrambling is A′-movement. Mahajan (1991) on the other hand, has claimed for Hindi that a certain type of scrambling, at least, has to be considered A-movement. Kiss (to appear b) proposes that topicalization in Hungarian is NP-movement, not Operator-movement or scrambling. Srivastav Dayal argues against these analyses of the Hindi data, presenting evidence that the positions to which NPs scramble in Hindi cannot be the antecedents for binding (one of the most important diagnostics for NPs in A-positions). On the other hand, scrambling cannot be considered to be a paradigmatic case of A′-movement either since it fails to show weak cross-over effects and is able to strand quantifiers. Instead, Srivastav Dayal argues for a three-way distinction in movement types based on the parameters of ±Case and ±H(ead)R(elated), depending on whether movement is to a Case-marked position and whether the landing site is an adjoined position or one related to a head, i.e., a specifier or complement position. This is an important claim since it expands the ontology of possible movement types within syntactic theory. Such an expansion, whether it is expressed within a GB theory or not, appears to be necessary to account for the phenomenon of scrambling in South Asian languages.

One of the classic debates prompted by 'free' word order languages is whether this relative freedom of linear precedence reflects a non-configurational syntactic structure, such as that often proposed for Warlpiri (Hale 1983). R. Bhatt in 'Word Order, Configurationality and the Structure of the Kashmiri Clause' argues that Kashmiri, a verb-second (V2) language, is configurational. Bhatt, building on work in Bhatt and Yoon 1992, proposes that V2 is the result of the parameterization of Mood and subordination marking. In Kashmiri, Mood is realized verbally in matrix and subordinate clauses: the finite element moves to Mood, resulting in V2 order once SpecMP is filled. This configurational structure is not restricted to that outside the VP. Instead, Bhatt argues that the subject must asymmetrically c-command the object in the VP to account for differences in their syntactic behavior. The existence of VP-internal and external hierarchical structure in Kashmiri, which has been previously analyzed as nonconfigurational, contributes to the debate as to whether universally all languages project their arguments configurationally (Speas 1990) and argues against the notion that 'free' word order is synonymous with nonconfigurationality.

T. Mohanan in 'Case OCP: A Constraint on Word Order in Hindi', argues that word order (linear precedence) relations are encoded at a level logically independent of syntactic hierarchical structure, and independent of lexical and phonological levels of linguistic representation. This organization in terms of precedence has access to information at the other levels and can be constrained by this information, but is logically independent of it. Mohanan argues that the Obligatory Contour Principle (OCP), well known for its effects in the domain of tonal and segmental phonology (Leben 1973, Yip 1988), can also operate more generally at the level of word order. In particular, she argues that identically case marked arguments of a predicate are prohibited when prosodically adjacent in the word string. The fact that the prohibited identical case formants are not phonologically adjacent (due to the intervening noun stem) makes this a particularly unusual adaptation of the OCP. The statement of this rule must make reference to syntactic, argument structure, and prosodic information for its correct formulation. Since Mohanan's formulation of the rule requires information from a number of levels, these data present a challenge to theories in which the interactions between different levels of representation are more constrained. The proposal in this paper is an interesting and compelling hypothesis on the independence and interdependence of word order (precedence) relations with respect to other modules of grammar, as well as being an intriguing argument for the linguistic generality of such principles as the OCP.

Word order differences in South Asian languages can also be shown to have interesting semantic and pragmatic effects. On the level of semantics, M. Singh in 'Thematic Roles, Word Order and Definiteness' shows that there are correlations between the scrambling possibilities of direct objects and the possibility of definite interpretations for those objects. Noun Phrases in Hindi do not always carry explicit morphological markers of definiteness, e.g., overt determiners. This means that in many contexts, an object is ambiguous between a definite and an indefinite interpretation. The interesting fact is that when such an object is scrambled out of its canonical position adjacent to the verb, it can no longer have an indefinite interpretation but must be interpreted as a definite. This Hindi data is intriguing from a number of perspectives. Mahajan (1990) has argued that Hindi has two different object positions which are correlated with a difference in specificity. The existence of distinct object positions with attendant differences in syntactic interpretation (usually specificity and/or definiteness and perfectivity) has been the subject of much recent work in the syntax-semantics literature (Travis 1991, Sportiche 1990). The consensus seems to be that these distinct phrase structural object positions exist and moreover, that they are correlated with a particular type of interpretation quite systematically across languages, although it has not been clear how to define this particular interpretation in a fully formal and general way. However one finally chooses to express this phrase structure variation (either by scrambling or by base generation of different orders), the data from South Asian languages must be accounted for in any more general analysis of this phenomenon.

Of course, some of the classical effects of word order differences in natural language are pragmatic and/or discourse based (Li 1976, Yokoyama 1986, Kiss to appear a). A collection of papers on word order in South Asian languages would not be complete without serious investigation of some of these effects, contributing to the current resurgence of interest in these matters and attempts to incorporate them into formal linguistic theory, both crosslinguistically and within South Asian languages. In 'Topicalisation in Hindi and the Correlative Construction' V. Dwivedi argues that topicalization in Hindi comprises two structures. The first of these, which she terms topic dislocation, involves a topic base generated under TopicP, outside of CP, and binds a pro within the CP. The other, termed topicalization, involves movement of an NP to a position adjoined to IP, which therefore binds a trace within the clause. Such a structural distinction is similar to Aissen's (1992) proposal that Mayan has external and internal topics, which are base generated and moved respectively. What is interesting about Dwivedi's proposal is the semantic difference she posits between the two positions: referential NPs are dislocated, while all other XPs and non-referential NPs are adjoined to IP. The difference between these positions interacts with topicalization out of correlative clauses. Left-adjoined correlatives are governed by the verb and hence allow trace binding; as a result, any phrase can topicalize out of left-adjoined correlatives. In contrast, right-adjoined correlatives do not allow trace binding, and their adjoined position prohibits binding of a pro by a dislocated topic. So, no topicalization is possible from these constructions. The paradigm is completed by embedded correlatives. Embedded correlatives do not allow trace binding. However, topicalization of referential NPs is permitted because the dislocated NP can bind a pro in the correlative. Topicalization out of correlatives in Hindi supports a syntactic and semantic distinction between the two topic positions, as well as a structural difference between the three types of correlatives.

In 'Bangla Correlative Pronouns, Relative Clause Order and Discourse Linking', T. Bagchi examines the different discourse properties of the correlative construction in Bangla depending on whether the correlative is expressed in a standard or right-dislocated structure. Not only are these distinct orders seen to have different semantics (as in similar phenomena for Hindi (Srivastav 1991)), but the interpretation of deictics and anaphors also varies depending on precedence relations. There are two types of pronouns in Bangla, which Bagchi labels 'anaphors' and 'deictics', both of which may appear in relation to the correlative pronoun in the correlative construction. However, the relative felicity of the anaphoric and deictic pronouns in Bangla is shown to be dependent on the respective precedence relations between the pronoun and the correlative. The analysis of these Bangla constructions is worked out in terms of the independent properties of the two different types of pronoun, discourse linking (D-linking), and the effects of precedence relations.

In 'Afterthoughts, Antitopics and Emphasis', S. Herring presents a theory of the different discourse functions associated with the exploitation of the post-verbal position in Tamil (a language whose base, or default order is verb-final). Herring argues that this post-verbal 'position' is not in fact one position but three *different* structural positions which show varying degrees of syntactic association with the sentence. The post-verbal position is associated with emphasis, backgrounding, and afterthoughts. However, Herring shows that these three functions are not only functionally distinct but are also positionally distinct, with the 'emphasis' position being most closely connected to the sentence as a whole, and the 'afterthought' being the furthest out and most loosely connected to the sentence. The distinctness of these positions is seen not only in prosodic differences between the post-verbal constituents, but also in their relative ordering when multiple constituents appear after the verb. Here we have a case where different pragmatic or semantic functions are in fact associated with *different* structural relations, even though the superficial word order relations might suggest otherwise.

The different papers in this collection present a constellation of different theoretical proposals and empirical effects. The collection does not attempt to unify all these facts into a full and precise theory of the status of word order relations within linguistic theory, for such an attempt would surely be premature. Much remains to be discovered about word order variability effects both in South Asian languages and in other languages of the world. However, in 'Issues in Word Order in South Asian Languages', K.P. Mohanan and T. Mohanan examine many of the crucial questions that arise from a discussion of the phenomenon of word order variability in these languages and present two main theoretical alternatives to capturing the basic facts. These alternatives involve the choice between an enriched phrase structure approach, which encodes a variety of syntactic information in a single phrase structure (e.g., GB), and a more multidimensional approach, which provides a number of different representations or modules for different types of information (e.g., LFG). The difficulty of a single level of representation, they argue, is that many different *kinds* of information must be encoded simultaneously, in one format. This often obscures both the modularity of the system and, for example, prevents phrase structure and precedence relations from being interpreted as logically separate. Mohanan and Mohanan then present a particular kind of multidimensional theory, which they argue represents most clearly and adequately the facts from a number of different South Asian languages.

What seems clear from the papers in this volume is that the facts exhibited by these languages have far reaching implications for the organization of grammar in general and for the interaction of the various modules. Considering analyses from the perspective of a variety of different theories can provide insight as to what the essential factors behind the phenomena are, and which issues are merely a reflection of idiosyncrasies of a given theory. The battle between adherents of 'movement' theories and the supporters of 'base generation' of different word orders will no doubt continue for some time to come. Similarly, the issue of how independent precedence relations are from hierarchical structure has yet to be resolved. We believe that the papers in this volume contribute to the general theoretical debate, and will stimulate further (heated) discussion on the issues. In editing this volume, however, we have found that the formal differences between theories and the task of deciding between them, has been secondary to the main issue of exposing this wide range of word order variation types, and simply attempting to analyze and incorporate their description into some formal linguistic framework. It seems clear that there are a large number of different types of deviation from default order in natural language, each with different linguistic effects. The problem of word order variation is a vastly complex and probably non-unified phenomenon, affecting many different aspects of linguistic theory. However the reader chooses to interpret these facts, or assess these theoretical proposals, we believe they cannot be ignored in any general analysis of the status of precedence relations and word order variability within languages.

References

Aissen, J. 1992. Topic and Focus in Mayan. *Language* 68:43–80.

Alsina, A. 1993. *Predicate Composition: A Theory of Syntactic Function Alternations.* PhD Dissertation, Stanford University.

Baker, M. 1988. *Incorporation: A Theory of Grammatical Function Changing.* Chicago, IL: University of Chicago Press.

Bhatt, R., and J. Yoon. 1992. On the Composition of Comp and Parameters of V2. In *Proceedings of the Tenth West Coast Conference on Formal Linguistics.* Stanford, CA: CSLI.

Bresnan, J. (Ed.). 1982. *The Mental Representation of Grammatical Relations.* Cambridge, MA: MIT Press.

Chomsky, N. 1981. *Lectures on Government and Binding.* Dordrecht, The Netherlands: Foris.

Déprez, V. 1989. *On the Typology of Syntactic Positions and the Nature of Chains: Move Alpha to the Specifier of Functional Projections.* PhD Dissertation, Massachusetts Institute of Technology.

Gazdar, G., E. Klein, G. Pullum, and I. Sag. 1985. *Generalized Phrase Structure Grammar.* Cambridge, MA: Harvard University Press.

Greenberg, J. 1966. Some universals of language with particular reference to the order of meaningful elements. In J. H. Greenberg (Ed.), *Language Universals, with Special Reference to Feature Hierarchies*, 73–113. The Hague, The Netherlands: Mouton.

Gurtu, M. 1985. *Anaphoric Relations in Hindi and English.* PhD Dissertation, Central Institute of English and Foreign Languages.

Hale, K. 1983. Warlpiri and the Grammar of Non-Configurational Languages. *Natural Language and Linguistic Theory* 1:5–47.

Kiss, K. to appear a. *Discourse Configurational Languages.* Oxford, England: Oxford University Press.

Kiss, K. to appear b. NP-Movement, Operator Movement, and Scrambling in Hungarian. In Kiss (Ed.), *Discourse Configurational Languages.* Oxford, England: Oxford University Press.

Leben, W. 1973. *Suprasegmental Phonology.* Bloomington, IN: Indiana University Linguistics Club.

Li, C. (Ed.). 1976. *Subject and Topic.* New York, NY: Academic Press.

Mahajan, A. 1990. *The A/A-bar Distinction and Movement Theory.* PhD Dissertation, Massachusetts Institute of Technology.

Mahajan, A. 1991. Clitic Doubling, Object Agreement and Specificity. In *Proceedings of the Twenty-first Annual Meeting of the North Eastern Linguistic Society* 21:263–277.

Pollard, C. and I. Sag. 1987. Head-driven Phrase Structure Grammar: An Informal Synopsis. Technical report CSLI-87-79, Stanford, CA.

Saito, M. 1985. *Some Asymmetries in Japanese and their Theoretical Implications.* PhD Dissertation, Massachusetts Institute of Technology.

Speas, M. 1990. *Phrase Structure in Natural Language.* Dordrecht, The Netherlands: Kluwer.

Sportiche, D. 1990. Movement, Agreement, and Case. Unpublished manuscript, UCLA.

Srivastav, V. 1991. The Syntax and Semantics of Correlatives. *Natural Language and Linguistic Theory* 9:637–686.

Travis, L. 1991. Derived Objects, Inner Aspect and the Structure of VP. In *Proceedings of the Twenty-second Annual Meeting of the North Eastern Linguistic Society.*

Yip, M. 1988. The Obligatory Contour Principle and Phonological Rules: A Loss of Identity. *Linguistic Inquiry* 19:65–100.

Yokoyama, O. 1986. *Discourse Function and Word Order.* Amsterdam, The Netherlands: John Benjamins.

2

Bangla correlative pronouns, relative clause order, and D-linking

TISTA BAGCHI

1 Relative Clauses and Correlative Pronouns

1.1 Introduction

Multiple word-order possibilities in relative-clause structures in a number of Indic languages raise certain interesting questions with regard to the semantics of relative clauses in relation to that of their head NPs. Some of these questions have been discussed for Hindi recently by Srivastav (1991, 1993, and to appear), who furthermore proposes that left-adjoined relative clauses in Hindi are generalized quantifiers (in the sense of Barwise and Cooper 1981) that bind the head NP in the matrix clause as if the latter were a variable. Evidence that Srivastav (1991) cites in support of her proposal are differences in the distribution of demonstrative determiners (singular *vo*, plural *ve* in colloquial Hindi), plural morphology on the head noun or pronoun, and bare definite NPs in Hindi relative-clause structures. In the counterparts of such phenomena in Hindi's sister language Bangla (a.k.a. Bengali), additional distinctions are found that support Srivastav's proposal for Bangla. Among these, the presence of two competing sets of pronouns/determiners for anaphoric reference in Bangla potentially allows for a wider choice as to what can occur in the head NP position of a relative clause. The choice is limited, however, by word order considerations. In this paper, I demonstrate that underlying these distributional differences — dependent on word order at a superficial level — are facts relating to what these pronouns (or determiners) re-

Theoretical Perspectives on Word Order in South Asian Languages
Miriam Butt, Tracy Holloway King, Gillian Ramchand (Eds.)

fer to. My discussion of reference issues will be based largely on Evans (1980), Heim (1988), and (regarding issues of discourse-linking) Pesetsky (1987).

1.2 Relative-clause Constructions and Correlative Pronouns in Hindi and in Bangla

A CORRELATIVE construction has a relative clause adjoined to the left of the main clause, with a pronoun — or a noun phrase with a demonstrative determiner — occurring in the main clause to indicate what the left-adjoined relative clause refers to. Relative clauses in (Modern) English are postnominal, i.e., they are adjoined to the nominal head immediately to its right. In the correlative construction, the relative clause not only is adjoined to the left of the main clause but also may or may not immediately precede the nominal head. The following are examples of both types of relative-clause constructions (i.e., correlative and postnominal) in Hindi, taken from Srivastav (1991) with a minor modification (viz., that of adding *vahãã* 'there', suggested by James D. McCawley), — subscripts indicate coreference:[1]

(1) a.

[*jo*	*laRkii*$_i$	vahãã	khaRii	hai]	[*vo*$_i$	lambii	hai].
rel.-sg.	girl	there	standing	is	dem.	tall	is

The girl who is standing there is tall.
(literally: Which girl is standing there, she is tall.)

b.

[*vo*	*laRkii*$_i$	*jo*$_i$	vahãã	khaRii	hai]	lambii	hai.
dem.-sg.	girl	rel.	there	standing	is	tall	is

The girl who is standing there is tall.

Notice the order of the relative expression *jo (laRkii)* 'which girl/who' with respect to the head NP/pronominal in the two examples (1a) and (1b). In (1a), the relative NP *jo laRkii* 'which girl' precedes, BUT DOES NOT IMMEDIATELY PRECEDE, the demonstrative pronoun *vo*. In (1b) the relative pronoun *jo* IMMEDIATELY FOLLOWS the demonstrative head NP *vo laRkii* 'that girl' (with *vo* as a demonstrative determiner this time). The mutual order of the relative and the demonstrative head expressions will be a key point in the discussion to follow. Following previous usage in the literature on the syntax of Indic languages, I shall use the term CORRELATIVE PRONOUN as a cover term for a demonstrative head NP (pronominal or otherwise) in either kind of construction. I shall thus use the terms "correlative pronoun" and "correlative construction" in very different senses that are not to be confused with one

[1] The following special symbols have been used in the transcription of the Bangla examples: *E O* are lower-mid vowels, *T D R* are retroflex stops and flap, *S* is a palato-alveolar sibilant, *N* is a velar nasal.

another: a correlative construction is a left-adjoined relative-clause construction, whereas a correlative pronoun is the pronominal head or determiner of the head in EITHER kind of relative-clause construction.

Bangla has three sets of third-person pronouns/determiners, viz., proximal-deictic, distal-deictic, and anaphoric. The second and third sets of pronouns/determiners (i.e., the distal-deictic and the anaphoric sets) are potentially available for use as correlative pronouns. This distinction is not present in Modern Standard Hindi, which uses the demonstratives *vo* and *ve* both deictically and anaphorically (although vestiges of the purely anaphoric set of pronouns remain in Dakkhini Hindi-Urdu: see Kachru 1973). In translating Srivastav's Hindi examples into Bangla one has to decide whether to render the Hindi demonstratives by distal-deictic or by anaphoric pronouns. I present the pronominal/determiner bases for each type (including the relative pronominal/determiner bases) in (2):[2]

(2)

	RELATIVE	CORRELATIVE	
		DISTAL-DEICTIC	ANAPHORIC
HONORIFIC	jini˜ jã-	uni˜ õ-	tini˜ tã-
NON-HONORIFIC	je(-)˜ ja(-)	o(-)	Se(-)˜ ta(-)

These bases are used also as relative, deictic, or anaphoric adverbs of time, place, manner ('the way in which', 'in that manner', etc.), and reason ('the reason why', 'since', 'for that reason', 'therefore', etc.). The bases listed in (2) under the heading of CORRELATIVE bases are the ones being discussed in this paper. Complicating matters, however, is the fact that in Standard Colloquial Bangla today the distal-deictic pronouns are often used anaphorically as well, thus seemingly taking over a lot of the functions that the anaphoric pronouns serve. One such function of these distal-deictics is that of occurring as correlative pronouns, a function that will be my primary concern here.

---

[2]The wavy hyphens connect distributional allomorphs of a single pronominal base. A hyphen in parentheses indicates that the form preceding it occurs either as a free morph or as a bound one. Gender is not specified at all in the pronominal system of Bangla, though honorific versus ordinary status is relevant for third-person pronouns and (along with an additional DESPECTIVE or FAMILIAR level) for second-person pronouns as well. Number is indicated in the endings rather than in the bases, though the choice of allomorph may be coincidentally governed by number: e.g., singular *Se* 'he/she' (ordinary), plural *ta-ra* 'they' (ordinary).

2 The Distributional Facts

2.1 Correlative Pronouns in Left-adjoined Relative-clause Structures

I now consider the correlative pronominal bases in Bangla examples parallel to the Hindi example (1a) seen above. These examples are given in (3) below. (A couple of features whereby the Bangla examples additionally differ are (i) the occurrence of a classifier suffix with the relative noun phrase, whose function is to indicate number in addition to definiteness of reference, and (ii) the absence of a copula in the present tense.)

(3) a.

[[*je*	*mee-Ti$_i$*	okhane	dãRie
rel.det.	girl-class.(def.sg.)	there(deict.)	stand-conj.ppl.
ache]	[*Se$_i$*	lOmba].]	
be-pres.-3	anaph.-3ord.	tall	

The girl who is standing over there is tall.

b.

?[[*je*	*mee-Ti$_i$*	okhane	dãRie
rel.det.	girl-class.	there(deict.)	stand-conj.ppl.
ache]	[*o$_i$*	lOmba].]	
be-pres.-3	deict.-3ord.	tall	

As one can see, there is a difference in acceptability when the anaphoric correlative pronoun *Se* in (3a) is replaced by the corresponding deictic pronoun *o* in (3b). Example (3a), with the anaphoric correlative pronoun, is perfect, while (3b), with the deictic, is not.

However, the deictic place adverbial *o-khane* '(over) there' in (3a,b) is likely to mitigate any oddness resulting from the occurrence of the deictic *o* as a correlative pronoun. If one replaces the deictic place adverbial *o-khane* by the anaphoric place adverbial *Se-khane* 'there (anaphoric)', the picture changes somewhat, as one can see in (4a,b):

(4) a.

[tumi	lOmba	mee	khûjcho?]	
you(ord.)	tall	girl	look-for-pres.cont.-2ord.	
[*Dalhausi*	*skoar-er*	*uttor*	*dik-er*	*bas-sTOp-e$_i$*
Dalhousie	Square-gen.	north	side-gen.	bus-stop-loc.
cole	jao.]	[[*je*	*mee-Ti$_j$*	
move-conj.ppl.	go-imperat.-2ord.	rel.	girl-class.	

Sekhane$_i$ dãRie ache] [*Se*$_j$
there(anaph.) stand-conj.ppl. be-pres.-3 anaph.-3sg.
lOmba].]
tall
Are you looking for a tall girl? Go over
to the bus stop on the north side of Dalhousie Square.
The girl who is standing there is tall.

b. [tumi lOmba mee khûjcho?] [*Dalhausi skoar-er* ...
...$_i$ cole jao.]
??[[*je* *mee-Ti*$_j$ *Sekhane*$_i$ dãRie ache]
rel. girl-class. there(anaph.)
[*o*$_j$ lOmba].]
deict.-3sg.

The final sentence in (4b) is somewhat worse than the example (3b), and it is considerably worse than the final sentence in (4a).[3] (The reason that a context has been provided in (4a,b) is to highlight the anaphoric nature of *Se-khane* there, which (in Standard Bangla) needs an overt antecedent NP whose referent is preferably beyond the speakers field of vision.) This strengthens the observation that in a Bangla correlative structure (i.e., a left-adjoined relative-clause structure) an anaphoric correlative pronoun is preferred over a deictic one.

2.2 Correlative Pronouns in Right-extraposed Relative-clause Structures

What are the possibilities of occurrence of pronouns in right-embedded and right-extraposed relative constructions? Right-embedded restrictive relatives (*i.e.*, non-final restrictive relatives in immediately post-nominal position) do not seem to be tolerated very well in Bangla[4] (unlike in Hindi, which seems to permit these quite readily: cf. (1b)). If one considers (5a), a right-extraposed version of (3b) in which the determiner of the head NP is deictic, one finds that this is acceptable. Example (5b), which has an anaphoric determiner in the head NP, is

[3]The final sentence in (4b) is somewhat more acceptable if the referent of *o* is someone whom the speaker knows — i.e., someone who is related to a context presupposed by the speaker.

[4]The examples that Morshed (1986) has as instances of right-embedded relative-clause structures in Bangla are actually utterances containing parenthetical non-restrictive relative clauses. In addition, medially embedded NP-complement clauses are also not tolerated in Bangla — perhaps the same processual constraint is responsible in the case of both relative and complement clauses. I am told that Probal Dasgupta mentions this fact in his 1990 manuscript entitled Relative anaphora in Bangla; unfortunately, I have not had access to his manuscript. I am also grateful to Alice Davison for drawing my attention to this fact.

also acceptable, though subject to certain restrictions on context, a matter that I shall discuss in Section 3.2.

(5) a. [[*oi* *mee-Ti*$_i$ lOmba,] [*je*$_i$ okhane
det.(deict.) girl-class. tall rel.-3ord. there(deict.)
dãRie ache].]
stand-conj.ppl. be-pres.-3
That girl is tall, the one who is standing over there.

b. [[*Sei* *mee-Ti*$_i$ lOmba,] [*je*$_i$ okhane
det.(anaph.) girl-class. tall rel.-3ord. there
dãRie ache].]
stand-conj.ppl. be-pres.-3
The girl who is standing there is tall.

For the time being, the point to note is that (5a) and (5b) are both acceptable, in sharp contrast to (3a), (3b), and (4a), (4b). It seems that a deictic pronoun is permitted much more readily as the head of a right-extraposed relative clause than as a correlative pronoun bound by a left-adjoined relative clause. The following piece of text serves to highlight this:[5]

(6) [[apni *o-der*$_i$ mokabila korun]
you(sg.hon.) deict.-pl.gen. confrontation do-imperat.-2hon.
[*ja-ra*$_i$ ei pepar-er pechone boSe
rel.-pl. this newspaper-gen. behind-loc. sit-conj.ppl.
ache].] [eboN [pechon-er pechon-e *ja-ra*$_j$
be-pres.-3 and behind-gen. behind-loc. rel.-pl.
ache] [∅ *ta-der*$_j$ ∅].]
be-pres.-3 anaph.-pl.ord.-gen.
'Confront the ones who are established behind [i.e., are responsible for the publication of] this newspaper. And (confront) the ones who are behind (even the ones who are) behind (it).' (Hussain 1989:29)

The first sentence in (6) — 'Confront the ones who are established behind this newspaper' — is an instance of a right-extraposed relative construction, while the second sentence is an instance of a correlative (i.e., left-adjoined relative) construction. One finds a deictic pronoun as head of the right-extraposed relative clause in the first sentence and an anaphoric pronoun as the correlative pronoun in the second (correlative) sentence — the subscript indices show coreference relations.

[5]This passage was pointed out to me by Clinton B. Seely. The forms in the first sentence that have been elided in the second sentence (*apni* 'you (sg. hon.)' and *mokabila korun* 'confront (honorific present imperative)') are indicated by the zeros.

Summarizing, one finds that a deictic, though potentially also anaphoric in function, is reluctant to occur as a correlative pronoun referring back to a left-adjoined relative clause: a correlative structure is thus odd when a deictic correlative pronoun occurs in it. A pure anaphoric, on the other hand, can readily occur as a correlative pronoun that refers back to a left-adjoined relative clause. In right-extraposed relative-clause structures, on the other hand, both deictics and anaphorics are permitted as correlative pronouns (or demonstratives). Given the kind of semantics that Srivastav (1991, 1993) proposes for right-adjoined and right-extraposed relative clauses in Hindi, this is as expected. The choice of pronouns is thus conditioned by word order. The question to be addressed at this point is what accounts for this conditioning.

3 The Formal Nature of Correlative Pronouns/Determiners

3.1 Correlative Pronouns in Left-adjoined Relative Structures

The formal character of the deictic and the anaphoric pronouns *qua* correlative pronouns is worth investigating, particularly in the light of Evans's (1980) taxonomy of pronouns and Heim's (1988) exploration of definite and indefinite NPs.

I focus on the anaphoric pronouns in correlative structures first. If, as Srivastav (1991) proposes, left-adjoined relative clauses (in correlative structures) are generalized quantifiers that bind correlative pronouns as variables, anaphoric correlative pronouns should be bound variables. I see no reason to challenge this view. However, if they are interpreted across the board as bound variables they should not be able to occur as heads of right-extraposed relative clauses, since, according to Srivastav, right-extraposed relative clauses have the semantics of noun modification, not of quantifiers, and moreover do not precede or c-command the anaphoric pronoun or determiner head. The facts indicate otherwise, as was seen in Section 2 above. Moreover, anaphoric pronouns are not always bound by a c-commanding quantifier expression, as the following example indicates:

(7) Few congressmen admire Kennedy, and they are very junior.

Evans (1980) calls these anaphoric pronouns "E-type pronouns". These are pronouns that take their reference from a preceding quantified antecedent but do not have the meaning of the quantified antecedent itself. The other three kinds of pronouns that he enumerates are the following (Evans 1980:337):

(i) "Pronouns used to make a reference to an object (or objects) present in the shared perceptual environment, or rendered salient in some other way," as in

(8) He's up early.

spoken about a man walking down a street;

(ii) "Pronouns intended to be understood as being coreferential with a referring expression occurring elsewhere in the sentence," as in the reading of (9) on which the pronoun *his* refers to *John*:

(9) John loves his mother.

(iii) "Pronouns which have quantifier expressions as antecedents, and are used in such a way as to be strictly analogous to the bound variables of the logician," as in (10):

(10) Every man loves his mother.

Unfortunately, it is unclear from Evans's taxonomy of pronouns which category of pronouns would include the most common use of anaphoric pronouns in everyday speech. This is illustrated by the following discourse fragment:

(11) My brother lives in New York. He's coming for a visit next week.

Does the pronoun *he* in this fragment belong to Evans's category (i) or to his category (ii)? This question is relevant to the determination of the nature of both deictic and anaphoric pronouns in spoken Bangla, since it is possible to use either kind of pronoun in a similar discourse fragment in Bangla:

(12) a.

amar	bhai	NewYork-e	thake.	Samner
my	brother	NewYork-loc.	live-pres.-3	ahead-gen.
SOptahe	**Se**	ekhane	bERate	aSche.
week-loc.	anaph.-3sg.	here	to-visit	come-pres.cont.-3

My brother lives in New York. He is coming here for a visit next week.

b.

amar	bhai	NewYork-e	thake.	Samner
my	brother	NewYork-loc.	live-pres.-3	ahead-gen.
SOptahe	**o**	ekhane	bERate	aSche.
week-loc.	deict.-3sg.	here	to-visit	come-pres.cont.-3

My brother lives in New York. He is coming here for a visit next week.

The pronouns in these examples cannot be called E-type pronouns, since their antecedent is a definite description, not a quantified expression. Nor are they bound by a referential expression within the sentence. On the other hand, they are not pure deictics either, since they refer back to a referential expression that has already been introduced in the discourse.

This is where the analysis of pronouns suggested by Heim (1988) may be put to use. Following a proposal made by Peter Geach, Heim claims that sentences in a coherent piece of discourse are dominated by a superordinate node that she calls T (for Text). Pronouns can then be bound by, or refer to, antecedents that occur in another sentence but are dominated by the same T node — or they can be unbound, i.e., purely deictic. In addition, there is a FILE for each discourse (a metaphor that Heim adopts from work on discourse referents by Karttunen). As novel NPs (which may denote individuals or sets) are introduced into the discourse, new cards are added to the file, and already existing file cards are updated whenever new information relevant to these existing file cards is added to the discourse.

It seems useful at this point to invoke Pesetsky's (1987) concept of D-LINKING to describe referents of NPs that are already given in the discourse. According to Pesetsky, D-linking (for "discourse-linking") distinguishes unselectively bound wh-expressions from wh-expressions that seem to be subject to Subjacency either syntactically or scopally, in languages as diverse as English, Japanese, and Polish. D-linked wh-expressions — which are already familiar in the discourse (i.e., "on file" in Heim's sense) at the time the sentence is uttered — are unselectively bound (like all indefinite noun phrases, as Heim proposes), while non-D-linked wh-expressions — which are novel to the discourse — are not. My specific proposal is that deictic pronouns, to the extent that they refer to an antecedent at all, most felicitously refer to a D-linked antecedent. In support of this claim I present the following pairs of examples:[6]

(13) a. *kon* *mee-Ti*$_i$ bhabche je
which girl-classif. think-pres.cont.-3 that
tar$_i$ bhai ekhane thakbe?
3sg.anaph.-gen. brother here stay-fut.-3
Which girl$_i$ thinks that her$_i$ brother will stay here?

b. ?*kon* *mee-Ti*$_i$ bhabche je
which girl-classif. think-pres.cont.-3 that
or$_i$ bhai ekhane thakbe?
3sg.deict.-gen. brother here stay-fut.-3

[6]I am grateful to Probal Dasgupta for his suggestion that Pesetsky's notion of D-linking may be at issue here and for the examples (13a,b) as possible illustrations of this notion. Following a suggestion by a reviewer, I might add here that (13b) and (14b) are both perfectly acceptable on a non-coreferential reading of the deictic pronoun *or*.

(14) a. *ke*$_i$ bhabche je *tar*$_i$ bhai
who think-pres.cont.-3 that 3sg.anaph.-gen. brother
ekhane thakbe?
here stay-fut.-3
Who$_i$ thinks that his$_i$/her$_i$ brother will stay here?

b. **ke*$_i$ bhabche je *or*$_i$
who think-pres.cont.-3 that 3sg.deict.-gen.
bhai ekhane thakbe?
brother here stay-fut.-3

The examples (13a) and (14a), with anaphoric pronouns bound by the (in situ) interrogative expressions *kon mee-Ti* 'which girl' and *ke* 'who', respectively, are both fairly acceptable. The difference is to be noted when the anaphoric pronoun is replaced by a deictic one, as in (13b) and (14b). To be felicitous, (13b) requires an elaborated discourse context (a "scenario") in which, as a minimum requirement, at least two girls are already "on file", so to speak, so that the questioned NP *kon mee-Ti* 'which girl' is sufficiently strongly D-linked. Example (14b), on the other hand, is unacceptable except purely as an echo question: the question word *ke* is (except on the echo-question reading) far too non-referential to be D-linked. The deictic pronoun cannot therefore comfortably refer back to it.

Having said this much by way of background, I shall now consider the nature of the deictic and anaphoric pronouns in the two kinds of relative-clause constructions described above. In a correlative construction, under the proposal made by Srivastav (1991), a left-adjoined relative clause is a generalized quantifier. An anaphoric correlative pronoun (or a NP with an anaphoric demonstrative) is therefore a bound variable that is preceded and (presumably) c-commanded by the quantifier relative clause as its antecedent. The other possibility is that anaphoric correlative pronouns are E-type pronouns. The referent (set or individual) of a left-adjoined relative clause is uniquely defined, however, and is never indefinite (see Srivastav 1991 for lambda-calculus representations of left-adjoined relative clauses: each of these has a definite description operator, i.e., the iota operator). An anaphoric correlative pronoun thus refers to an antecedent that is already a definite description, which is not the case with the antecedent of an E-type pronoun. I therefore conclude that anaphoric correlative pronouns are not E-type pronouns. (This is not to say, however, that anaphoric pronouns can never be E-type pronouns: on the contrary, they are often E-type pronouns in ordinary discourse, just as pronouns like *it, she, they* can be in English.)

It has been seen that a deictic pronoun has a referential interpretation, with the requirement that its referent — which may or may not have a previously mentioned antecedent that is somehow salient in the discourse — be strongly D-linked in Pesetsky's sense. It has also been seen that its occurrence as a correlative pronoun in a correlative construction is facilitated by the presence of a deictic adverb of place such as *okhane* 'over there', which helps bring the referent of the deictic pronoun more immediately into the shared perceptual environment of the speaker and the addressee. I now suggest that whether a deictic pronoun can occur as a correlative pronoun that refers to a preceding left-adjoined relative-clause antecedent depends on how strongly the antecedent is D-linked, just as in any other construction. In illustration, I present the following examples:

(15) a. [[*je* *mee-Ti*$_i$ bEam kOre] [*Se*$_i$ utphullo
rel. girl-classif. exercise do-pres.-3 anaph. cheerful
thake].]
stay-pres.-3
The girl who exercises (regularly) remains cheerful.

b. ?/*[[*je* *mee-Ti*$_i$ bEam kOre] [*o*$_i$
rel. girl-classif. exercise do-pres.-3 deict.
utphullo thake].]
cheerful stay-pres.-3

There is disagreement amongst native speakers as regards the degree of unacceptability of (15b), but the difference of opinion concerns how strongly *je mee-Ti* 'which (rel.) girl' must be established in the discourse for (15b) to be felicitous. The consensus is that *je mee-Ti* 'which girl' has to be established in the discourse, i.e., D-linked, at least to a certain degree — an effect that is hard to achieve with this particular example. In contrast, consider the examples below:

(16) a. [[baRi-te *je* *mee-Ti*$_i$ kaj kOre]
house-loc. rel. girl-classif. work do-pres.-3
[*tar*$_i$ bhiSon OSukh].]
anaph.-gen. terrible illness
The girl/woman who works at (my/our) house is terribly sick.

b. [[baRi-te *je* *mee-Ti*$_i$ kaj kOre]
house-loc. rel. girl-classif. work do-pres.-3
[*or*$_i$ bhiSon OSukh].]
deict.-gen. terrible illness
(same reading as (a))

The relative clause in examples (16a,b) seems to be able to establish the referent of the correlative pronoun sufficiently strongly in the discourse scenario, i.e., to D-link it strongly enough, for the deictic pronoun to be able to refer to it without difficulty.

There are a couple of predictions[7] that this analysis makes, and indeed it turns out that the facts for Bangla fulfill these predictions. The first is that the distal-deictic pronoun should be ruled out as a bound pronoun referring to an indefinite quantifier NP, in a position analogous to that of the bound pronoun *he* in (17a) and *they* in (17b):

(17) a. *Every man*$_i$/*No man*$_i$ thinks that *he*$_i$ is smart.
b. *Most men*$_i$/*Few men*$_i$ think that *they*$_i$ are smart.

When translated into Bangla, these examples rule out the distal-deictic (on a coreferential reading) in the position of the bound pronoun, allowing only an anaphoric pronoun (the focusing emphasizer *-i* 'alone' makes the quantified NP unequivocally generic):

(18) a. *prottek lok-i* bhabe je
each person-emph. think-pres.-3 that
*Se/**o calak.
3sg.anaph/3sg.deict. clever
Every person$_i$ thinks that he$_i$/she$_i$ is clever.

b. *kono lok-i* bhabe na je
any person-emph. think-pres.-3 neg. that
*Se/**o calak.
3sg.anaph./3sg.deict. clever
No one$_i$ thinks that he$_i$/she$_i$ is clever.

c. *beSirbhag lok-i* bhabe je
most person-emph. think-pres.-3 that
*tara/**ora calak.
3pl.anaph./3pl.deict. clever
Most people$_i$ think that they$_i$ are clever.

d. *khub kOm lok-i* bhabe je
very few person-emph. think-pres.-3 that
*tara/**ora calak.
3pl.anaph./3pl.deict. clever
Very few people$_i$ think that they$_i$ are clever.

The other prediction is that a correlative structure in which the left-adjoined relative clause is generic in reference should permit an anaphoric but not a deictic as the bound pronoun in the "matrix" clause. As Srivastav (to appear) points out, a Hindi sentence such as (19), because of the combination of the focusing element *bhii* and the

[7] I am grateful to a reviewer for CSLI-Stanford for suggesting these.

"generic" verb form *hotii hai* (as opposed to the epistemic *hai*) yields a free-choice reading for the left-adjoined relative:

(19) jo-bhii laRkii sundar hotiihai ravii usse milnaa
whichever girl pretty is Ravi her to-meet
caahtaa hai.
wants is
Ravi wants to meet any girl who is beautiful.

The prediction is that Bangla should render the Hindi pronoun *usse* by an anaphoric, not a distal-deictic pronoun, and indeed the Bangla counterpart of (19) reveals such a restriction:

(20) *je mee-i* Sundori hOe robi
rel. girl-emph. beautiful occur-pres.-3 Ravi
*tar/*or* SONge-i alap
3sg.anaph.-gen./3sg.deict.-gen. with-gen. acquaintance
korte cae.
do-imperf.participle want-pres.-3
Ravi wants to make the acquaintance of any girl who happens to be beautiful.

Bangla prefers the emphasizer *-i* 'only, alone' as a clitic that marks its host NP as being generic in reference, rather than the emphasizer *-o* 'also', which in other uses is a more direct counterpart of the Hindi *bhii*. Bangla also lacks a present-tense copula in the epistemic sense, and the opposition is between a zero copula and a generic form of 'be, occur', namely, *hOe*. Both these elements impart an unequivocally generic reading to the left-adjoined relative clause, which can bind the anaphoric *tar* but not the deictic *or* in the matrix clause. The analysis in terms of D-linking thus turns out to be consistent with the distinction made independently by other elements in Bangla between a generic and a referential reading.

3.2 Correlative Pronouns in Right-extraposed Relative Structures

The pronominal heads of right-extraposed relative clauses have a different character from the correlative pronouns discussed above. To remind the reader of the word order relations that hold for these, I repeat the examples (5a,b) below as (21a,b):

(21) a. [[*oi* *mee-Ti*$_i$ lOmba,] [*je*$_i$ okhane
det.(deict.) girl-class. tall rel.-3ord. there(deict.)
dãRie ache].]
stand-conj.ppl. be-pres.-3
That girl is tall, the one who is standing over there.

b. [[*Sei* *mee-Ti*$_i$ lOmba,] [*je*$_i$ okhane
det.(anaph.) girl-class. tall rel.-3ord. there
dãRie ache].]
stand-conj.ppl. be-pres.-3
The girl who is standing there is tall.

Uttering (21a) is appropriate when the referent of the deictic head is in the shared perceptual environment of the speaker and the addressee. D-linking of the referent is not a sufficient condition by itself, in this case, for the deictic element to refer to it. In other words, the deictic head has the character of a "pure" deictic, more so than a deictic correlative pronoun does. Under the assumption that a right-extraposed relative clause has the semantics of a noun modifier, not that of a quantifier, this is as expected. Unfortunately, the information expressed by the relative clause is then somewhat redundant, given that the deictic head has already picked out the individual in question from the shared perceptual environment.

As it turns out, the relative clause in both (21a) and (21b) serves to provide information that is meant to help the addressee figure out which girl is being talked about. This information may or may not already be obvious from the perceptual environment or "on file". In the case of (21b), which has an anaphoric head, this makes a difference as to whether the anaphoric head has the status of an E-type pronoun or a definite description that is a focus of contrast. If the information provided by the relative clause is already on file in the form of the proposition *A girl is standing there* at the time that (21b) is uttered, the anaphoric head, including the relative clause modifying it, has the status of an E-type pronoun. If, on the other hand, the relative clause introduces new information, the anaphoric head has the status of a definite description whose uniqueness follows from the information expressed by the relative clause. In neither case does the anaphoric head have the interpretation of a bound variable, unlike an anaphoric correlative pronoun.

3.3 Does a Classifier Suffix D-link the Head of a Relative Clause?

I would now like to focus on a matter that is somewhat peripheral to the main issue of this paper, but relevant to the issue of D-linking, viz., the role of the classifier suffix *-Ti* that has occasionally appeared with a relative or head NP in the examples in regard to D-linking. The classifier suffix *-Ta/-Ti* , when it attaches to the head noun of a (singular) NP, usually marks the NP as being definite and of "individual aggregation" (for detailed descriptions of classifier suffixes in Bangla, and for an exposition of the feature "aggregation" as pertaining to Bangla nouns and classifiers, see Dasgupta 1983, 1985). However, a demonstrative such as *Sei* or *oi*[8] may additionally occur to mark the NP as being deictic or anaphoric in reference, or to mark a relative NP. Examples (22a)–(22c) illustrate the different possibilities:[9]

(22) a. *mee Ti* dãRie ache.
girl-classif. stand-conj.ppl. be-pres.-3
The girl is standing.

b. *oi* *mee-Ti* dãRie ache.
det.(deict.) girl-classif. stand-conj.ppl. be-pres.-3
That girl (over there) is standing.

c. *Sei* *mee-Ti* dãRie ache.
det.(anaph.) girl-classif. stand-conj.ppl. be-pres.-3
The (aforementioned) girl is standing.

A singular relative NP has two options: it can either be bare, as in (23a), or it can take the classifier suffix *-Ta/-Ti*, as in (23b):

(23) a. [*je* mee_i bEam kOre] [*Se* $(mee)_i$ utphullo thake].
rel. girl exercise do-pres.-3 anaph. girl cheerful remain-pres.-3
Any girl who exercises (regularly) remains cheerful.

b. [*je* $mee\text{-}Ti_i$ bEam kOre] [*Se* $(mee\text{-}Ti)_i$ utphullo thake].
rel. girl-classif. exercise do-pres.-3 anaph. girl-class. cheerful remain-pres.-3
(Among a specific group of people being talked about:)
The girl who exercises (regularly) remains quite cheerful.

The suffix *-Ti* in (23b) has the function of making the NP referential (see Ramchand 1991). The bare NP in (23a) has a somewhat different

[8]The demonstratives *Sei* and *oi* are the anaphoric base *Se* and the deictic base *o*, respectively, with the emphasizer clitic *i* attached to them: the emphatic force of these demonstratives has almost disappeared.

[9]Example (22a) might be compared with (i), in which the suffix *-Ti* does not occur:

(i) mee dãRie ache.
girl stand-conj.ppl. be-pres.-3
A/The girl is standing (there).
(Some) girls are standing (there).

The reference of *mee* in (i) seems to be unspecified with regard to definiteness, specificity of reference, or plurality. The reading that (i) does *not* permit, however, is the reading 'The girls are standing there'.

semantics, perhaps that of a "generic" NP in the sense that Carlson (1977) uses the term in the context of bare plurals in English, perhaps that of a universal quantifier that is best translated by English 'free choice' *any*. This is an issue that would take me too far afield from the point. I would like to concentrate on, namely, the role of the classifier suffix *-Ti*. I suggest, however, that this suffix is by itself not strong enough to D-link an NP to the extent that a deictic pronoun can refer to it in the capacity of a correlative pronoun: cf. the problematic example (13b) in Section 3.1, in which a deictic correlative pronoun is of questionable acceptability even though its antecedent carries the classifier suffix *-Ti*.

4 Conclusion

In this paper, I have sought to demonstrate how word order differences in relative-clause structures in Bangla affect the semantic interpretation of correlative pronouns. The issue of D-linking raised by Pesetsky (1987) to explain the behavior of wh-expressions has been found useful also in accounting for the behavior of deictic correlative pronouns in correlative structures, and in differentiating their behavior from that of deictic heads in right-extraposed relative structures. The formal nature of anaphoric correlative pronouns is also found to differ with word order: in correlative structures they have the semantics of bound variables, while as heads of right-extraposed relative structures they have the semantics of either E-type pronouns or definite descriptions, depending on the discourse status of the information expressed by the right-extraposed relative clause. Word order is thus found to be strongly linked to both formal semantic interpretation and discourse features of relative-clause constructions in Bangla.

Acknowledgements

Several of the participants of SALA XIV made valuable comments and suggestions on the theme of this paper, for which I am duly grateful. I would also like to thank Probal Dasgupta and the anonymous reviewers for CSLI-Stanford who read an earlier version of this paper, for their very helpful criticism and suggestions. Any errors remaining are, of course, mine.

References

Barwise, J., and R. Cooper. 1981. Generalized quantifiers and natural language. *Linguistics and Philosophy* 4:191–219.

Carlson, G. 1977. A unified analysis of the English bare plural. *Linguistics and Philosophy* 1:415–457.

Dasgupta, P. 1983. The Bangla classifier *Ta,* its penumbra, and definiteness. *Indian Linguistics* 44:11–26.

Dasgupta, P. 1985. On Bangla nouns. *Indian Linguistics* 46:37–65.

Evans, G. 1980. Pronouns. *Linguistic Inquiry* 11:337–362.

Heim, I. 1988. *The semantics of definite and indefinite noun phrases.* (Series: Outstanding dissertations in linguistics.) New York: Garland.

Hussain, S. H. 1989. *Sokun* [in Bangla: 'The Vulture']. Dhaka: Sabyasachi.

Kachru, Y. 1973. Some aspects of pronominalization and relative clause construction in Hindi-Urdu. *Studies in the Linguistic Sciences* 3:87–103.

Morshed, A. K. M. 1986. *Relativization in Bengali.* Dhaka: University of Dhaka.

Pesetsky, D. 1987. *Wh*-in-situ: movement and unselective binding. In E. J. Reuland and A. G. B. ter Meulen (Eds.), *The Representation of (In)definiteness,* 98–125. Cambridge, MA: MIT Press.

Ramchand, G. 1991. Bangla nominals, predication, and small clauses. Paper presented at the Thirteenth South Asian Languages Analysis Roundtable, University of Illinois at Urbana-Champaign, May 25–27, 1991.

Srivastav, V. 1991. The syntax and semantics of correlatives. *Natural Language and Linguistic Theory* 9:637–86.

Srivastav, V. 1993. Restrictive relativization in Hindi. *South Asian Language Review* Volume 3(1).

Srivastav, V. To appear. Quantification in correlatives. E. Bach et al. (Eds.), *Cross-Linguistic Quantification,* Dordrecht: Kluwer.

3

Word Order, Configurationality and the Structure of the Kashmiri Clause

RAKESH MOHAN BHATT

1 Introduction

One of the properties commonly associated with nonconfigurational structures is freedom of word order. In Kashmiri,[1] a sentence like (1) can be written/spoken in as many as *120* different ways (given the appropriate pragmatic conditions) as long as the verb occupies the clause second position.[2]

(1) raath **dyut** Tiicar-an laRk-as yenaam klaasas-manz
yesterday gave teacher(E) boy(D) prize(N) class-in
The teacher gave the boy a prize in the class.

[1]Kashmiri is an Indo-Aryan language spoken mainly in the Kashmir province of the state of Jammu and Kashmir.

[2]Note: The capital letter in the transcription indicates retroflex sound. The capital 'N' after a vowel indicates nasalization. The abbreviations used in this paper are:

CP = Conjunctive Participle;	Perf = Perfective
NPerf = Nonperfective	E = Ergative
N = Nominative	A = Accusative
D = Dative	O = Oblique
G = Genitive	Q = Question marker
Pass = Passive marker	Neg = Negative marker
Fut = Future	Subj = Subjunctive
Inf = Infinitive marker	aux = Finite auxiliary verb
1 = First person	2 = Second person
3 = Third person	m = Macsculine
f = Feminine	s = Singular
p = Plural	

Theoretical Perspectives on Word Order in South Asian Languages
Miriam Butt, Tracy Holloway King, Gillian Ramchand (Eds.)

The empirical correlation between free word order and nonconfigurationality forces us to investigate the structure of Kashmiri clause. Superficially, Kashmiri does give an illusion of Walpiri since it too has the constraint of the Aux to be at the clause second position (Hale 1982). The natural question to ask in this regard is: Does Kashmiri have a nonconfigurational structure (à la Hale 1982)? Recently, Raina (1991) has claimed that Kashmiri is a nonconfigurational language: the subject and the object mutually c-command each other. She assumes (2) as the underlying structure of a Kashmiri clause: the VP projection dominates a series of inflectional phrases which host grammatical relations in an unordered way.

(2)

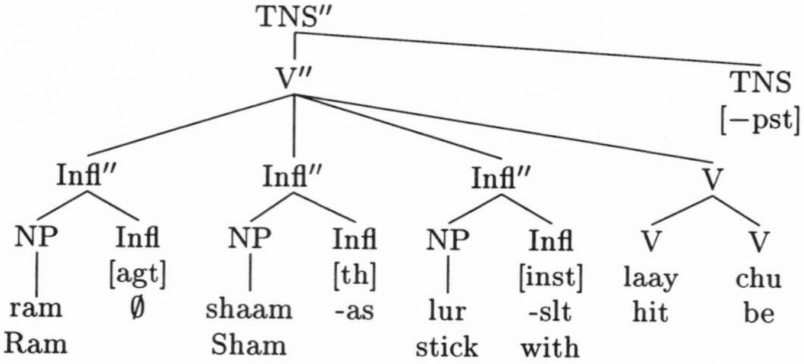

In the first part of this paper then, I will present evidence to show that Raina's claim cannot be maintained for Kashmiri. I argue that in spite of the fact that Kashmiri allows considerable freedom in the order of its constituents, there is sufficient evidence to claim that Kashmiri does not have a nonconfigurational structure like (2), as suggested by Raina (1991); but rather that there is a VP projection in the Kashmiri clause structure which is asymmetrically c-commanded by the IP-Spec.

This brings us to the second problem with respect to the clause structure of Kashmiri: What is the underlying constituent order of main and subordinate clauses? Grierson (1919), Kachru (1969), Masica (1976) and Syeed (1984) have suggested S–V–O, while Hook (1984), based on the functional theory of "communicative dynamism", and Subbarao (1984), based on gapping facts, contend that underlyingly Kashmiri is S–O–V. In this paper I will claim that the phrase structure of Kashmiri is as given in (3): the lexical projections {NP, VP, AP, PP}[3] are head final while functional projections {CP, IP} are head initial.

[3]I assume the category P to be lexical (for an extended discussion on the categorial status of P, see Grimshaw 1991).

(3)

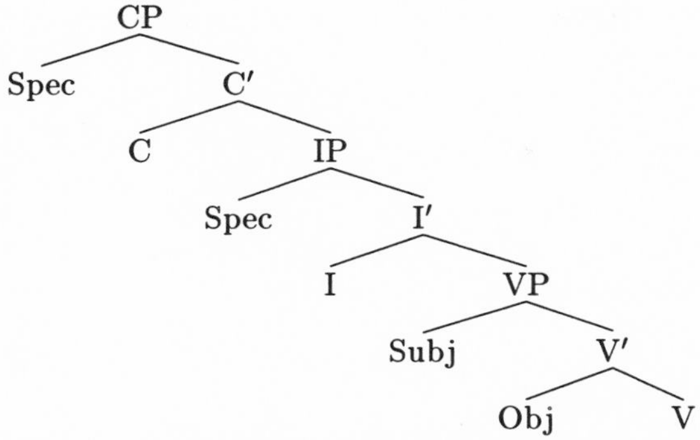

The surface S–V–O order results from the movement of the inflected verb to the clause second position. Specifically, I will claim that the landing site of finite verb movement is not Comp, as is assumed for German, Dutch, etc, rather it is Mood — the functional projection used for clause-type marking — as is suggested in Bhatt (1993) and Bhatt & Yoon (1992). Also, I will briefly discuss the position of complement *ki* clauses in the Kashmiri phrase structure: These *ki* clauses are always excluded from sentence internal position.

This paper is organised into three major sections. Section 2 discusses the notion of configurationality, and then presents evidence against Raina's claim showing that Kashmiri is a configurational language. Section 3 examines the phrase structure order of Kashmiri. Arguments are presented to support the claim that the verb phrase of Kashmiri is head final. Section 4 presents a parametric theory of verb-second.

2 Kashmiri is Not "Nonconfigurational"

Ever since Chomsky (1981) and Hale (1982, 1983), it has been necessary to acknowledge the existence of the typological distinction between configurational and nonconfigurational languages. In configurational languages (e.g., English) subjects and objects are uncontroversially non-sisters; subject is hierarchically higher than the other complements of the verb. However, in nonconfigurational languages (e.g., Walpiri) the clause structure is constrained neither by the familiar X′-theoretic principles (Chomsky 1981, Jackendoff 1977) nor by any structural conditions on predication (Williams 1980). The phrase structure rule responsible for generating nonconfigurational languages, according to Hale (1982), is given in (4); it makes the specific prediction that languages with structures like (4) will not show any subject/object asymmetry.

(4) S ⟶ W* [W* is a string of concatenated words without internal structure]

With this background, we turn to the surface diagnostics proposed in the literature to motivate a proposal for a nonconfigurational structure like (2) for Kashmiri. In (5) below, I list the diagnostics most commonly associated with languages that have been considered nonconfigurational (cf. Hale 1982, 1983, Farmer 1984, Mohanan 1983, Jelinek 1984, Webelhuth, 1984, Speas 1990):

(5)
a. free word order
b. ability to pro drop
c. no overt expletives
d. rich Case system
e. presence of discontinuous constituents
f. no NP-movement

At first glance it seems rather difficult to determine whether Kashmiri is configurational or not, since on the surface Kashmiri displays some of the criteria but lacks other. With respect to word order, Kashmiri allows considerable freedom with the exception of the "Aux Second" constraint. In Kashmiri, a sentence like (6) can perhaps be written/spoken in as many as *six* different ways (given appropriate contexts), as long as the verb occupies the clause second position.

(6)
a. raath khyav tem batI
yesterday ate he(E) food(N)
He ate food yesterday.

b. raath khyav batI tem
yesterday ate food he

c. tem khyav raath batI
he ate yesterday food

d. tem khyav batI raath
he ate food yesterday

e. batI khyav tem raath
food ate he yesterday

f. batI khyav raath tem
food ate yesterday he

In addition, Kashmiri also allows both subject and object to *pro-drop*. This is seen in (7). In both (7a) and (7b), the arguments (subject and object) of the verb are missing. This points to a nonconfigurational structure of Kashmiri.

(7) a. dop-n-am pagah yiiz-na
said-3s-1s tomorrow come-not
He told me not to come tomorrow.

b. naav prutsh-th-as-aa
name asked-2s-3s-Q
Did you ask his/her name?

Also, like other Indic languages, Kashmiri does not have overt expletives[4] (in the sense of English, e.g., *It is raining* or *There is a snake in the toilet.*) and it can therefore be counted as a language which has a fairly rich Case system. It makes use of nominative (agreeing non-overt morphological Case), accusative (non-agreeing non-overt morphological Case), dative, ergative and ablative.

There are, however, some properties that Kashmiri does not share with other nonconfigurational languages. For example, Kashmiri does not allow discontinuous expressions, as Walpiri does.[5]

Another property that Kashmiri does not share with other nonconfigurational languages is that it allows NP movement as shown in the passive construction in (8) below. In (8a) only the subject *maasTar*, and not the object, controls the reflexive. In (8b), on the other hand, it is shown that the passive subject is now able to control the reflexive.

(8) a. maasTar-an$_i$ looy raath laRk-as$_j$ paninyi$_{i/*j}$
teacher(E) hit yesterday boy(D) self's

---

4 The ungrammaticality of (i) and (ii) suggests that Kashmiri does not allow overt expletives as English does. The demonstrative pronoun yi "this" is used pleonastically sometimes as in extraposed clauses (iii).

(i) *yi chu ruud pyav-aan
this is rain falling
It is raining.

(ii) *tetyi chu soruph Techyi-manz
there is snake toilet-in
There is a snake in the toilet.

(iii) yi kor-na tem-is khosh ki su tsol
this did-Neg her(D) happy that he ran away
It upset her that he ran away.

5 Kashmiri does show some symptoms of nonconfigurationality at the phrase level. It allows NPs and PPs to be discontinuous, just as Hungarian. In (i) below, I show an example of a discontinuous genitive construction: the genitive and the governing noun are separated.

(i) tem-sund chu asyi makaan baDI pasand
he-of aux us(D) house(N) very like
We like his house very much.

fuuT-as siithyi
ruler-of with
Yesterday the teacher$_i$ hit the boy$_j$ (student) with his$_{i/*j}$ ruler.

b. laRk-as$_i$ aav raath laay-ni paninyi$_i$
boy(D) came yesterday hit-Pass self's
fuuT-as siithyi
ruler-of with
The boy$_i$ (student) was hit yesterday with his$_i$ ruler.

To sum up, of the six properties that are commonly associated with nonconfigurational languages, Kashmiri has four of them but it clearly lacks the other two. In the remainder of this section, I will show that the arguments for nonconfigurationality that Raina (1991) presents do not hold when the facts are carefully scrutinized — subject/object asymmetries do indeed exist in Kashmiri.

Raina proposes a nonconfigurational syntactic representation for Kashmiri based on the claims (a) that there are no asymmetries between the subject and the other arguments of the verb, and (b) that there are no asymmetries between the verb's direct object and the postpositional (indirect) object. Basically, Raina claims that Kashmiri does not have a VP constituent and therefore no c-commanding asymmetries hold between arguments of the verb. She uses verbal agreement, reflexive-antecedent relationship, and the distribution of PRO to show that the notion of subject is not motivated in the grammar of Kashmiri. She claims that in Kashmiri "verb agrees with any NP without an overt inflection" (ibid: 29). This is, however, an incorrect generalization as the Kashmiri data in (9) shows — it is always the subject with which the verb agrees if both subject NP and object NP are without an overt inflection.

(9) a. tse ch-u-k yim kitaabI par-aan
you(N) aux-(m,2s) these book(A,f,p) read-NPerf
You are reading these books.

b. ba ch-a-s yi Thuul khyv-aan
I(N,f,s) aux-(f,1s) this egg(A,m,s) eat-NPerf
I am eating this egg.

In both (9a) and (9b), the subjects as well as the objects are not overtly Case-marked. The nominative NP in Kashmiri is never overtly Case-marked, and the stem always appears in what is called the direct (uninflected) form. The direct object, on the other hand, whenever overtly Case-marked, changes the shape of the stem to what is known as the oblique form. In the examples above, both the subject and the object are in the direct form, yet the verb agrees with the subject, and not with the object. Besides, verbal agreement cannot be used to motivate the notion of subject in Kashmiri, since Kashmiri, like other Indic languages, displays a split ergative system — the verb agrees with the subject in non-perfective clauses, and with the object in unaccusative clauses (i.e., ergative and psych constructions).

I now turn to her other argument, i.e., reflexive antecedent relationship. I discuss in detail the relevant binding theoretic facts of Kashmiri to show that there is indeed a need to posit a hierarchical structure in which the subject asymmetrically c-commands the verb and its complement.

2.1 Binding Theory — A

Raina claims, among other things that the reflexive does not always choose subject as its antecedent and therefore nothing crucial hinges on the notion of subject in Kashmiri grammar. We discuss some restrictions on the appearence of anaphors and show that the Binding-theoretic data indicate the existence of a configurational structure in Kashmiri. In the framework assumed here (Chomsky 1981), Principle A of the Binding Theory [BT-A] states that the anaphors have to be bound in their governing category, i.e., there is a c-commanding antecedent in that domain binding the anaphors. This principle makes different predictions for configurational vs. nonconfigurational languages with respect to the distribution of subject and object anaphors. Under a nonconfigurational analysis, the contrast in (10) and (11) is unexpected: both the subject and object c-command each other and therefore the anaphor is bound in its governing category (=IP), so there should be no violation of BT-A in either (10a, 11a) or (10b, 11b).

(10) a. tim$_i$ chi-na akh ekyi-sinz$_i$ kath boozaan
they aux-not each other-of story listen
They$_i$ do not listen to each other's$_i$ story.

b. *akh ekyis$_i$ chi-na tihanz$_i$ kath boozaan
each other aux-not them-of story listen
Each other$_i$ do not listen to their$_i$ story.

(11) a. timav$_i$ kor paanvInyi$_i$ khaandar
they did each other marriage
They married each other.

b. *paanvInyi$_i$ kor timav$_i$ khaandar
each other did they marriage
Each$_i$ other married them$_i$.

In assuming a configurational structure, however, the contrast in (10) and (11) follows straightforwardly, given that in configurational structures the subject asymmetrically c-commands the object. In (10b), the antecedent in the object position *tihanz* is unable to A-bind the *akh ekyis* in the subject position, yielding the ungrammaticality of the sentence. A similar explanation holds for (11b).

Another piece of evidence for the hierarchical structure of Kashmiri comes from the binding facts of reflexive possessives like *panun*. In Kashmiri any NP can be the antecedent for *panun* (as Raina maintains), as long as it is not itself a proper part of an NP or a PP (see Hook & Koul 1992). Thus, while (12a) is ambiguous, both *ba* and *su* acting as possible antecedents for *panun* (12b) is disambiguated by moving ("scrambling" à la Mahajan 1990) the phrase containing the reflexive possessive over the direct object *su*. In so doing, the direct object *su* no longer c-commands (and therefore A-binds) the anaphor, which of course explains the impossibility of the second interpretation in (12b).

(12) a. ba$_i$ nyiman su$_j$ panun$_{i/j}$ gar kaaryi manz
I take-Fut he self's house car in
I will take him to my/his house in the car.

b. ba$_i$ nyiman panun$_{i/*j}$ gar su$_j$ kaaryi manz
I take-Fut self's house he car in
I will take him to my/*his house in the car.

It can be conjectured that the contrasts in (12) follow from the hypothesis that binders must preceede their bindees. This hypothesis, however, is not able to account for the data in (13): The precedence effect hypothesis does not predict the behavior of the Kashmiri reflexive pronoun *panunpaan* 'own's self'. As the data in (13a) shows, these are typically subject oriented reflexives. In (13b), the reflexive *panun* 'self' only takes the clausal subject as its antecedent and nothing else.

(13) a. tem$_i$ hoov me$_j$ shiishas-manz panunpaan$_{i/*j}$
he(E) showed me(D) mirror-in self's self
He showed me his self (his image) in the mirror.

b. tem$_i$ kor ramesh$_j$-sinz paarTiiyas-manz panun$_{i/*j}$
he(E) did Ramesh-of party-in self's
booy badnaam
brother insult
He$_i$ insulted his$_{i/*j}$ brother in Ramesh's$_j$ party.

2.1.1 Binding Theory — C

Some more robust evidence for configurationality in Kashmiri comes from data on Binding Theory C. If Kashmiri were indeed nonconfigurational, as Raina argues, then the grammaticality of (14) is unexpected, given the indexation (data from Raina 1991:128; Ex. 103).

(14) raam-sinz$_i$ maaj chi temis$_i$ tshaanDaan
Ram(G) mother aux him look for
Ram's mother is looking for him.

Under Raina's nonconfigurational account, (14) should be ungrammatical as a violation of BT-C — an R-expression is bound by the c-commanding pronoun. However, if we assume a configurational structure like (3) for Kashmiri, then the grammaticality of (14) is expected. The subject, 'Ram's mother' is higher in the structure than the coindexed pronominal 'him' — the latter does not c-command the former, rendering R-expression free and thereby accounting for the grammaticality of (14).

2.2 Distribution of PRO

Raina merely observes that in some languages like Kashmiri, Hindi and Oriya, etc. PRO can only be an agentive and an experiencer subject, but not an instrumental subject. While Raina does not provide any data to support her claim, there is evidence contrary to her claim. I show in (15) that in Kashmiri, both the controllee in the nonfinite clauses and the controller in the finite matrix clauses are always the subjects.

(15) [PRO$_{i/*j}$ batI khya-th] vach laRk-an$_i$ kuur$_j$
food eat-CP saw boy(E) girl(N)
After the boy finished eating the food, he saw the girl.
*After the girl finished eating the food, the boy saw her.

2.3 Additional Evidence

Additional evidence against the nonconfigurational analysis of Kashmiri phrase structure shown in (2), and in favor of the configurational structure in (3) can be derived by the well-known phenomena of Weak Crossover [WCO], and Constituent Fronting [CF]. I will show, based on evidence of WCO effects and CF, that subjects in Kashmiri asymmetrically c-command objects. Implicit in Raina's proposal (2) is the assumption that there are no adjunct-argument asymmetries. I provide data from Superiority-like Effects to show that Kashmiri does indeed exhibit adjunct-argument asymmetries, which are unexpexted in a flat structure like (2).

2.3.1 Weak Crossover (WCO)

Another argument for configurationality in Kashmiri can be developed based on the facts of Weak Crossover. WCO is a property of only those languages in which the subject c-commands the object but the object does not c-command the subject. The contrast in *wh*-extraction facts in (16) receive a natural explanation if the subject is assumed to c-command objects, and not vice-versa.

(16) a. Who_i t_i loves his_i mother?
  b. *Who_i does his_i mother love t_i?

In (16a), the trace of the moved *wh*-phrase is locally A′-bound and the possessive is locally A-bound by t_i. In (16b) however, the *wh*-trace is not A-bound by the pronoun 'his' since it does not c-command the trace t_i. The ungrammaticality of (16b) is a result of the violation of the Bijection Principle [BP] given in (17) below:

(17) The Bijection Principle: (cf. Koopman & Sportiche 1982)
  (a) Every variable must be bound by exactly one operator;
  (b) Every operator must bind exactly one variable. A variable is defined as a locally A′-bound category and an operator is defined as any XP in Comp.

The ungrammaticality of (19b) is a violation of the second clause of the Bijection Principle (17): one (*wh*-phrase) operator binds two variables.

The contrast in (16) is not predicted if we assume a nonconfigurational structure for English. Under a nonconfigurational analysis, both (16a) and (16b) should be grammatical and no WCO effects should be noticed since the t_i (in 16b) could c-command and therefore bind the pronoun 'his', which would then not lead to a BP violation. Thus, in a flat structure like (2), where subject and object mutually c-command each other, contrasts such as (16) are unexpected.

A similar subject/object asymmetry also obtains with quantifier phrases. The subject quantifier phrase coindexed with a possessive pronoun yields the wellformed sentence in (18a). The sentence is ill-formed if the quantifier phrase is in the object position and is coindexed with a possessive pronoun in the subject position, as in (18b).

(18) a. Everyone_i loves his_i mother.
  b. *His_i mother loves everyone_i.

The assumption of a configurational structure for English (subject asymmetrically c-commanding object) will yield the contrast shown in (18). The wellformedness of (18a) is explained in the following manner: at LF, *everyone* moves to the operator-position A′-binding its trace, which A-binds the possessive pronoun. (18b) will be ruled out at LF since at that level *everyone* will bind two variables (its own trace and the possessive pronoun) in violation of the BP. Again, if we assume a nonconfigurational structure for (18), such a contrast will not be predicted, since at LF the trace of *everyone* could bind *his*, hence no violation of BP and no WCO effects.

In Kashmiri we do notice WCO effects, as shown in (19).

(19) a. raath kemyi$_i$ kor t$_i$ temsinz$_i$ maajyi phoon
yesterday who did his mother phone
Who$_i$ called his$_i$ mother yesterday?

b. *raath kemyis$_i$ kor temsinz$_i$ maajyi t$_i$ phoon
yesterday whom did his mother phone
Who$_i$ did his$_i$ mother call?

The contrast in (19) would be unavailable if Kashmiri were analysed as nonconfigurational. Assuming a nonconfigurational analysis, (19a) and (19b) would be equivalent in their c-command relations at LF: the possessive pronoun in each case will be locally A-bound, and hence not a variable. The BP will not be violated since only the trace (variable) is associated with the *wh*-operator. This, of course, would leave the ungrammaticality of (19b) unexplained.

On the other hand, if a configurational structure is assumed for Kashmiri, then the contrast in (19) follows straightforwardly. In (19a) the possessive pronoun *temsinz* is not a variable locally operator-bound, rather it is A-bound (c-commanded) by the subject trace. In (19b), on the other hand, the possessive pronoun *temsinz* does not have an A-antecedent: it is a variable bound by the operator *kemyis.* In such a configuration, then, the *wh*-operator binds two variables — *temsinz* and t$_i$, which results in the ungrammaticality of the sentence as a violation of the BP.

Another subject/object asymmetry is observed with quantifier phrases, as shown by the contrast in (20).

(20) a. saaryii$_i$ chi temsendis$_i$ baayis pyaar karaan
everyone aux his brother-to love does
Everyone$_i$ loves his$_i$ brother.

b. *temsund$_i$ booy chu saaryini$_i$ pyaar karaan
his brother aux everyone love does
His$_i$ brother loves everyone$_i$.

Again the contrast in (20) cannot be explained by assuming a nonconfigurational structure like (2). Under a nonconfigurational structure, (20a) and (20b) are predicted to be grammatical, since in each sentence the trace of LF movement of QP can c-command, and therefore A-bind the possessive pronoun.

The contrast in (20) can be explained only by assuming a configurational structure where the subject NP asymmetrically c-commands the object NP. In (20a), when *saaryi* moves at LF, the trace it leaves behind A-binds the possessive pronoun *temsendis*. The trace itself is A′-bound by the moved quantifier. In (20b), on the other hand, the LF movement of the quantifier creates another variable (its trace). The moved QP locally A′-binds its trace as well as the possessive pronoun, resulting in a BP violation.

2.3.2 Constituent Fronting

Earlier in this paper I presented evidence to show (see (6) above) that in Kashmiri, a finite verb in second position can be preceded by any major constituent in sentence initial position. There are restrictions as to how many constituents the finite verb can follow. The restriction is that exactly one constituent, but not more than one constituent, is fronted.[6] Thus (21), in which two object NPs appear before the finite verb, is ungrammatical.

(21) *laRk-as kitaab dits tem
boy(D) book(N) gave he(E)
He gave a book to the boy.

The constraint that only a single constituent can be fronted makes for a good test for constituentcy in Kashmiri. In Kashmiri, if two items can occur together (without a pause between them) in pre-verbal main clause position, then they are elements of a single constituent; if they cannot then they belong to separate constituents. So, the direct object of a verb can be topicalized with a participle as shown in (22b, 23b), while any attempt to do so with the subject and a participle leads to ungrammaticality (22c, 23c).

(22) a. su chu dohay panun phoTuu vuchaan
he aux daily self's picture sees
He looks at his picture everyday.

b. panun phoTuu vuchaan chu su dohay
self's picture sees aux he daily
He looks at his picture everyday.

[6]The exception to this generalization is found in interrogative clauses wherein the finite verb is immidiately preceded by *Wh*-words which can be preceded by one topic NP.

c. *su vuchaan chu dohay panun phoTuu
he sees aux daily self's picture
He looks at his picture everyday.

(23) a. temsund mool oos habkadalas nish kitaabI kanaan
his father aux Haba bridge near books sells
His father used to sell books near Haba bridge.

b. kitaabI kanaan oos temsund mool habkadalas nish
books sells aux his father Haba bridge near
His father used to sell books near Haba bridge.

c. *temsund mool kanaan oos habakadalas nish
his father sells aux Haba bridge near
kitaabI
books
His father used to sell books near Haba bridge.

The data in (22b) and (23b) thus clearly shows that the verb and the object form a single constituent. The ungrammaticality of (22c, 23c) shows that the subject and the participle belong to separate constituents.

2.4 Argument-adjunct Asymmetries

In Kashmiri there is also some evidence that suggests adjunct-argument asymmetries. For example, in multiple questions with adjuncts, as in (24) below, we find Superiority-like effects.

(24) a. (me prutshmas) kos kitaab kyaazi/kithpaThyi par
I asked which book why/how read
tem
he
(I asked him) which book he read why/how?

b. *(me prutshmas) kyaazi/kithpaThyi kos kitaab par
I asked why/how which book read
tem
he
(I asked him) why/how he read which book?

In (24) we notice that the adjunct *wh*-phrase needs to be next to the finite verb or the sentence is ungrammatical. In Kashmiri the finite verb indicates which element is the one that moves first; it is the one that immidiately precedes the finite verb. Now if the adjunct moves first, which is the case in (24a), it assigns its (non-referential) index to the Spec of the projection it moves to, thereby ensuring antecedent government. In (24b), the object *wh*-phrase has moved first giving the Spec its (referential) index. Now when the adjunct moves it fails to antecedent govern its trace resulting in the ECP violation. The ungrammaticality of (24b) thus further supports my claim that the structure of the Kashmiri clause is configurational as shown in (3).

To sum up, the data presented above in Sections 2.1 through 2.4 cannot receive an explanation without positing ad hoc filters, etc. if a nonconfigurational structure is assumed for Kashmiri along the lines proposed by Raina (1991). I have argued that a nonconfigurational structure of the type in (2) *cannot* be maintained for Kashmiri since it cannot account for all the subject/object asymmetries as well as argument/adjunct asymmetries noticed above. These asymmetries can *only* find an explanation in a configurational structure like (3), which has the subject position asymmetrically c-commanding the object position.

Having established that Kashmiri is configurational, I now turn to Kashmiri phrase structure to determine precedence relations.

3 Word Order Constraints: Kashmiri Phrase Structure

Under the assumptions of some versions of Government-Binding (GB) theory (Chomsky 1981, 1986, 1989), D-structure is characterized as having a welldefined underlying linear order of constituents to which Move-α applies to yield a change in the linear order at the S-structure. Languages like Kashmiri, which have relatively flexible word order, pose a challenge in accurately determining the D-structure order of heads and their complements. I will claim here that Kashmiri is underlyingly a head final language. My argument is that the direction in which a lexical head discharges its θ-role and assigns Case (=direction of government) will determine the respective order of a head and its complement at D-structure and the S-structure. This is consistent with the assumptions of the theory (Koopman 1983):

(25) (i) D-structure is not merely an X-bar theoretic projection of argument structure to which θ-roles are assigned but that they also include specifications about the direction in which these θ-roles are assigned, and
(ii) the assignment of Case involves a directional parameter.

Given these assumptions, I will describe word order facts in Kashmiri examining both head-complement relations within NPs, PPs, APs and word order relations among constituents at the IP (=S) level. The evidence will show that the head of a lexical projection appears to the right, and that the canonical government relation is [___ X].

3.1 N-complements

Given the constraints of X′ system, it has been claimed that dominance relations are constant, and that languages vary only in terms of precedence relations. In NPs, e.g., specifiers, genitives, and complement of a noun always precede the head, as shown in (26).

(26) a. yi laRk chu myon booy
this boy is my brother
This boy is my brother.

b. TuurisTan hund makaan
tourists of house
Tourist's house.

c. akh baD thod katsur laRk
one very tall blonde boy
A very tall blonde boy.

These examples (26a–c) can be accounted for if one assumes that NPs are head-final. Particularly, in (26b) the genitive *hund* 'of' appears to the left of the head. This observation is stated in terms of the following generalization for Kashmiri:

(27) Heads discharge θ-roles to their left.

However, while the generalization in (27), correctly predicts (28a) to be ungrammatical, it wrongly predicts (28b) to be grammatical.

(28) a. *makaan myoon booy
house my brother
My brother's house.

b. *myon booy makaan
my brother house
My brother's house.

The order of the complements and head in (28) follows from (27), yet (28) is ungrammatical because the noun *booy* 'brother' is in the complement position and is unable to receive Case. A genitive adposition that reflects the θ-role (possessor) associated with its complement is required to assign Case to it (i.e., *booy*). The only two places where the adposition can occur is either to the right or to the left of the complement noun. If it is placed to the left, the phrase is ungrammatical as shown in (29a) and (29b), but if it is placed after the complement noun, the phrase becomes grammatical as shown in (29c).

(29) a. *sund myon booy makaan
of my brother house
My brother's house.

b. *myan-is sund booy makaan
my(O) of brother house
My brother's house.

c. myan-is booy sund makaan
my(O) brother of house
My brother's house.

The ungrammaticality of (29a) and (29b) and the grammaticality of (29c) can be attributed to the fact that in (29a) and (29b) the genitive marker *sund* 'of' cannot assign Case to the right, and thus the complement noun remains Caseless and violates the Case Filter. This observation allows us to hypothesize that in Kashmiri

(30) Case is assigned to the left by a Case assigner.

If hypothesis (30) is correct, then the Case assigning adposition should immediately follow the complement noun in order for Case to be correctly assigned. Sentence (29c) in fact confirms our hypothesis (30) since the Case assigner *sund* occurs to the right of the nominal *booy* bearing the thematic role of "possessor". The sentence is grammatical because at this position *sund* correctly assigns Case to *booy*.

3.2 Postpositions

In Kashmiri, the complement-head order inside an adpositional phrase is consonant with the head-final character of Kashmiri. The adposition always occupies the phrase-final position, and the complements always precede their head. The evidence for the head-final character of postpositional phrases in Kashmiri is presented in (31a, 31a′).

(31) a. tem an zanaan maal-is khaatr
he(E) brought wife father(O) for
He brought (his)wife for the (sake of his) father.

a.′ tem on zanaan-i khaatr mool
he(E) brought wife(O) for father(N)
He brought father for the (sake of his) wife.
He brought the wife for the (sake of his) father.

In (31a) the PP *khaatr* 'for' assigns oblique Case to *mool* 'father', which is realised as *maalis* in the oblique case. If the PP *khaatr* is moved between the two nomimals *zanaan* 'wife' and *mool* 'father', as in (31a′), the meaning changes, since the PP will now be interpreted (semantically) as associated with the preceding noun to which it assigns the oblique Case (cf. hypothesis 30). The second reading in (31a′) is, therefore, impossible. Also, the verb *on* 'brought' in (31a′) agrees with the direct object *mool* (PPs in Kashmiri block agreement) and the verb an in (31a) shows agreement with *zanaan*, the direct object.

3.3 Adjectives

Adjective projections (herafter, AP) also provide evidence about [___ X] as the possible canonical government structure. In Kashmiri APs too, the complements always precede their heads (cf. 32a,b).

(32) a. huun-is hyuu
dog(O) like
Like a dog.

b. kanana-khaatr taiyaar
sale for ready
Ready for business.

In addition, certain adjectives appear to have the lexical property of taking clausal complements, as shown below in (32c). The ungrammaticality of (32c′) confirms the head-final character of the adjective projection.

(32) c. [PRO ilekshan khabar bozni khaatr] beetaab luukh
election news hear for impatient people
People impatient to hear the election news.

c.′ *beetaab [PRO ilekshan khabar bozni khaatr] luukh

3.4 V Projections

The verb phrase (VP) facts are similar to those of other phrases. The hypotheses in (27) and (30) predict that Kashmiri is head-final within VP given that the assignment of theta roles and Case to the argument NPs is to the left. On the surface, however, the hypotheses (27) and (30) do not seem to hold for the Kashmiri clauses as the examples in (33) below indicate: The word order at the IP (=S) level is the same as the one we find for English, viz., Subject–Verb–Object.

(33) a. laRk-an par kitaab
boy(E) read(f,s) book(N,f,s)
The boy read the newspaper.

b. laRk-an khe-yi tsoT
boy(E) ate(f,s) bread(N,f,s)
The boy ate the bread.

c. kus gav kamar-as manz
who(N) went room(O) in
Who went in the room.

It is perhaps reasonable to assume at this point that Kashmiri VP is head initial. There, however, seem to be several problems with this assumption. First, in assuming head initial VP, I will have to motivate a movement of the nonfinite verb to the end of the clause for (34): it is not possible to motivate such a movement in Kashmiri.

(34) ba chu-s laRk-as kitaab div-aan
I(N) aux(m,sg) boy(D) book(A) give-NPerf
I give a book to the boy.

Second, I shall have to assume that within VP, the directionality of theta- and Case assignment is opposite of what we found for other lexical heads. There is reason to believe that verb does indeed assign Case to its left. Consider again the data in (34). Given that the order of objects is unmarked, and assuming that VP is head initial, and also assuming that verb assigns accusative Case to its direct complement under adjacency condition, the sentence (34) should be ungrammatical since the verb is unable to assign Case to the direct object. An analogous English sentence like (35) is indeed ungrammatical.

(35) *I gave to the boy a book.

Since (34) is grammatical, the most reasonable analysis will be to assume that the direct object has Case, and the only way it could get Case is from the verb which is to its right. A head final VP provides a simple explanation for the grammaticality of (34): the verb assigns Case to its direct complement under government. In so doing, I maintain that in Kashmiri the canonical government direction is leftward. In assuming head final VP, all I need to do to account for the word order is to motivate the finite verb movement to clause second position, which we do in Section 4 of this paper.

Third, and the final problem in assuming a head initial VP for Kashmiri is the clause final appearence of the verbal complex and the relative order of the elements of the verbal complex in relative and adverbial subordinate clauses as shown in (36a) and (36b), respectively.

(36) a. [RC yi ba khyv-aan chus] su chuyi-aa tse
what I eat-NPerf aux that aux-Q you
khosh karaan
like does
Do you like what I eat.

b. [AdvC yelyi su baat gyvaan oos] kamras manz aas
when he song sings aux room in aux
tshop gatsaan
quiet goes
It used to get quiet in the room when he would sing.

Assuming a head initial VP, we will need to account for the main verb–auxiliary verb order in relative and adverbial clauses as in (36). Motivating these movements and ensuring the main verb–finite verb clause final order will require adding some stipulations and thereby complicating the grammar of Kashmiri. On the other hand, if I assume a head final VP, I only have to block the finite verb movement to clause second position in relative and adverbial clauses.

In conclusion, then, a more elegant account of the Kashmiri VP can be made if we assume that, like other lexical projections discussed above, Kashmiri VP is head final. This assumption, coupled with the VP-internal subject hypothesis (Koopman & Sportiche 1988, Speas 1990), leads to a fairly simple mechanism of theta role assignment: all theta roles are assigned/discharged to the left by the verb to all its arguments within the VP projection. I quickly summarize below in (37) the Case and θ-theoretic facts observed so far:

(37)

	θ assignment	Case assignment
N (Gen)	Left	Left
P (Obl)	Left	Left
A (Obl)	Left	Left
V (Acc)	Left	Left

3.5 The Functional Projections

First, let us remind ourselves the word order facts in Kashmiri. I have so far argued that Kashmiri is a verb final language. The presence of the finite verb in the clause second position must then be a result of its movement from the clause final position. If so, then I make the plausible assumption that the head of the functional projection which hosts the finite verb must be head initial, otherwise the word order facts in Kashmiri will not receive an account. I suggest that the finite verb moves to the head of a functional projection, MP (=Mood Phrase) via head to head movement (see Section 4, for details), respecting the Head Movement Constraint (Baker 1988, Travis 1984). I further assume that the structure of all of the functional projections in Kashmiri is the one given in (38) below:

(38)

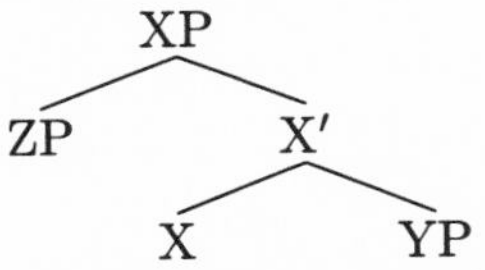

It is not uncommon for a language to exhibit both head final and head initial projections. German and Dutch are S–O–V languages yet the Comp projection in both languages is systematically analysed as head initial (cf. Haider and Prinzhorn 1986, Weerman 1989). There is some evidence from optional verb movement in relative clauses that in Kashmiri the heads of functional projections above the VP (which serves as landing sites for verb movement) must be head initial.

(39) a. yus laRk dohay panyis kamraz manz batI khyvaan
which boy daily self's room in food eats
chu
aux
The boy who eats his food in his room.

b. ?yus laRk dohay panyis kamraz manz chu batI
which boy daily self's room in aux food
khyvaan
eats
The boy who eats his food in his room.

c. ??yus laRk dohay chu panyis kamraz manz batI
which boy daily aux self's room in food
khyvaan
eats
The boy who eats his food in his room.

d. *yus laRk chu dohay panyis kamraz manz batI
which boy aux daily self's room in food
khyvaan
eats
The boy who eats his food in his room.

The examples (39b) and (39c) indicate various places where the finite verb can optionally appear. (39d) indicates that in relative clauses, verb second is prohibited. The only logical way to account for the data in (39b) and (39c) is to assume that the functional projections above the VP are head initial and are possible landing sites for finite verb movement.

3.6 Complement *ki* Clauses

In this section, I explore the distribution of the finite complement clauses that always appear to the right of the matrix clause, as we find in right branching languages like English. The finite complement clauses in Kashmiri, introduced by a complementizer *ki*, are systematically excluded from appearing in sentence internal position. Consider the contrast in (40): In spite of the fact that the preverbal object position is the unmarked position for objects, *ki* complements cannot occur preverbally. Similarly, like object complements, subject complements of predicate adjectives (41) also show that these *ki* complements, interpreted as arguments of a predicate, do not occur in the syntactic positions where other arguments occur. These clauses must occur external to the matrix clause.

(40) a. *laRk-as chI [ki swa yii-na] khabar
boy(D) aux that she(N) come-Fut-Neg knowledge
The boy knows that she will not come.

b. laRk-as chI khabar [ki swa yii-na]
boy(D) aux knoweledge that she(N) come-Fut-Neg
The boy knows that she will not come.

(41) a. *[(yi) ki su chu lingvistikis paraan]] chu
this that he aux linguistics studies aux
mahatavpurn
important
The fact that he studies linguistics is important.

b. yi chu mahatavpurn ki [su chu lingvistikis
this aux important that he aux linguistics
paraan]
studies
The fact that he studies linguistics is important.

The ungrammaticality of the (a) examples in (40) and (41) above shows that in Kashmiri the finite complement clauses cannot be internal to the matrix clause. These finite complements, as the (b) examples in (40) and (41) show, are always external adjuncts. The interesting generalization about these finite complements is that they are possible only in non-Case positions. This contrasts with the nonfinite complements which appear in governed (Case-marked) positions. Consider the contrast in (42) below.

(42) a. laRk chu yets-aan [ki su kheyi-hee batI]
boy(N) aux want-NPerf that he ate-Subj food
The boy wants that he should eat food.

b. *laRk chu [ki su kheyi-hee batI] yets-aan
boy(N) aux that he ate-Subj food want-NPerf
The boy wants that he should eat food.

c. laRk chu [PRO batI khy-on] yets-aan
boy(N) aux food eat-Inf want-NPerf
The boy wants to eat food.

More evidence for this distributional difference between finite and nonfinite complements comes from the fact that certain verbs like *majbuur karun* 'to force' require lexical Case on their clausal complements. As shown in (43) below, the (Oblique) postpositional Case appears on the nonfinite infinitive gerund (43a) but not on its finite counterpart (43b) which appears right adjoined to the matrix clause. Instead the postpositional Case in (43b) appears on the NP which appears in the argument position, to the left of the verb. The finite complement gets its theta role and Case indirectly by virtue of coindexation with the NP in the argument position.

(43) a. raam-an kor me [PRO batI khya-nI] khaatr
Ram(E) did I(D) food eat-Inf-(O) for
majbuur
force
Ram forced me to eat food.

b. raam-an kor me [ath kathyi pyaath]$_i$ majbuur [$_i$ ki
Ram(E) did I(D) this matter on force that
ba khyam-haa batI]
I(E) eat-Subj food
Ram forced me to eat food.

One plausible hypothesis that emerge from the data in (40)–(43) is that finite complement clauses do not occur in governed positions. Since the argument positions to which Case can be assigned are governed, finite complement clauses are systematically excluded from these positions. The incompatibility of finiteness and Case is presumably due to Stowell's (1981:146) Case Resistance Principle [CRP], which states that:

(44) Case Resistance Principle: Case may not be assigned to a category bearing a Case-assigning feature.

Stowell has argued that the feature [+Tense] resides in Comp and carries Case assigning properties. While the nonfinite clauses can appear in argument positions, however, as a result of the CRP, finite clause cannot appear in the Case-marked position. The finite complement clause in (42b) will not receive Case in argument position which will make it invisible for theta marking, and thus yield an ungrammatical result.

To sum up, finite *ki* clauses are prohibited to occur in governed, Case-marked positions, and therefore necessarily occur as adjuncts outside the domain of a governor/Case assigner. I suggest, following Stowell (1981), that although the finite complement clauses have argument interpretation, they are syntactically external to the normal argument position. With respect to the externalization of these complement clauses, there are two alternatives. One is that proposed by Stowell (1981) for English: that finite complement clauses originate in A-positions and are later extraposed leaving a coindexed gap (or a pronoun). The argument interpretation is derived by reconstruction at LF. The other alternative is to assume that finite clauses are base generated as right or left syntactic adjuncts of IP (cf. Webelhuth 1989,

Bayer 1990, and Davison 1991). We adopt the latter alternative; that in Kashmiri finite complement clauses are base generated as syntactic adjuncts of IP.

This alternative has at least one big advantage over the movement analysis. In assuming a movement analysis, we have no explanation for the differences in the extraction of finite and nonfinite clauses. Nonfinite clauses, unlike finite clauses, do not leave a (resumptive) pronoun at the extraction site (45). Finite clauses, on the other hand, are interpreted with a pronoun or a gap, as shown in (46).

(45) a. laRk chu t_i yetsh-aan [$_i$ PRO batI khy-on]
boy(N) aux want-NPerf food eat-Inf
The boy wants to eat food.

b. *laRk chu yi_i yetshaan [$_i$ PRO batI khy-on]
boy(N) aux this want-NPerf food eat-Inf
The boy wants to eat food.

(46) a. laRk chu yi_i yetsaan [$_i$ ki su kheyi-hee
boy aux this want-NPerf that he(N) ate-Fut-Subj
tsuuNTh]
apple
The boy wants to eat an apple.
Lit. The boy wants this that he may eat an apple.

b. laRk chu pro_i yetsaan [$_i$ ki su kheyi-hee
boy aux want-NPerf that he(N) ate-Fut-Subj
tsuuNTh]
apple
The boy wants to eat an apple.

In assuming a movement analysis of finite complements, the contrast between (45) and (46) remains unexplained. The right adjunct finite clauses are not instances of move alpha; they are base generated as right adjuncts of IP. These adjunct clauses are associated semantically with a NP in the nearest argument position. As Davison (1992:55) correctly notes, these complements are "subject to linear processing constraint on the lambda extraction or identity account of argument clauses."

I suggest that nonfinite clauses move from a Case-marked argument position to a right adjoined A′-position via a syntactic rule of extraposition, leaving variable-bound empty category. The interpretation of extraposed nonfinite clauses is mediated either by Case, or by A′ binding of an empty category.

4 Verb-Second [V2]

4.1 Germanic V2

The bulk of generative research in Germanic has been devoted to explaining the complementary distribution between the presence of the complementizer and V2. For example, in German the finite verb occupies the clause-second position in matrix clauses and clause-final position in subordinate clauses that are introduced by a lexical complementizer.[7] The *standard* account of V2 for German (see Haider & Prinzhorn 1986) assumes that in matrix clauses (47a) the finite verb moves to Comp (via the head of IP). In embedded clauses (47b) where the Comp position is filled by a complementizer, verb movement is blocked, hence no V2: the inflected verb appears in the clause-final position. This analysis thus correctly predicts the complementary distribution of V2 and appearence of complementizers.

(47) a. Johann **aß** einen Apfel
John ate an apple
John ate an apple.

b. Ich weiß daß Johann einen Apfel **aß**
I know that John an apple ate
I know that John ate an apple.

Other Germanic languages like Dutch (Weerman 1989), Swedish (Platzack 1986) and Norwegian (Taraldsen 1986) have been similarly analyzed (see Haider & Prinzhorn 1986). In all of these languages, V2 is assumed to occur "mechanically" whenever an empty Comp node is available as a landing site for the verb. The structures for main and subordinate clauses in German, e.g., is given in (48a) and (48b), respectively.

(48) a.

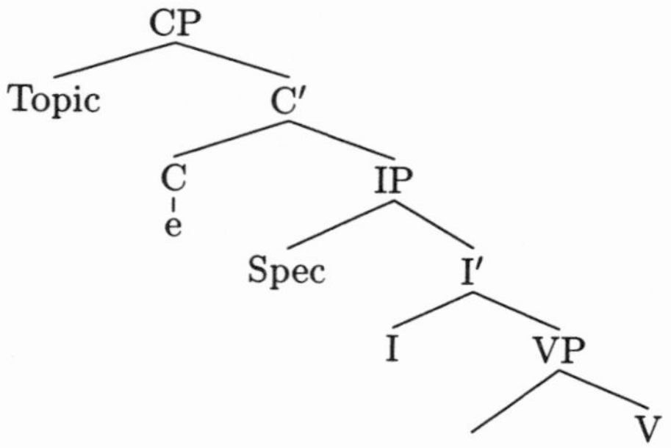

[7] Thanks to the reviewer for bringing this point out.

b.

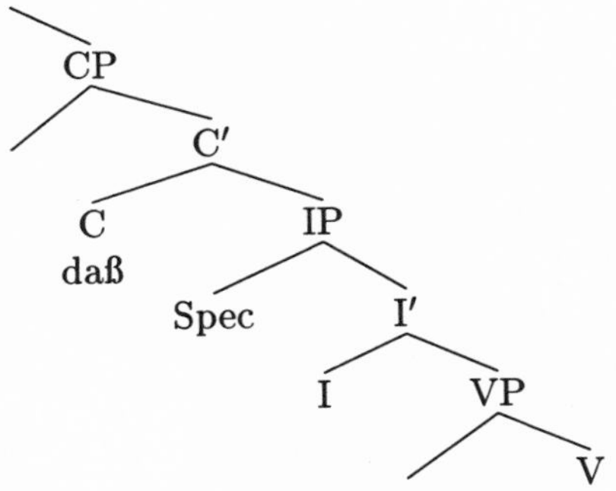

4.2 Kashmiri V2

Kashmiri poses problems for the standard account (cf. German) of verb movement in that it does not exhibit the main/subordinate asymmetry with respect to the position of the finite verb, as shown with the compound verb *deeryith dyun* 'to throw (away)' in (49) below:

(49) a. laRk-an **dyut** tshawTh daar-yith
boy(E) give-Perf trash throw-CP
The boy threw (away) the trash.

b. tem dop ki laRk-an **dyut** tshawTh daar-yith
he(E) said that boy(E) give-Perf trash throw-CP
He said that the boy threw (away) the trash.

4.3 Diesing 1990

Diesing, adopting the VP-internal subject Hypothesis (Fukui & Speas 1986, Kitagawa 1986, Koopman & Sportiche 1988) argues that in Yiddish V2 is achieved by V-movement to Infl, rather than to Comp. That is why in embedded clauses V2 is possible even in the presence of the complementizer *az*, as shown in (50).

(50) Avrom gloybt **az** Max **shikt** avek dos bukh
Avrom believes that Max sends away the book
Avrom believes that Max send the book away.

Diesing proposes that Infl is able to assign nominative Case rightward which accounts for the fact that subjects can remain in their base generated position, while any non-subject can occupy the topic position, IP-Spec. As this position is usually assumed to be the position of subjects, she proposes that Yiddish allows IP-Spec to function either as an A or an A′ position. She holds the ECP responsible for the obligatory filling of the Spec of IP position: complementizers in

Yiddish are not lexical governers, thus empty topics are ruled out as ECP violations.

Since Infl is free for the verb to move into even in embedded clauses, one gets the desired V2 even in those clauses. Thrainsson (1986) reaches similar conclusions for V2 phenomena in Icelandic. I show in (51) the V2 phenomena in Yiddish.

(51)

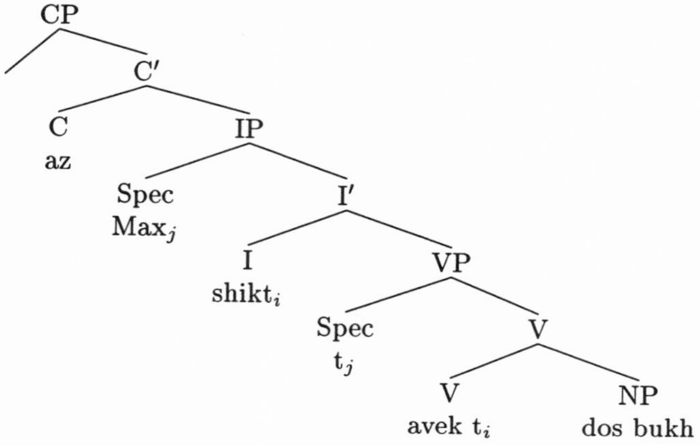

4.4 The Structure of V2 Clause

With respect to the structure of V2 clauses, Diesing's analysis of V2 as movement to Infl depends crucially on the assumption that in matrix clauses there *must not* be any Comp or the projection of Comp. She shows that with a CP the facts of Yiddish will not receive an account, because if matrix clauses had CPs, one would wrongly predict that Topics and *Wh*'s could co-occur in direct questions and that V3 order will obtain. However, this begs the question why Yiddish matrix clauses *cannot* have a CP projection, especially in view of the fact that other Germanic V2 clauses *must* have a CP.[8]

In what follows, I will propose a parametric approach to V2, which accounts for the range of variation found in V2 languages

[8]Diesing (1990:55) proposes what might appear to be the principle banning the projection of CP in Yiddish main clauses which stipulates that "only the *minimal amount* of A-bar structure" should be generated. She claims that this guarantees that a CP will not be generated in matrix clauses in Yiddish. The problem with this stipulation is that it is rather vague. For example, under one interpretation of this principle, main clauses should have both CP and IP if there is both a Topic and a *WH*-element, since the minimal amount of A-bar structure needed in this case appears to for both the Spec of IP and of CP. Other problems with her proposal are discussed at length in (Bhatt 1993).

(German/Dutch/Swedish vs. Kashmiri/Yiddish/Icelandic). Following Bhatt (1993), and Bhatt and Yoon (1992), I assume the following:

(52) a. Mood marking (=clause-type marking) is obligatory in all clauses, main and subordinate.
b. The strategies of Mood marking in Universal Grammar may be verbal (empty mood attracting V-movement) or non-verbal (through lexical complementizers).
c. The category known as "Comp" should be decomposed into Mood and Subordinators. Some languages (like German) lexicalize/conflate the two, whereas others (like Kashmiri) lexicalize them separately.

The choice of options in (52b,c) interact to yield the typological distinction in V2 languages, viz., the German type and Kashmiri type. V2 arises in subordinate clauses when a language has an empty Mood that hosts verb movement to make mood marking visible. However, this is possible only if the language (like Kashmiri) lexicalizes Mood and Subordinator separately. There is overt evidence in Kashmiri for the dissociation of Mood(verbal) and Subordination, as suggested in the example given below:

(53) a. tem dop **ki** swa gatshi-**hee**
he(E) said that she(N) go-Subj
He said that she should go.
b. tem prutsh **ki** swa gatshy-**aa**
he(E) asked that she(N) go-Q
He asked whether she should go?

On the other hand, if Mood and Subordinator are lexicalized together as Comp, another means of Mood-marking must be sought, one that crucially does not involve verb movement. This is the situation with embedded clauses in German.

This analysis provides an immediate answer to a fundamental question for any V-raising account of V2 — namely, why the impossibility of V2 in the presence of lexical Comps in German does not lead to ungrammaticality. It is because the function performed by V2 is fulfilled by the lexical complementizer, which also indicates mood/clause-type distinctions. This also answers the question why verb movement can fulfill this function in V2 clauses — mood is verbal.

To sum up, we must recognize in UG at least *two* general ways in which mood marking can be made visible: verbal and non-verbal. V2 clauses employ verbal mood identification, whereas non-V2 clauses headed by lexical complementizers choose non-verbal mood identification. Also, I assume that the lexical complementizer of V2 languages may either be pure *Subordinators* (or *subordinator comps*), or may indicate *both* the clause type/mood *and* subordinate status. The term "complementizer" is reserved to refer to the latter category. Distinct from this newly defined category of *Comp*, we also recognize lexemes whose sole function is mood-marking, *Mood.* In the former languages, e.g., Kashmiri, the structure of embedded clauses will be as in (54a),[9] while in the latter, e.g., German, it will be as in (54b).

(54) a.

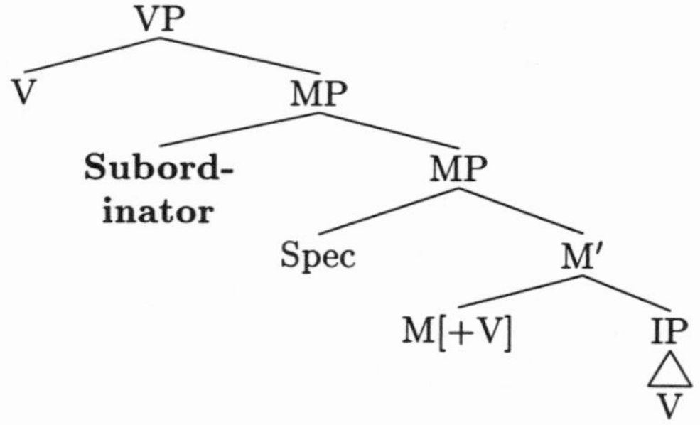

b.

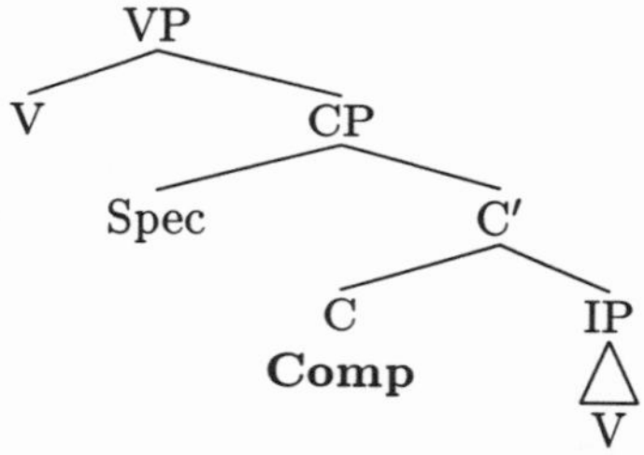

One of the desirable consequences of this account is that a principled explanation now emerges as to why the clausal structures of main and subordinate clauses in languages like Kashmiri and Yiddish *have to be* different, a result Diesing wanted for Yiddish but could not explain. The element Diesing analyzed as Comp (*az*) in Yiddish is taken to be a simple marker of subordination in my account; it cannot be available in a *root* context, by hypothesis, while it must be available in an embedded context, yielding different structures for root and embedded contexts.

[9]I have treated the subordinator as being adjoined to MP and not heading its own projection. I might have to allow subordinators to project a full X-bar theoretic structure in order to account for some subtleties of *wh*-movement differences between Kashmiri and Yiddish. I shall leave that issue for future research.

4.5 Deriving Word Order(s) in Kashmiri

4.5.1 V2 Order

In Section 4.2 it was observed that Kashmiri allows V2 in both root and embedded clauses. We present below some more data to illustrate verb movement in both root and non-root contexts.[10]

(55) a. laRkan **por** az akhbaar
boy(E) read-Perf today newspaper
The boy read the newspaper today.

b. az **por** laRkan akhbaar
today read-Perf boy(E) newpaper
The boy read the newspaper today.

c. akhbaar **por** laRkan az
newpaper read-Perf boy(E) today
The boy read the newspaper today.

d. me chi patah **ki** laRkan **por** az
I(D) aux know that boy(E) read-Perf today
akhbaar
newspaper
I know that the boy read the newpaper today.

e. me chi patah **ki** az **por** laRkan
I(D) aux know that today read-Perf boy(E)
akhbaar
newspaper
I know that the boy read the newpaper today.

f. me chi patah **ki** akhbaar **por** az
I(D) aux know that newspaper read-Perf today
laRkan
boy(E)
I know that the boy read the newpaper today.

---

[10]V1 orders, restricted in use to only Yes/No questions and Imperatives as shown in (i) and (ii), are not discussed. Nothing in the analysis hinges on this data.

(i) Speaker A: **khyoon-aa** batI **khyooth-aa** batI
ate-3sg-Q rice ate-2sg-Q rice
Did s/he eat rice? Did you eat rice?

Speaker B: aa, **khyoon** **aa, khyoom**
Yes, ate-3sg Yes, ate-2sg
Yes, s/he ate. Yes, I ate.

(ii) **kar** panin kaam
do self's work
(Do your work!)

Unlike root clauses, embedded clauses with V2 begin with the lexeme *ki*, which is taken to be the complementizer in most accounts of Kashmiri and other Indic languages. We propose here that *ki* is a simple marker of subordination. Therefore, only the subordinate clause has an additional layer of structure above the MP, but both clauses possess a verbal M node, which is responsible for the observed V2 in both root and subordinate clauses.

(56)

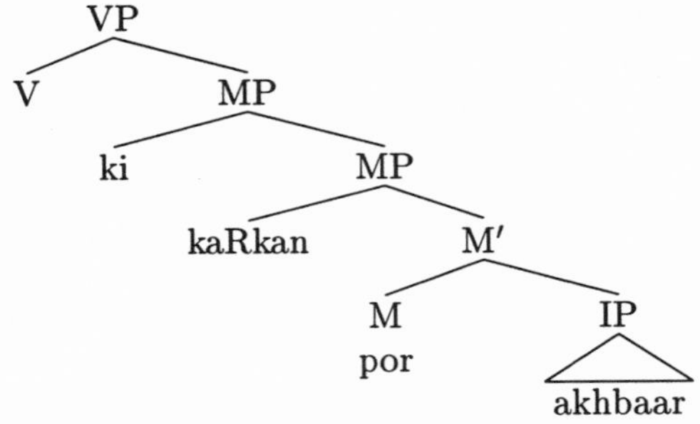

4.5.2 *Wh*-movement: V3 Order

In Kashmiri, the element *ki* has always proved problematic when viewed as an item parallel to the comlementizer 'that', for in indirect questions, the *wh*-word *follows* these lexemes rather than preceding it (as it should under the CP analysis). I show an example of the relative ordering of the *wh*-phrase and the subordinator in Kashmiri to illustrate this point.

(57)	a.	tse	chay	khabar	**ki**	**kyaa**	kor	tem
		you	aux	know	that	what	did	he
		Do you know what he did?						
	b.	*tse	chay	khabar	**kyaa**	**ki**	kor	tem
		you	aux	know	what	that	did	he

We can account for this contrast in the following manner. It is natural to assume that the *wh*-phrase, when it moves in syntax, moves to the Spec of the head that carries Mood information, since the *wh*-phrase is sensitive to clause-type, and we can assume that this sensitivity is reflected as Spec-Head agreement. Therefore, in Kashmiri, where Mood and Subordinator are kept apart in embedded clauses, the *wh*-phrase should move to the Spec of M, as shown in (58) below. This is also the head to which V moves in V2. This gives rise to *ki*–*wh*–*Vf* order, as desired.

(58)

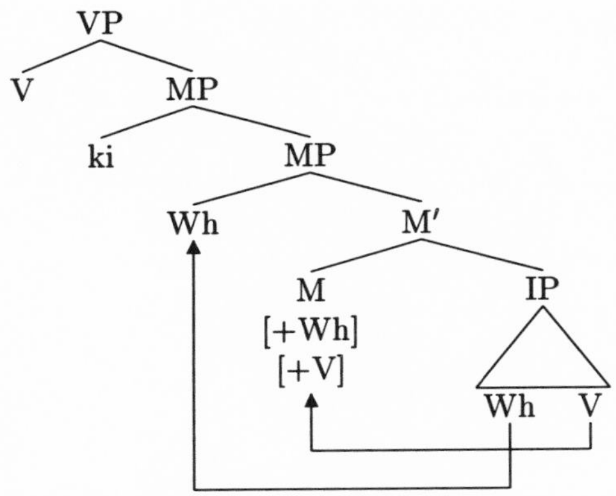

In addition to the V2 order found in declarative clauses in Kashmiri, we find other orders as well. V3 order is typically found with direct and indirect questions. Kashmiri *permits* direct and indirect questions to co-occur with topics yielding the surface V3 — Topic–*WH*–V — orders as shown below in (59). I suggest that the V3 order, found in topicalized structures like (59), are derived simply by adjoining some XP to MP.[11]

(59) a. tem **kyaa** kor
he what did
What did he do?

b. tse chay khabar **ki** tem **kyaa** kor
you aux know that he what did
Do you know what he did?

4.5.3 V-final Order

Another aspect of Kashmiri syntax which would otherwise remain a puzzle receives an explanation in our approach. While we have treated Kashmiri as a language that exhibits V2 even in subordinate contexts, there are, however, two situations where V2 is prohibited. This is in relative clauses and certain adverbial clauses.

(60) yus laRk tshawTh deer-yith **dyii**
which boy(N) trash throw-CP give-Fut
The boy who will throw (away) the trash.

[11]Kashmiri disallows multiple topics. In *Wh*-questions, only one constituent can adjoin to the pre-verbal focus position, which is occupied by the *Wh*-phrase. The preverbal ordering that Kashmiri allows is the following: Topic-Focus-V. I refrain from an elaborate discussion of this issue due to space restrictions; interested readrers are referred to Bhatt (1993).

(61) yelyi ba tshawth deeryith **dyim**
when I(N) trash throw-CP give-Fut
When I throw (away) the trash.

I believe it is possible to give a principled account of this behavior in my system. The relative clause is introduced by a *wh*-element and the adverbial clauses are introduced by the lexeme *yelyi*. I propose that while Kashmiri dissociates Mood and Subordinator in *ki*-clauses, the introducers of RCs and AdvCs are lexemes which conflate both Mood and Subordinator. If this is the case, I predict these clauses to behave like embedded clauses in German, showing no V2, since no Mood is available separately.[12]

5 Conclusion

In this paper I presented evidence from Binding, Weak-Crossover, and Constituent Fronting to argue that despite of the relative freedom in word order, Kashmiri has, contrary to Raina's claims, a configurational structure underlyingly: the IP-Spec asymmetrically c-commands the VP. I then examined the phrase structure order of Kashmiri and concluded that Kashmiri is underlyingly a verb-final (S–O–V) language. I proposed that the V2 order in main clauses is derived as a result of two operations: (i) finite verb movement to Mood, and (ii) some XP moving to the Spec of Mood. To account for the verb final order in relative clauses (RCs) and adverbial clauses (AdvCs), it was proposed that the introducers of RCs and AdvCs are lexemes which conflate both Mood and Subordinator. These clauses, therefore, behave like embedded clauses in German, showing no V2, since no Mood is available separately.

Acknowledgements

I wish to thank Alice Davison, Peter Hook, Tracy King, Beatrice Santorini, James Yoon, and the four anonymous reviewers for their comments, suggestions, and help in various ways.

References

Baker, M. 1988. *Incorporation: A Theory of Grammatical Function Changing.* Chicago: University of Chicago Press.

Bayer, J. 1990. *Directionality of Government and Logical Form: A Study of Focussing Particles and Wh-Scope.* PhD dissertation, University of Konstanz.

[12]To account for the data in (39) I shall have to assume an optional verb movement to Infl in relative and adverbial clauses.

Bhatt, R.M. 1993. *Word Order and Case in Kashmiri.* PhD dissertation, University of Illinois, Urbana.

Bhatt, R.M., and J. Yoon. 1992. On the Composition of Comp and Parameters of V2. In D. Bates (Ed.), *Proceedings of the Tenth West Coast Conference on Formal Linguistics.*

Chomsky, N. 1981. *Lectures on Government and Binding.* Dordrecht: Foris.

Chomsky, N. 1986. *Barriers.* Cambridge: MIT Press.

Chomsky, N. 1989. Some Notes on Economy of Derivation and Representation. In I. Laka and A. Mahajan (Eds.), *MIT Working Papers in Linguistics* 10:43–74.

Davison, A. 1991. Feature percolation and Agreement in Hindi-Urdu. Presented at the *South Asian Conference*, University of Wisconsin.

Davison, A. 1992. Lexical Projection, Case and Clause Adjunction: Another View of 'Case Resistance'. Ms., University of Iowa.

Diesing, M. 1990. Verb Movement and the Subject Position in Yiddish. *Natural Language and Linguistic Theory* 8:41–79.

Farmer, A. 1984. *Modularity in Syntax.* Cambridge: MIT Press.

Fukui, N., and M. Speas. 1986. Specifiers and Projections. *MIT Working Papers in Linguistics* 8:128–172.

Grierson, G.M. 1919. *The Linguistic Survey of India* Vol. VII, Part II. Calcutta, India.

Grimshaw, J. 1991. Extended Projections. Ms., Brandeis University.

Haider H., and M. Prinzhorn (Eds.). *Verb Second Phenomena in Germanic Languages.* Dordrecht: Foris.

Hale K. 1982. Preliminary Remarks on Configurationality. *Proceedings of the North Eastern Linguistics Society* 12:86–96.

Hale, K. 1983. Walpiri and the Grammar of Non-configurational Languages. *Natural Language and Linguistic Theory* 1:5–47.

Hook, P.E. 1984. Further Observations on Kashmiri Word Order. In O.N.Koul and P.E. Hook (Eds.), *Aspects of Kashmiri Linguistics*, 145–153. New Delhi: Bahri.

Hook, P.E., and O.N. Koul. 1992. Reflexive Possessives in Kashmiri and Hindi-Urdu: Evidence for an Antecedency and Hierarchy. *South Asian Language Review* 2(1):68–83.

Jackendoff, R. 1977. *X-Bar Syntax: A Study of Phrase Structure.* Cambridge: MIT Press.

Jelinek, E. 1984. Empty Categories, Case, and Configurationality. *Natural Language and Linguistic Theory* 2:39–76.

Kachru, B. B. 1969. *A Reference Grammar of Kashmiri.* Illinois: University of Illinois Press.

Kitagawa, Y. 1986. *Subjects in Japanese and English.* PhD dissertation, University of Massachusetts, Amherst.

Koopman, H. 1983. *The Syntax of Verbs.* Dordrecht: Foris.

Koopman, H., and D. Sportiche. 1982. Variables and the Bijection Principle. *The Linguistic Review* 2:139–160.

Koopman, H., and D. Sportiche. 1988. Subjects. Ms., University of California, Los Angeles.

Mahajan, A. 1990. *The A/A' Distinction and Movement Theory.* PhD dissertation, MIT.

Masica, C. 1976. *Defining a Linguistic Area: South Asia.* Chicago: University of Chicago Press.

Mohanan, K.P. 1983. Lexical and Configurational Structures. *The Linguistic Review* 3:113–139.

Platzack, C. 1986. The Position of the Finite Verb in Swedish. In H. Haider and M. Prinzhorn (Eds.), *Verb Second Phenomena in Germanic Languages*, 27–48. Dordrecht: Foris.

Raina, A. 1991. *An S-Selection Approach to Grammar: Some Issues in Kashmiri Syntax.* PhD dissertation, Indian Institute of Technology.

Speas, M. 1990. *Phrase Structure in Natural Language.* Dordrecht: Kluwer.

Stowell, T. 1981. *Origins of Phrase Structure.* PhD dissertation, MIT.

Subbarao, K.V. 1984. Word Order in Kashmiri: Some Further Evidence. In O.N. Koul and P.E. Hook (Eds.), *Aspects of Kashmiri Linguistics*, 136–144. New Delhi: Bahri.

Syeed, S. M. 1984. *Morphological Causatives and the Problems of the Transformational Approach.* PhD dissertation, Indiana University, Bloomington.

Taraldsen, K.T. 1986. On Verb Second and the Functional Content of Syntactic Categories. In H. Haider and M. Prinzhorn (Eds.). *Verb Second Phenomena in Germanic Languages*, 7–26. Dordrecht: Foris.

Thrainssen 1986. In H. Haider and M. Prinzhorn (Eds.). *Verb Second Phenomena in Germanic Languages.* Dordrecht: Foris.

Travis, L. 1984. *Parameters and Effects of Word Order Variation.* PhD dissertation, MIT.

Webelhuth, G. 1989. *Syntactic Saturation Phenomena and the Modern Germanic Languages.* PhD dissertation, University of Massachusetts, Amherst.

Weerman, F. 1989. *The V2 Conspiracy.* Dordrecht: Foris.

Williams, E. 1980. Predication. *Linguistic Inquiry* 11:203–238.

4

Complex Predicate Scrambling in Urdu

MIRIAM BUTT

1 Introduction

Complex Predicates in Urdu pose a problem for theories of syntax in that they challenge usual conceptions of the relationship between grammatical functions and phrase structure. The Urdu permissive, in particular, is difficult with regard to word order and constituency.[1] No clear consensus has been reached in the literature as to the exact defining characteristic of a complex predicate (Cattell 1984, Rosen 1989, Alsina 1993, Manning 1992), but the Urdu permissive is surprising because the data which suggest a complex predicate analysis are independent and orthogonal to facts about its phrase structure. I argue that the defining characteristic of a complex predicate must be stated in terms of grammatical functions: a complex predicate has only a single subject, contains no embedded grammatical functions, and thus parallels a simple predicate.

The Urdu permissive is illustrated in (1).[2] With regard to verb agreement, anaphora, and control, the infinitive *banaane* 'make' and

[1] I restrict myself to the dialect of Urdu spoken in Lahore. This dialect differs from other varieties of Urdu or Hindi (these two South Asian languages are so closely related that some researchers refer to them as Hindi-Urdu) found in India and Pakistan in some interesting ways. Not all of the scrambling data presented in this paper, for example, are possible for speakers of other dialects. The data in this paper are based primarily on two speakers from Lahore: Nadya Shah and Mumtaz Shahnawaz. I would like to thank them for serving as, more or less, patient informants.

[2] Abbreviations are as follows. F = feminine; M = masculine; Erg = ergative; Nom = nominative; Gen = genitive; Dat = dative; Acc = accusative; Inf = infinitive; Obl = oblique; Perf = perfect; Impf = imperfect; Fut = Future; Stat = stative;

Theoretical Perspectives on Word Order in South Asian Languages
Miriam Butt, Tracy Holloway King, Gillian Ramchand (Eds.)

the finite verb *diyaa* 'let' function as a single unit. Data from scrambling, negation, and coordination, on the other hand, present conflicting evidence as to what the phrase structure representation of (1) should be: the two predicates can form a constituent at phrase structure, but they need not.

(1) anjum=ne saddaf=ko haar
Anjum.F=Erg Saddaf.F=Dat necklace.M=Nom
banaa-ne di-yaa
make-Inf.Obl give-Perf.M.Sg
'Anjum let Saddaf make a necklace.'

The *Tell Construction* in (2) is superficially very similar to the Urdu permissive. However, it is not a complex predicate.

(2) anjum=ne saddaf=ko haar
Anjum.F=Erg Saddaf.F=Dat necklace.M=Nom
banaa-ne=ko kah-aa
make-Inf.Obl=Acc say-Perf.M.Sg
'Anjum told Saddaf to make a necklace.'

Unlike the permissive, the two predicates *banaane=ko kahaa* 'told to make' in (2) do not function as a single unit with regard to verb agreement, anaphora, and control. However, just as for the permissive, the data concerning the phrase structure of the Tell Construction are ambiguous. Scrambling, negation, and coordination suggest that the two verbs can be a constituent, but they can also head separate clauses.

This paper argues that a Lexical-Functional Grammar (LFG) approach allows a relatively simple analysis of the permissive vs. the Tell Construction. For one, LFG inherently allows for the possibility of flat structure. This is desirable as Urdu has fairly free word order, and scrambling is much more tractable under a flat structure approach than within a configurational approach. LFG also defines grammatical functions (subject, object, etc.) at a separate level from phrase structure. Information about phrase structure is represented at the level of c(onstituent)-structure. Grammatical functions, on the other hand, are defined at f(unctional)-structure. This separation of information provides the key to understanding the nature of the permissive in contrast to the Tell Construction in Urdu.

Pron = pronoun; Sg = Singular. A '-' indicates a morpheme boundary, while a '=' separates a clitic from a lexical item.

2 Complex vs. Single Predicate

2.1 Agreement

The agreement facts for simple sentences in Urdu are illustrated in (3). The basic pattern (see T. Mohanan (1990) for details) is that the verb agrees with its highest nominative (unmarked) argument.[3] When there is no nominative argument in the clause, the verb is inflected with the default masculine singular *-aa*.[4]

(3) a. **anjum** xat **lik^h-tii** hai
Anjum.**F**=Nom letter.M=Nom write-Impf.**F**.Sg is
'Anjum writes a letter.'

b. anjum=ne **xat** **lik^h-aa** hai
Anjum.F=Erg letter.**M**=Nom write-Perf.**M**.Sg is
'Anjum wrote a letter.'

c. anjum=ne **ciṭṭ^{h}ii** **lik^h-ii** hai
Anjum.F=Erg note.**F**=Nom write-Perf.**F**.Sg is
'Anjum wrote a note.'

d. anjum=ne ciṭṭ^{h}ii=ko **lik^h-aa** hai
Anjum.F=Erg note.F=Acc write-Perf.**M**.Sg is
'Anjum wrote the note.'

In (3a) the verb *lik^{h}tii* 'write' agrees in gender and number with the nominative feminine subject *Anjum*. When the case on the subject is non-nominative, as in (3b) and (3c), the verb agrees with the nominative object. In (3d) both the subject and the object have overt case; so the verb does not agree with either.

Agreement in Urdu is clause bound.[5] The sentences in (4) contain an embedded participial adverbial headed by *kar* 'having'. This participial adverbial must always be controlled by the subject of the matrix clause (see Davison (1985)). The pattern of verb agreement for the sentences in (4) indicates very clearly that the matrix verb only agrees with one of its own nominative matrix arguments. If there are no nominative matrix arguments, the verb carries the default inflection *-aa*. Thus, the matrix predicate *diyaa* 'gave' in (4c) does not agree with the nominative embedded argument *ṭofii* 'candy'.

---

[3]The "highest" here makes reference to grammatical functions. For example, subject is higher than object. It should also be noted that the nominative case in Urdu is phonologically null.

[4]Auxiliaries agree with nominative arguments in person, and number. The aspectual morphology on finite verbs reflects number and gender agreement. As auxiliaries are often optional, I do not include a discussion of auxiliary agreement in this paper.

[5]For analyses showing that "long distance" agreement in Urdu/Hindi is actually a case of local agreement see Butt (1993b), Davison (1991), and Mahajan (1989).

(4) a. **anjum** [naan xariid kar]
Anjum.F=Nom bread.M=Nom buy having
ciṭṭ^{h}ii saddaf=ko **de-gii**
note.F=Nom Saddaf.F=Dat give-Fut.F.Sg
'Anjum, having bought bread, will give Saddaf the note.'

b. anjum=ne [naan xariid kar]
Anjum.F=Erg bread.M=Nom buy having
ciṭṭ^{h}ii saddaf=ko **d-ii**
note.F=Nom Saddaf.F=Dat give-Perf.F.Sg
'Anjum, having bought bread, gave Saddaf the note.'

c. anjum=ne [**ṭofii** xariid kar] ciṭṭ^{h}ii=ko
Anjum.F=Erg toffee.F=Nom buy having note.F=Acc
kamre=mẽ saddaf=ko **di-yaa**
room=in Saddaf.F=Dat give-Perf.M.Sg
'Anjum, having bought candy, gave Saddaf the note
in the room.'

The patterns of agreement in (3) and (4) contrast a simple sentence and a sentence with an embedded participial adverbial, and provide a basis of comparison for the Tell Construction and the permissive. As shown in (5), the Tell Construction behaves exactly the same as the sentences in (4), which contain an embedded clause. Crucially, in (5b) the finite verb *kahaa* 'told', as in (4c), does not agree with the nominative feminine *ciṭṭ^{h}ii* 'note'. This indicates that the object *ciṭṭ^{h}ii* 'note' cannot be a matrix argument. Rather, it must be the argument of the embedded predicate *lik^{h}ne=ko* 'to write'.

(5) a. **anjum** saddaf=ko [xat
Anjum.F=Nom Saddaf.F=Dat letter.M=Nom
lik^{h}-ne=ko] **kah-tii** hai
write-Inf.Obl=Acc say-Impf.F.Sg is
'Anjum tells Saddaf to write a letter.'

b. anjum=ne saddaf=ko [**ciṭṭ^{h}ii**
Anjum.F=Erg Saddaf.F=Dat note.F=Nom
lik^{h}-ne=ko] **kah-aa**
write-Inf.Obl=Acc say-Perf.M.Sg
'Anjum told Saddaf to write a note.'

The permissive in (6), on the other hand, is exactly parallel to the simple sentences in (3). Examples (6b) and (6c) provide the crucial data. In (6b), the object *xat* 'letter' is masculine and so is the inflection on the verb. It could be argued that the masculine *-aa* on the verb is the default agreement marker, however, this argument is immediately refuted by (6c). Here the verb agrees with the feminine nominative object *ciṭṭ^{h}ii* 'note' Since the verb agrees with the object, the object cannot be embedded; it must be a matrix object. The permissive thus behaves as if it is a single clause headed by a single predicate, as in (3), and not as if it contains an embedded constituent, as in (4).

(6) a. **anjum** saddaf=ko xat
Anjum.F=Nom Saddaf.F=Dat letter.M=Nom
lik^h-ne **de-gii**
write-Inf.Obl give-Fut.F.Sg
'Anjum will let Saddaf write a letter.'

b. anjum=ne saddaf=ko **xat**
Anjum.F=Erg Saddaf.F=Dat letter.M=Nom
lik^h-ne **di-yaa**
write-Inf.Obl give-Perf.M.Sg
'Anjum let Saddaf write a letter.'

c. anjum=ne saddaf=ko **ciṭṭ^{h}ii** lik^h-ne
Anjum.F=Erg Saddaf.F=Dat note.F=Nom write-Inf.Obl
d-ii
give-Perf.F.Sg
'Anjum let Saddaf write a note.'

The permissive and the Tell Construction thus differ with respect to agreement. As will be seen, the agreement facts presented here remain constant under scrambling. The permissive and the Tell Construction turn out to have exactly the same scrambling possibilities, but no matter which possibility is examined, the agreement facts remain the same. Under the assumption that equivalent scrambling behavior is an indication of equivalent phrase structure, the invariability of the agreement facts demonstrates that the status of the permissive as a complex predicate cannot be represented at phrase structure. Although it is logically possible to argue that the permissive and the Tell Construction do have differing phrase structures, I maintain that the analysis presented in this paper provides a more straightforward theory of the structure of complex predicates.

2.2 Control

As already mentioned, the subject of a participial adverbial headed by *kar* 'having' must always be controlled by the matrix subject. It is only *Anjum*, the subject, who opens the door in (7), and never *Saddaf*, the object.

(7)

anjum=ne$_i$	saddaf=ko$_j$	[___$_{i,*j}$	darvaazaa	
Anjum.F=Erg	Saddaf.F=Acc		door.M=Nom	
k^{h}ol	kar]	andar	bula-yaa	
open	having	inside	call-Perf.M.Sg	

'Anjum, having opened the door, called to Saddaf to come in.'

The Tell Construction in (8) contains the participial adverbial *darvaazaa k^{h}ol kar* 'having opened the door'. Example (8) differs from the simple sentence in (7) in that both the matrix subject *Anjum* and the indirect object *Saddaf* are possible controllers of the participial adverbial.

(8)

anjum=ne$_i$	saddaf=ko$_j$	[___$_{i,j}$	darvaazaa	k^{h}ol
Anjum.F=Erg	Saddaf.F=Dat		door.M=Nom	open
kar]	samaan=ko	kamre=mẽ	rak^h-ne=ko	
having	luggage.M=Acc	room.M.Obl=in	put-Inf.Obl=Acc	
kah-aa				
say-Perf.M.Sg				

'Anjum told Saddaf to put the luggage in the room, after having opened the door.'

Recall from the previous section on agreement that the Tell Construction seems to have an embedded infinitive predicate. The data in (8) then are not surprising. Since *Anjum* is the subject of the matrix verb, and *Saddaf* controls the subject of the embedded infinitive *rak^{h}ne* 'to put', there are two possible controllers for the participial adverbial.

The permissive again differs from the Tell Construction. Example (9) is exactly parallel to the simple case in (7). As in (7), the object *Saddaf* cannot be a possible controller of the participial adverbial. This indicates that *Saddaf* in the permissive is not controlling a subject of the infinitive *rak^{h}ne* 'to put'; so, there is no embedded subject contributed by the infinitive predicate.[6]

(9)

anjum=ne$_i$	saddaf=ko$_j$	[___$_{i,*j}$	darvaazaa	
Anjum.F=Erg	Saddaf.F=Dat		door.M=Nom	
k^{h}ol	kar]	samaan=ko	kamre=mẽ	rak^h-ne
open	having	luggage.M=Acc	room.M=in	put-Inf.Obl
di-yaa				
give-Perf.M.Sg				

'Anjum, having opened the door, let Saddaf put the luggage in the room.'

[6] An anonymous reviewer points out that I could have used less complicated examples. However, as the reviewer points out, the control facts in Urdu/Hindi are also influenced by linear precedence and pragmatic factors. The examples in this section were chosen to control for this.

The permissive again exactly parallels the behavior of a simple predicate, while the Tell Construction behaves as if it contained a matrix verb and an embedded infinitive. Although the exact placement of the participial adverbial results in differing interpretations as to which of the possible controllers is preferred, the control facts essentially remain constant under scrambling as well.

2.3 Anaphora

A final bit of evidence for the view that only the permissive is a complex predicate comes from anaphora. The Urdu reflexive *apnaa* can only take a subject as its antecedent. The antecedent of the pronominal *us=kaa*, on the other hand, cannot be a subject.[7] T. Mohanan (1990) states this restriction at the level of f-structure: the antecedent for a pronominal cannot be an f-structure subject within the same minimal nucleus; the antecedent of the reflexive must be an f-structure subject within the same minimal nucleus. The examples in (10) illustrate this for a simple sentence.[8] In (10a) the reflexive *apnii* can only refer to the subject *Anjum*. The pronoun *us=kii* in (10b), on the other hand, can have anything but the subject as an antecedent.

(10) a. **anjum=ne**$_i$ adnaan=ko$_j$ **apn-ii**$_{i,*j}$ gaaṛii=mẽ
Anjum.F=Erg Adnan.M=Acc self's-F car.F=in
dek^h-aa
see-Perf.M.Sg
'Anjum saw Adnan in her (Anjum's) car.'

b. anjum=ne$_i$ **adnaan=ko**$_j$ **us=kii**$_{*i,j,k}$ gaaṛii=mẽ
Anjum.F=Erg Adnan.M=Acc Pron=Gen.F car.F=in
dek^h-aa
see-Perf.M.Sg
'Anjum saw Adnan in his (Adnan's or somebody else's) car.'

Contrasting the behavior of the permissive with that of the Tell Construction once again demonstrates clearly that the permissive is a complex predicate while the Tell Construction is not. In (11a) the

[7] This simple generalization is, of course, not all there is to Urdu anaphora but is sufficient for my purposes. For more detailed discussions of Hindi anaphora see Gurtu (1985), Subbarao (1984), and Davison (1990). An anonymous reviewer disputes the judgements presented here. While anaphora judgements are notoriously subject to much variation, I should point out that the judgements in this section are not only based on the Lahori dialect, but have been confirmed by speakers of various Hindi dialects.

[8] Both the reflexive *apnaa* and the pronominal *us=kaa* agree in number and gender with the noun they modify. The reflexive *apnaa* can also refer to *logical subject* within the same minimal domain of predication (T. Mohanan 1990). This does not directly concern me here.

reflexive *apnii* cannot refer to matrix subject *Anjum.*[9] The indirect object *Adnan* is the antecedent of *apnii* 'self' because it controls the subject of the embedded infinitive *calaane* 'to drive'.

(11) a. anjum=ne$_i$ **adnaan=ko**$_j$ [____ **apn-ii**$_{?*i,j}$
Anjum.F=Erg Adnan.M=Dat self's-F
gaaṛii calaa-ne=ko] kah-aa
car.F=Nom drive-Inf.Obl=Acc say-Perf.M.Sg
'Anjum told Adnan to drive self's (Adnan's) car.'

b. **anjum=ne**$_i$ **adnaan=ko**$_j$ [____ **us=kii**$_{i,j,k}$
Anjum.F=Erg Adnan.M=Dat Pron=Gen.F
gaaṛii calaa-ne=ko] kah-aa
car.F=Nom drive-Inf.Obl=Acc say-Perf.M.Sg
'Anjum told Adnan to drive his/her car.'

Unlike in (10b), the pronominal *us=kii* in (11b) can have either the matrix subject *Anjum*, or the indirect object *Adnan* as an antecedent. Because *Adnan* is a matrix argument (as well as the controller of the embedded subject), the pronominal *us=kii* has two possible referents outside of its domain: the matrix subject *Anjum* and the indirect matrix object *Adnan*. The pattern in (11) contrasts with the pattern for simple sentences in (10); so, it follows that the Tell Construction cannot be analyzed as a simple sentence. The permissive in (12), on the other hand, once again behaves like a simple sentence.

(12) a. **anjum=ne**$_i$ adnaan=ko$_j$ **apn-ii**$_{i,*j}$ gaaṛii
Anjum.F=Erg Adnan.M=Dat self's-F car.F=Nom
calaa-ne d-ii
drive-Inf.Obl give-Perf.F.Sg
'Anjum let Adnan drive self's (Anjum's) car.'

b. anjum=ne$_i$ **adnaan=ko**$_j$ **us=kii**$_{*i,j,k}$ gaaṛii
Anjum.F=Erg Adnan.M=Dat Pron=Gen.F car.F=Nom
calaa-ne d-ii
drive-Inf.Obl give-Perf.F.Sg
'Anjum let Adnan drive his car.'

Just as in (10a), the *apnii* 'self' in (12a) can refer to the subject *Anjum.* And in (12b), just as in (10b), the pronominal *us=kii* cannot refer to the subject *Anjum.* Possible antecedents for *us=kii* are either the non-subject argument *Adnan*, or another person specified in a previous

[9] Some speakers allow the reflexive to refer to the matrix subject under certain conditions. Harbert and Srivastav (1988) suggest that the data can be accounted for systematically by a distinction between argument and adjunct infinitival complements.

utterance. Thus, the permissive again behaves as if it is monoclausal, while the Tell Construction does not.

3 Phrase Structure Ambiguities

3.1 Scrambling

Word order in Urdu is relatively free.[10] T. Mohanan (1990) assumes that Hindi (Urdu) has a flat structure and accounts for scrambling as follows: only direct daughters of S can scramble freely. I follow T. Mohanan (1990) in assuming that Urdu has a flat structure. I further assume that Urdu has no VP node and analyze the Urdu predicate as a $\overline{\text{V}}$. The possible permutations of a simple Urdu sentence are shown in (13). The three elements in the sentence (*Anjum*, *Saddaf* and *dek^h aa* 'see') can appear in any order.

(13) a. [$_{NP}$ anjum=ne] [$_{NP}$ saddaf=ko] [$_{\overline{V}}$ dek^h-aa]
Anjum.F=Erg Saddaf.F=Acc see-Perf.M.Sg
'Anjum saw Saddaf.'

b. [saddaf=ko] [anjum=ne] [dek^h-aa]

c. [anjum=ne] [dek^h-aa] [saddaf=ko]

d. [dek^h-aa] [anjum=ne] [saddaf=ko]

e. [dek^h-aa] [saddaf=ko] [anjum=ne]

f. [saddaf=ko] [dek^h-aa] [anjum=ne]

As (14) demonstrates, lexical items cannot freely scramble out of or within phrasal constituents.[11] In (14a), the $\overline{\text{V}}$ contains three elements: a main verb *banaa* 'make', an aspect marker *rahii*, and an auxiliary *hai*. As (14b-f) show, any attempt to scramble the three elements within or out of the $\overline{\text{V}}$ produces an illformed result. Although not demonstrated here, the same is true for items contained within an NP.

(14) a. [$_{NP}$ anjum] [$_{NP}$ haar] [$_{\overline{V}}$ **banaa**
Anjum.F=Erg necklace.M=Nom make

---

[10]See Gambhir (1981) for a detailed discussion on Hindi word order and Mahajan (1990) for a configurational account for Hindi scrambling in terms of three different types of movements: X^0 Shift, Argument Shift, and Adjunction to XP. These movement mechanisms are not directly relevant to the issues in this paper because they do not attempt to account for complex predicate phenomena.

[11]It is possible to scramble out of finite embedded clauses as well. However, such 'long distance scrambling' is not the same type of scrambling observed in (13), or in the remainder of this paper. Mahajan (1990) and Srivastav (1991) distinguish topicalization from scrambling. Topicalization is claimed to occur across a clause boundary, while scrambling takes place within a clause. Gurtu (1985) in earlier work makes a similar distinction. Also see Dwivedi (1993) for a detailed examination of topicalization in Hindi.

rah-ii **hai]**
Stat-Perf.F.Sg is
'Anjum is making a necklace.'
b. *anjum haar [**rah-ii banaa hai**]
c. *anjum haar [**rah-ii hai banaa**]
d. *anjum [**hai**] haar [**banaa rah-ii**]
e. *anjum [**rah-ii hai**] haar [**banaa**]
f. *anjum [**banaa**] haar [**rah-ii hai**]
g. anjum [**banaa rah-ii hai**] haar

The only wellformed scrambled sentence is shown in (14g). In conjunction with the illformed examples in (14b-f), (14g) shows that it is only possible to scramble the entire $\overline{\mathrm{V}}$ within a finite clause. Under the assumption that scrambling depends on constituency, the data in (13) and (14) follow from the phrase structure I posit, and the generalization that only direct daughters of S can scramble. The next two sections compare the scrambling facts of the Tell Construction and the permissive with the facts presented for simple clauses in this section.

3.1.1 Tell Construction

Data from agreement, anaphora, and control indicated that the Tell Construction in (15a) should be analyzed as a matrix verb which takes an infinitival complement. Given these data, the assumption that Urdu does not have a VP, and the fact that infinitival clauses in Urdu/Hindi have the external distribution and characteristics of an NP (see Butt 1993a), the constituency structure indicated in (15a) is predicted for the Tell Construction. And indeed, as (15b) and (15c) show, the infinitive complement *ciṭṭ^{h}ii lik^{h}ne=ko* 'to write a note', does scramble as a constituent. Also notice that the agreement facts remain constant under scrambling: the matrix verb *kahaa* 'said' in (15) never agrees with the embedded *ciṭṭ^{h}ii* 'note'.

(15) a. [$_{NP}$anjum=ne] [$_{NP}$saddaf=ko] [$_{NP}$ciṭṭ^{h}ii
Anjum.F=Erg Saddaf.F=Dat note.F=Nom
lik^h-ne=ko] [$_{\overline{V}}$ **kah-aa]**
write-Inf.Obl=Acc say-Perf.M.Sg
'Anjum told Saddaf to write a note.'
b. anjum=ne **kah-aa** saddaf=ko [ciṭṭ^{h}ii **lik^h-ne=ko**]
c. anjum=ne [ciṭṭ^{h}ii **lik^h-ne=ko**] saddaf=ko **kah-aa**

However, as (16) shows, the infinitive and the finite verb can also scramble as a unit. Since the Tell Construction is not a complex predicate, there is no reason why the two predicates *lik^{h}ne=ko kahaa* 'told to write' should form a unit.

(16) a. anjum=ne saddaf=ko **[lik^{h}-ne=ko kah-aa]** ciṭṭ^{h}ii
b. anjum=ne **[lik^{h}-ne=ko kah-aa]** saddaf=ko ciṭṭ^{h}ii

It could be argued that the assumption that scrambling is a test for constituency is wrong. Perhaps it is the case that in sentences involving infinitive complements, anything can appear anywhere. The data in (17), however, show that this is not the case. If anything were allowed to appear anywhere, there is no explanation for why the sentences in (17) are ungrammatical.

(17) a. *anjum=ne saddaf=ko **lik^{h}-ne=ko** ciṭṭ^{h}ii **kah-aa**
b. *anjum=ne saddaf=ko ciṭṭ^{h}ii **kah-aa lik^{h}-ne=ko**
c. *anjum=ne **kah-aa** ciṭṭ^{h}ii saddaf=ko **lik^{h}-ne=ko**

A close examination of (15)–(17) reveals that scrambled versions of the Tell Construction are only wellformed under two circumstances: 1) if the infinitive complement is a constituent, as in (18a); 2) if the two predicates form a constituent, as in (18b).

(18) a. [$_{NP}$ anjum=ne] [$_{NP}$ saddaf=ko] [$_{NP}$ **ciṭṭ^{h}ii lik^{h}-ne]=ko** [$_{\overline{V}}$ kah-aa]
b. [$_{NP}$ anjum=ne] [$_{NP}$ saddaf=ko] [$_{NP}$ ciṭṭ^{h}ii] [$_{\overline{V}}$ **lik^{h}-ne=ko kah-aa**]

As the next section shows, the permissive patterns just like the Tell Construction with respect to scrambling.

3.1.2 Permissive

Example (19a) illustrates the constituency structure expected for the permissive as a complex predicate. Since the two predicates in the permissive were seen to function as a single predicate, one would expect them to behave as a unit in terms of phrase structure. However, as the data in (19)–(21) show, the scrambling pattern for the permissive is exactly the same as that of the Tell Construction in (15)–(17). And as with the Tell Construction, the permissive agreement facts are not affected by scrambling: the matrix verb *dii* 'let' always agrees with the nominative object *ciṭṭ^{h}ii* 'note'. This shows that *ciṭṭ^{h}ii* 'note' must be a matrix object.

(19) a. [$_{NP}$ anjum=ne] [$_{NP}$ saddaf=ko] [$_{NP}$ ciṭṭ^{h}ii]
Anjum.F=Erg Saddaf.F=Dat note.F=Nom
[$_{\overline{V}}$ **lik^{h}-ne d-ii**]
write-Inf.Obl give-Perf.F.Sg
'Anjum let Saddaf write a letter.'
b. anjum=ne **d-ii** saddaf=ko [ciṭṭ^{h}ii **lik^{h}-ne**]
c. anjum=ne [ciṭṭ^{h}ii **lik^{h}-ne**] saddaf=ko **d-ii**

In (19b) and (19c), the infinitive *likʰne* 'to write' scrambles as a unit with *ciṭṭʰii* 'note', the argument it contributes to the complex predicate. On the other hand, as (20) shows, the two predicates *likʰne dii* 'let write' can also be scrambled together as a unit. The pattern in (20) is what would be expected of a complex predicate. The pattern in (19) is not.

(20) a. anjum=ne saddaf=ko [**likʰ-ne d-ii**] ciṭṭʰii
     b. anjum=ne [**likʰ-ne d-ii**] saddaf=ko ciṭṭʰii

And as with the Tell Construction, it is not the case that any item can simply appear anywhere in a sentence. The examples in (21) are illformed precisely because neither the two predicates, nor the infinitive and its argument form a unit.

(21) a. *anjum=ne saddaf=ko **likʰ-ne** ciṭṭʰii **d-ii**
     b. *anjum=ne saddaf=ko ciṭṭʰii **d-ii likʰ-ne**
     c. *anjum=ne **d-ii** ciṭṭʰii saddaf=ko **likʰ-ne**

Just as for the Tell Construction, then, there seem to be two possible c-structure realizations for the permissive. Data from negation and coordination in the next sections provide further evidence that there are two possible c-structures for the permissive and the Tell Construction.

I should note that while the scrambling data presented here is not agreed on by every speaker of Urdu/Hindi, some dialects of Hindi (T. Mohanan, p.c.) and other dialects of Urdu (Dalrymple, p.c.) do confirm the pattern established above. An anonymous reviewer reports that in his/her dialect the permissive and the Tell Construction do not conform to the above pattern. However, this reviewer also reports that all the scrambled varieties in examples (14)–(21) are possible. This dialect would therefore seem to be an instance of 'anything can move anywhere'. I have no immediate analysis that would unify this dialect with the Lahori dialect reported here.

Aside from the dialect variations, I take it to be significant that the 'constituency paradox' described here has also been noticed for German infinitival complements (see Reape (1992) for a survey).[12] Furthermore, the German *lassen* 'let' has long been problematic because it is ambiguous in its "syntactic behaviour with respect to mono- and bisententiality" (see McKay (1985:12)). In particular, *lassen* 'let' patterns differently from other predicates taking infinitival complements in terms of reflexivization, negation, extraposition, and clitic movement (see McKay (1985)). I would argue that the constituency para-

[12] I thank an anonymous reviewer for drawing my attention to this fact.

dox found for German infinitival complements can be accounted for by positing two possible c-structure realizations, and that the particular properties of *lassen* 'let' can be attributed to the fact that it participates in complex predicate formation, just as the Urdu permissive.

3.2 Negation

The negative *nahĩĩ* can be used both for phrasal and clausal negation in Urdu/Hindi (see T. Mohanan (1992) and Dwivedi (1991) for details). The clausal, or sentential, negation illustrated in (22) is the one relevant to this paper.

(22) [anjum] [haar] [nahĩĩ [banaa
Anjum.F=Nom necklace.M=Nom not make
rah-ii hai]]
Stat-Perf.F.Sg is
'Anjum is not making a necklace.'

T. Mohanan's analysis, which I adopt, is that the negative appears to the left within a $\overline{\mathrm{V}}$ in sentential negation. For the Tell Construction, the prediction is that it should be possible to negate either of the two predicates. This prediction is borne out. The *nahĩĩ* 'not' can negate either the matrix verb, as in (23a), or it can negate the embedded infinitive, as in (23b). It can also be ambiguous as to which predicate is negated. This is illustrated in (23c).

(23) a. anjum saddaf=ko [haar
Anjum.F=Nom Saddaf.F=Dat necklace.M=Nom
banaa-ne=ko] nahĩĩ **kah-egii**
make-Inf.Obl=Acc not say-Fut.F.Sg
'Anjum will not tell Saddaf to make a necklace.'

b. anjum [haar nahĩĩ
Anjum.F=Nom necklace.M=Nom not
banaa-ne=ko] saddaf=ko **kah-egii**
make-Inf.Obl=Acc Saddaf.F=Dat say-Fut.F.Sg
'Anjum will tell Saddaf not to make a necklace.'

c. anjum saddaf=ko [nahĩĩ
Anjum.F=Nom Saddaf.F=Dat not
banaa-ne=ko kah-egii] haar
make-Inf.Obl=Acc say-Fut.F.Sg necklace.M=Nom
'Anjum will tell Saddaf not to make a necklace.'
'Anjum will not tell Saddaf to make a necklace.'

The permissive as a complex predicate pattern differently. Since the two predicates in the permissive appear to function as a unit, the prediction with regard to negation is that the negative should only be able to appear to the left of *both* the infinitive and the finite verb, as in (24c). However, the negative can appear between the two verbs and negate only the finite verb *degii* 'will let'. This is shown in (24a). In (24b), the negative can negate the infinitive separately when the infinitive and its argument form a constituent.[13]

(24) a. anjum saddaf=ko [haar
Anjum.F=Nom Saddaf.F=Dat necklace.M=Nom
banaa-ne] nahĩĩ **de-gii**
make-Inf.Obl not give-Fut.F.Sg
'Anjum will not let Saddaf make a necklace.'

b. anjum [haar nahĩĩ **banaa-ne**]
Anjum.F=Nom necklace.M=Nom not make-Inf.Obl
saddaf=ko **de-gii**
Saddaf.F=Dat give-Fut.F.Sg
'Anjum will let Saddaf not make a necklace.'

c. anjum saddaf=ko [nahĩĩ **banaa-ne**
Anjum.F=Nom Saddaf.F=Dat not make-Inf.Obl
de-gii] haar
give-Fut.F.Sg necklace.M=Nom
'Anjum will not let Saddaf make a necklace.'
'Anjum will let Saddaf not make a necklace.'

The fact that the two predicates in the permissive function as a single unit with respect to agreement, anaphora and control is again not reflected in the phrase structure. With regard to negation, as well as scrambling, the infinitive and the finite verb may form a constituent, but they need not.

3.3 Coordination

Anything that is a constituent can be coordinated in Urdu. If something is not conjoinable, then it is not a constituent. However, it is not necessarily true that if something can be coordinated it must form a constituent. The constraint on coordination must be stated as: If something is a constituent, it can undergo coordination. The examples in (25) illustrate a simple case. In (25a), two NPs are coordinated and the result is wellformed. One NP consists of an adjective and a noun, *garm anḍe* 'hot eggs', while the other consists of only the noun *roṭii* 'bread'. In (25b), on the other hand, items from different constituents

[13]It is furthermore possible to negate both the infinitive and the finite verb simultaneously by placing a *nahĩĩ* 'not' in front of each predicate separately. That is, it is possible for the sentences in (23) and (24) to contain two negatives, where each negative takes scope over one of the predicates.

have been conjoined and the sentence is illformed. Here the object *haar* 'necklace' and a part of the predicate, the main verb *banaa* 'make', are conjoined with the object *xat* 'letter' and the verb *lik*^{h} 'write'. Each main verb forms a constituent with the auxiliaries *rahii hai*. As the auxiliaries are not included in the coordination, the result is illformed.

(25) a. anjum [[garm anḍe] aur
Anjum.F=Nom hot eggs.M.Obl=Nom and
[roṭii]] xariid-tii hai
bread.F=Nom buy-Impf.F.Sg is
'Anjum buys hot eggs and bread.'

b. *anjum [haar banaa] aur
Anjum.F=Nom necklace.M=Nom make and
[xat lik^h] rah-ii hai
letter.M=Nom write Stat-Perf.F.Sg is
'Anjum is making a necklace and writing a letter.'

The Tell Construction and the permissive both contrast with the data in (25b). As (26) shows, the Tell Construction allows two possibilities for coordination. In (26a) the infinitival complements (*haar banaane* 'make necklace' and *xat lik*^{h}*ne* 'write letter') can be conjoined. This is as expected, given that the Tell Construction is not a complex predicate. However, in (26b) two predicates, an infinitive and a finite matrix verb, are coordinated with another two predicates. It would appear that the infinitive and the finite verb form a $\overline{V}$, and that in (26b) two $\overline{V}$s are coordinated.

(26) a. anjum=ne saddaf=ko [[haar
Anjum.F=Erg Saddaf.F=Dat necklace.M=Nom
banaa-ne=ko] aur [xat
make-Inf.Obl=Acc and letter.M=Nom
lik^h-ne=ko]] kah-aa
write-Inf.Obl=Acc say-Perf.M.Sg
'Anjum told Saddaf to make a necklace and write a letter.'

b. anjum=ne saddaf=ko roṭii
Anjum.F=Erg Saddaf.F=ko bread.F=Nom
[[xariid-ne=ko kah-aa] aur [k^{h}aa-ne=ko
buy-Inf.Obl=Acc say-Perf.M.Sg and eat-Inf.Obl=Acc
kah-aa]]
say-Perf.M.Sg
'Anjum told Saddaf to buy and eat bread.'

The permissive again displays exactly the same kind of pattern as the Tell Construction. The wellformedness of (27b) is not surprising because the infinitive and the finite verb are expected to form a constituent. However, it is not clear why (27a) should be possible, when (25b) is not. If the permissive is really functioning as a single predicate, its behavior with respect to coordination should be like that of the single predicate in (25b), and not like that of the two predicate Tell Construction in (26a).

(27) a. anjum=ne saddaf=ko [[haar
Anjum.F=Erg Saddaf.F=Dat necklace.M=Nom
banaa-ne] aur [xat lik^h-ne]]
make-Inf.Obl and letter.M=Nom write-Inf.Obl
di-yaa
give-Perf.M.Sg
'Anjum let Saddaf make a necklace and write a letter.'

b. anjum=ne saddaf=ko roṭii [[xariid-ne
Anjum.F=Erg Saddaf.F=Dat bread.F=Nom buy-Inf.Obl
d-ii] aur [k^{h}aa-ne d-ii]]
give-Perf.F.Sg and eat-Inf.Obl give-Perf.F.Sg
'Anjum let Saddaf buy and eat bread.'

The coordination data thus provide more evidence for two differing possible phrase structure realizations of both the permissive and the Tell Construction. Along with the scrambling and negation data, they show that the Tell Construction and the permissive cannot be differentiated in terms of phrase structure. In each case, the behavior of the permissive is exactly that of the Tell Construction. And yet the Tell Construction is not a complex predicate, while the permissive clearly is.

4 Analysis

The crucial difference between the permissive and the Tell Construction must be expressed in terms of grammatical functions. As LFG defines grammatical functions at a separate level from phrase structure, the differences and similarities between the permissive and the Tell Construction can be accounted for in terms of f-structure and c-structure properties. The fact that the permissive is a complex predicate while the Tell Construction is not is expressed at the level of f-structure. An abbreviated f-structure representation for the permissive in (28) is shown in (29).[14]

[14]The f-structure is abbreviated in the sense that I have only included the basic necessities. A complete f-structure would list such things as number, case, gender, tense, etc.

(28)

anjum=ne	saddaf=ko	ciṭṭ^{h}ii	lik^h-ne
Anjum.F=Erg	Saddaf.F=Dat	note.F=Nom	write-Inf.Obl
d-ii			
give-Perf.F.Sg			

'Anjum let Saddaf write a note.'

(29)

$$\left[\begin{array}{ll} \text{SUBJ} & [\ \text{PRED}\ \ \text{'Anjum'}\ ] \\ \text{OBJgo} & [\ \text{PRED}\ \ \text{'Saddaf'}\ ] \\ \text{PRED} & \text{'let-write} < \_\_ , \_\_ , \_\_ > \text{'} \\ \text{OBJ} & [\ \text{PRED}\ \ \text{'note'}\ ] \end{array}\right]$$

The f-structure of the permissive in (29) has a single PRED 'let-write'. There is only one subject, one object, and one indirect object. The permissive thus has a flat f-structure. The f-structure in (31) for the Tell Construction, on the other hand, contains two PREDs. Here the PRED 'say' takes an XCOMP as one of its arguments. This XCOMP in turn contains another argument taking PRED ('write'). The Tell Construction therefore has a complex f-structure. The data from agreement, anaphora, and control are accounted for completely at the level of f-structure. Recall that the permissive and the Tell Construction differ in that the Tell Construction has an embedded subject, while the permissive has no embedded arguments.

(30)

anjum=ne	saddaf=ko	ciṭṭ^{h}ii
Anjum.F=Erg	Saddaf.F=Dat	note.F=Nom
lik^h-ne=ko	kah-aa	
write-Inf.Obl=Acc	say-Perf.M.Sg	

'Anjum told Saddaf to write a note.'

(31)

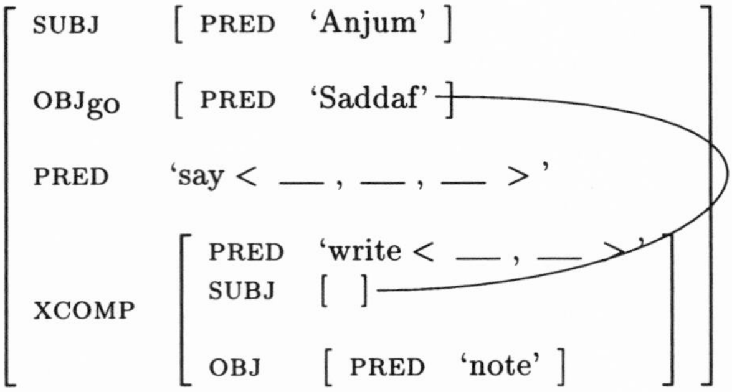

Although the permissive and the Tell Construction behaved exactly the same with regard to scrambling, negation, and coordination, these phenomena also suggested two differing phrase structures for both of the constructions. The separation of grammatical function information from phrase structure in LFG makes it possible for a given sentence to have more than one c-structure realization, as long as the requirements of completeness and coherence are met at f-structure. I therefore propose that the permissive and the Tell Construction simply be viewed as having two possible c-structure realizations. So both (32a) and (32b) are possible representations of the Tell Construction, and both (33a) and (33b) are possible realizations of the permissive. If it is granted that the permissive and the Tell Construction can be realized as either of the c-structures below, then their behavior with respect to scrambling, coordination, and negation is completely accounted for as well. Note that in the interests of space, the notations S, O, and XC have been used to indicate SUBJ, OBJ, and XCOMP in (32.

(32) a.

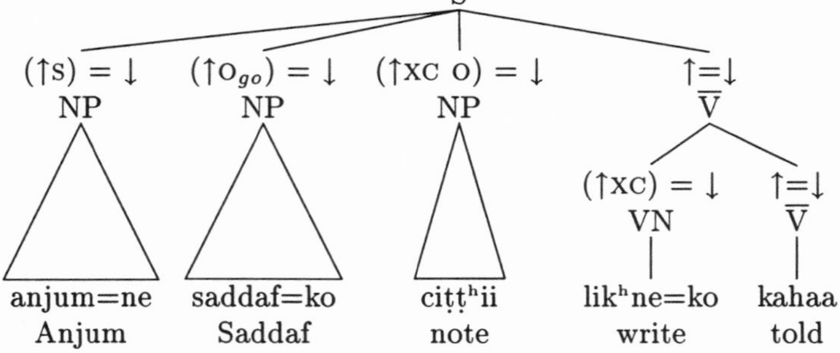

b.

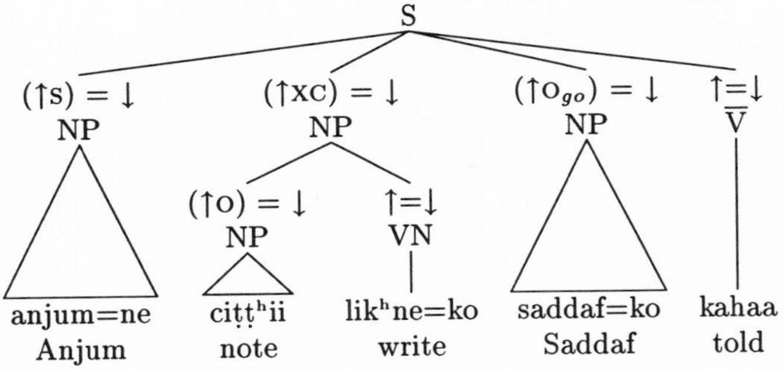

(33) a.

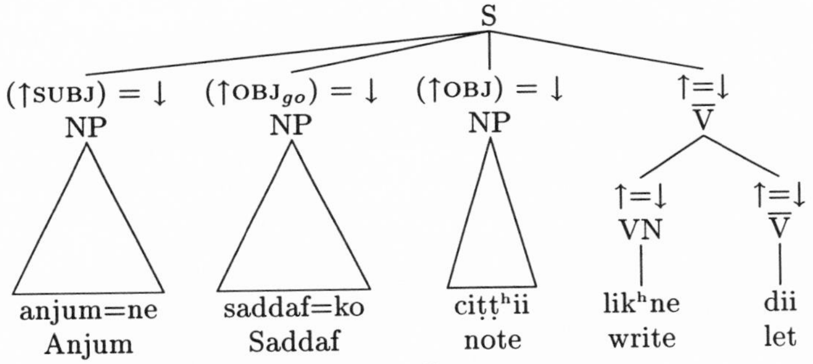

b.

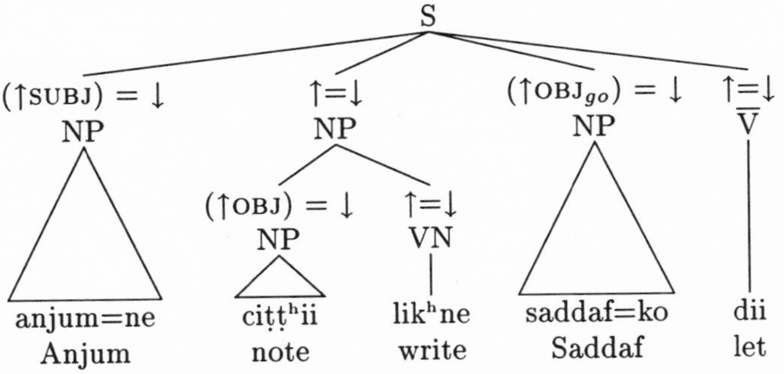

The fragment of phrase structure rules needed to produce the c-structures in (32) and (33) is shown in (34).

(34) a. S ⟶ NP*, (↑XCOMP* GF) = ↓   (NP), (↑XCOMP*) = ↓   V̄

b. V̄ ⟶ VN (↑XCOMP*) = ↓   V̄

c. $\overline{\text{V}} \longrightarrow$ V

d. NP $\longrightarrow$ NP* VN
$(\uparrow \text{GF}) = \downarrow$

These rules are, of course, only a subset of the phrase structure rules needed to account for the syntax of Urdu. But even for this small set of rules, some explanation is required. For one, I assume Urdu is flat and that only direct daughters of S can scramble. As (34a) allows direct daughters of S to appear in any order, no machinery other than (34a) is needed to account for scrambling in Urdu. A further point about (34a) and (34d) is that the notation $(\uparrow \text{XCOMP}^* \ \text{GF}) = \downarrow$ allows for recursion (see Ishikawa 1985 and Matsumoto 1992) and therefore also for the scrambling of arguments of more than one infinitive predicate. The notation 'GF' stands for 'grammatical function' and is used when the grammatical function a given NP is underdetermined. 'GF' thus ranges over subject, object, thematic (indirect) objects, and complements (XCOMP). This notation may at first glance appear to be too powerful, however, it is desirable as the scrambling behavior discussed in this paper is not restricted to the arguments of one infinitive and a finite verb, but applies to sentences like (35), in which more than one infinitive occurs, as well. As can be seen, the permissive agreement facts also hold in a more complex situation like (35): the finite verb *dii* 'let' agrees with the nominative argument *gaarii* 'car', which is subcategorized for by the predicate *calaane* 'drive'.

(35) anjum=ne saddaf=ko adnaan=ko gaarii
Anjum.F=Erg Saddaf.F=Dat Adnan.M=Dat car.F=Nom
calaa-ne de-ne di-yaa
drive-Inf.Obl give-Inf.Obl give-Perf.M.Sg
'Anjum let Saddaf let Adnan drive a car.'

As mentioned, the Urdu infinitives in this paper must be analyzed as verbal nouns which have been nominalized in the syntax. Infinitive constituents have the external distribution of an NP, but the infinitive predicate behaves like a V constituent internally (see Butt 1993c for a more detailed treatment). Lacking the space for an in-depth discussion of verbal nouns, I simply represent the infinitive predicate with the category label VN, and the infinitive constituent in the trees in (32b) and in (33b) as an NP.

The c-structures for the permissive in (33) ostensibly have two heads: the infinitive and the finite verb. Both predicates must combine in some way to form the single PRED 'let-write' at f-structure (see (29)). LFG, as originally formulated (Bresnan 1982), does not allow the combination of two c-structure predicates into a single f-structure PRED.

As such, the permissive poses a challenge for LFG despite the fact that the separation of grammatical function and constituency information into f-structure and c-structure provides the key for an analysis that can accurately account for the differences and similarities between the permissive and the Tell Construction. The ultimate solution to this problem lies at the level of a(rgument)-structure.[15] It is at this level that the argument structures of the infinitive and the finite verb combine to result in a single predicate at f-structure. Similar processes are suggested by Alsina and Joshi (1991) for causatives, and by Alsina (1993) and Rosen (1989) for Romance complex predicates.

A full analysis of complex predicate formation at a-structure and a theory of linking between a-structure, f-structure, and c-structure in LFG are worked out in Butt (1993c). Space limitations do not allow a detailed discussion here; so, I confine myself to a brief description. On the basis of evidence from another type of Urdu complex predicate, I argue for the need to adopt an elaborated a-structure based on Jackendoff's (1990) theory of Conceptual Semantics. Within this level of elaborated a-structure, I take the defining characteristic of a light verb like the Urdu permissive *de* 'let' to be that it contains a *transparent Event* at a-structure. The presence of a transparent Event at a-structure triggers complex predicate formation, which results in the fusion of two or more separate argument structures. The arguments of such a fused a-structure are mapped onto a flat (simple) f-structure, such as the one for the permissive in (29). A single PRED at f-structure, like *let-write*, indicates that complex predicate formation has taken place.

The verb *kah* 'say', on the other hand, subcategorizes for a 'real', non-transparent *Event* argument. Because the Event is not transparent, complex predicate formation is not triggered, and argument fusion does not take place. Correspondingly, there will be a PRED which subcategorizes for an XCOMP at f-structure. In this case there is an embedding of one argument structure within another, rather than a fusion of the argument structures, as with the permissive.

[15] Although a mechanical solution at the level of f-structure would at first seem more desirable, any such proposal is inadequate in the long run. An anonymous reviewer suggested having a H(eavy)-PRED versus a L(ight)-PRED distinction at f-structure to account for the permissive. Thus, an L-PRED *de*- 'give' would subcategorize for an H-PRED like *likʰ* 'write'. This type of solution breaks down as soon as more than one infinitive predicate, as in the sentence in (35), is encountered. In such sentences, there would then be two L-PRED's, one of which would somehow have to subcategorize for the other. One could fix this problem by introducing some new machinery, but in my opinion the mechanical mess that results is not a desirable solution.

In this way, both the permissive and the Tell Construction are accounted for. Both contain two predicates which each contribute an argument structure. In the case of the Tell Construction, one argument structure is embedded in the other. In the case of the permissive, two argument structures are fused. The Tell Construction and the permissive are therefore both complex at a-structure. As there is no difference between the two at c-structure, it is the level of f-structure which directly expresses the distinction between the complex predicate permissive and the non-complex predicate Tell Construction. A complex predicate is thus characterized by a complex a-structure which maps onto a flat f-structure. The precise c-structure realization of a complex predicate may or may not be complex.

5 Conclusion

This paper has examined two Urdu constructions: the permissive and the Tell Construction. The permissive was shown to be a complex predicate. The Tell Construction cannot be analyzed as a complex predicate despite its surface similarity to the permissive. Rather, it must consist of a matrix verb and an embedded infinitival complement. Furthermore, evidence from scrambling, negation, and coordination showed that the difference between the Tell Construction and the permissive cannot be expressed in terms of phrase structure. Rather, the notion of a complex predicate must be defined in terms of a-structure and f-structure: a given construction is a complex predicate only when it a complex argument structure corresponds to a flat f-structure.

Acknowledgements

Many thanks go to Joan Bresnan, Peter Sells, Tara Mohanan and Gillian Ramchand, and to several anonymous reviewers for their insightful comments.

References

Alsina, A. 1993. *Predicate Composition: A Theory of Syntactic Function Alternations.* PhD thesis, Stanford University.

Alsina, A., and S. Joshi. 1991. Parameters in Causative Constructions. In *Papers from the 27th Regional Meeting of the Chicago Linguistic Society* Part One: 1–16.

Bresnan, J. (Ed.). 1982. *The Mental Representation of Grammatical Relations.* Cambridge, MA: MIT Press.

Butt, M. 1993a. Hindi/Urdu Infinitives as NPs. *South Asian Language Review: Special Issue on Studies in Hindi-Urdu,* ed. Y. Kachru, Vol. 3(1):51–72.

Butt, M. 1993b. A Reanalysis of Long Distance Agreement in Urdu. To appear in *Proceedings of the 19th Annual Meeting of the Berkeley Linguistics Society.*

Butt, M. 1993c. *The Structure of Complex Predicates.* PhD thesis in progress, Stanford University.

Cattell, R. 1984. *Composite Predicates in English.* Syntax and Semantics, Volume 17. Sydney: Academic Press Australia.

Davison, A. 1985. Case and Control in Hindi-Urdu. *Studies in the Linguistic Sciences* 15(2):9–23.

Davison, A. 1990. Long distance syntactic anaphors in Hindi-Urdu. Presented at *Delhi University Conference on Pronouns and Anaphors.*

Davison, A. 1991. Feature percolation and agreement in Hindi-Urdu. Presented at the *South Asian Conference*, University of Wisconsin.

Dwivedi, V. 1991. Negation as a Functional Projection in Hindi. In *Proceedings of the 21st Western Conference on Linguistics*: 88–101.

Dwivedi, V. 1993. *Syntactic Dependencies and Relative Phrases in Hindi.* PhD thesis in progress, University of Massachusetts at Amherst.

Glassman, E. H. 1977. *Spoken Urdu.* Lahore: Nirali Kitaben.

Gambhir, V. 1981. *Syntactic Restrictions and Discourse Functions of Word Order in Standard Hindi.* PhD thesis, University of Pennsylvania.

Gurtu, M. 1985. *Anaphoric Relations in Hindi and English.* PhD thesis, Central Institute of English and Foreign Languages.

Harbert, W., and V. Srivastav. 1988. A Complement/Adjunct Asymmetry in Hindi and Other Languages. *Cornell Working Papers in Linguistics* 8:79–106.

Ishikawa, A. 1985. *Complex Predicates and Lexical Operations in Japanese.* PhD thesis, Stanford University.

Jackendoff, R. 1990. *Semantic Structures.* Cambridge, MA: The MIT Press.

Mahajan, A. 1989. Agreement and Agreement Phrases. *MIT Working Papers in Linguistics* 10:217–252.

Mahajan, A. 1990. *The A/A-Bar Distinction and Movement Theory.* PhD thesis, MIT.

Manning, C. 1992. Romance is so complex. Technical Report CSLI-92-168, CSLI: Stanford, CA.

Matsumoto, Y. 1992. *On the Wordhood of Complex Predicates in Japanese.* PhD thesis, Stanford University.

McKay, T. 1985. *Infinitival Complements in German.* Cambridge: Cambridge University Press.

Mohanan, T. 1990. *Arguments in Hindi.* PhD thesis, Stanford University.

Mohanan, T. 1992. Wordhood and lexicality: Noun Incorporation in Hindi. To appear in *Natural Language and Linguistic Theory.*

Reape, M. 1992. Getting Things in Order. Ms., University of Edinburgh.

Reape, M. 1990. A Theory of Word Order and Discontinuous Constituency in West Continental Germanic. In E. Engdahl and M. Reape (Eds.), *Parametric Variation in Germanic and Romance: Preliminary Investigations*, 25–40. DYANA Deliverable R1.1.A, Centre for Cognitive Science, University of Edinburgh.

Rosen, S. 1989. *Argument Structure and Complex Predicates.* PhD thesis, Brandeis University.

Subbarao, K.V. 1984. *Complementation and Hindi Syntax.* Delhi: Academic Publications.

Srivastav, V. 1991. *WH Dependencies in Hindi and the Theory of Grammar.* PhD thesis, Cornell University.

5

Topicalization in Hindi and the Correlative Construction

VEENA DWIVEDI

1 Introduction

The goal of this paper is to account for the topicalization paradigm that exists with respect to the different relative clause constructions in Hindi. Examples (1)–(3) show that there are three ways to translate the English sentence 'The girl who is standing is tall' in Hindi, (NB: the relative clause in each construction is italicized).[1]

(1) Left-adjoined:

jo	*laRkii*	*khaRii*	*hai*	**vo**	lambii	hai
REL	girl	standing	is	DEM	tall	is

(2) Right-adjoined:

vo	laRkii	lambii	hai	*jo*	*khaRii*	*hai*
DEM	girl	tall	is	REL	standing	is

(3) Embedded:

vo	laRkii	*jo*	*khaRii*	*hai*	lambii	hai
DEM	girl	REL	standing	is	tall	is

'The girl who is standing is tall.'
(taken from Srivastav 1991a:23)

I will show that the left-adjoined relative clause is transparent for topicalization constructions, in direct contrast to the right-adjoined relative clause, which is completely opaque. When the topic is a ref-

[1] The relative *j-* morpheme in Hindi is distinct from the interrogatives, which are k-words, e.g., *kisKO* 'who', *kahaaN* 'where'. In nominative case it is *jo* for singular and plural; in oblique case, *jis* and *jin*, respectively. The forms of the demonstrative are *vo* and *ve* in the nominative and *us* and *un* in the oblique. I follow Srivastav and gloss the relative morpheme as REL, and the demonstrative morpheme as DEM.

Theoretical Perspectives on Word Order in South Asian Languages
Miriam Butt, Tracy Holloway King, Gillian Ramchand (Eds.)

erential NP, the embedded relative supports the topicalization construction. Thus, there is a three way asymmetry in the topicalization paradigm I examine.

I make two crucial assumptions in accounting for the above mentioned paradigm. First, I assume the syntactic structures that Srivastav (1991a,b) assigns to (1)–(3).[2] Second, I assume that the syntactic analysis of the topicalization construction in Hindi is potentially ambiguous between a movement and non-movement relation. I assume that "topicalization" of referential NPs is another form of Left Dislocation, which I term *Topic Dislocation.* The "resumptive pronoun" is small pro that is bound by a topic in a non-argument position. The empty category associated with all other XP topics (including non-referential NPs) is a trace. This type of topicalization, referred to simply as *Topicalization*, is an instance of trace-binding, in contrast to the former type just mentioned, which is pro-binding. For a more detailed exposition of these assumptions, see Dwivedi (forthcoming, Chapter 2). Table 1 summarizes the differences between these two types of topics.

Table 1: Topic Dislocation vs. Topicalization

Topic Dislocation	Topicalization
Referential NP	Non-ref. NP, other XPs
Binds pro	Binds trace
Base generated	Moved
TopP (Ex. (7))	Adjoined to IP (Ex. (8))

The organization of this paper is as follows: Section 2 will go over further assumptions about Hindi syntax. In Section 3, I account for the topicalization facts with respect to trace binding for the three different types of relative clauses. There I appeal to a theory of government in the Government Binding theory of Chomsky (1986). In Section 4, I account for the topicalization facts of pro-binding, where I adopt the Path Theory of Pesetsky (1982). Section 5 concludes this paper.

[2]See Dwivedi (forthcoming, Chapters 3 and 4) where I rely on a different analysis than the one I present in this paper. There, I modify the structures of Srivastav (1991a,b). I claim that the correlative is a type of co-ordinate structure. Further, I posit that the right-adjoined relative is a type of afterthought restrictor, which is syntactically disconnected from the main clause.

2 Assumptions

2.1 The Syntax of Correlatives and Relatives

Srivastav (1991a,b) distinguishes the left adjoined relative clause (the correlative construction) from the right adjoined and embedded constructions. She claims that the left adjoined relative clause is a quantificational phrase, whereas the other two are modifier phrases. She captures the semantic similarity of the latter two clauses by assigning them related syntactic structures: the right adjoined clause is transformationally derived from the embedded construction. The structures she assigns to (1)–(3) are shown in (1a)–(3a):[3]

(1) a. Left-Adjoined

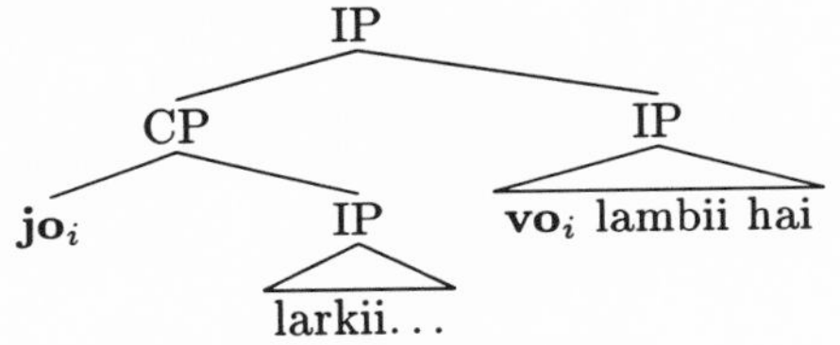

(2) a. Right-Adjoined

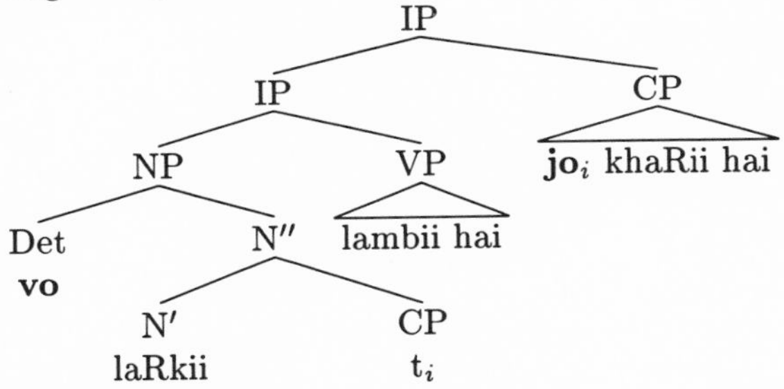

[3]The structure of the correlative construction in Indic languages has been subject to much investigation in the literature (cf. Verma 1966; Kachru 1973, 1978; Bach and Cooper 1978; Subbarao 1984, among others. See Srivastav 1991b for a complete list of references).

(3) a. Embedded

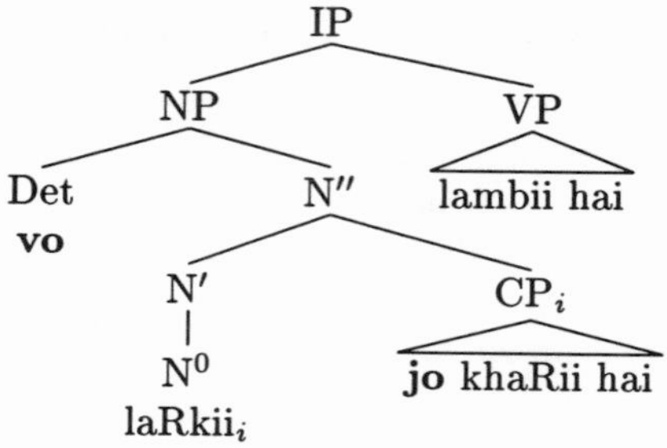

In (1)′ the left adjoined CP clause quantificationally binds the argument *vo*, which acts as a variable in the main IP clause. This is indicated by co-indexing.[4] The right adjoined and embedded relatives originate inside the noun phrase and restrict the interpretation of the head. Unlike the left adjoined relative, these relatives involve ordinary noun modification. This is a predication relation, indicated by co-indexing the relative clause with the head noun.[5] [6]

[4] *Jo* 'REl', does not actually bind the demonstrative *vo*. It is an operator that moves to an A′ position from its IP internal position. It binds its trace created by this movement only. Srivastav (1991b:677) maintains that it cannot bind *vo* for two reasons. First, as an operator it already is binding its trace, a variable. It cannot bind another variable under the Bijection Principle (Koopman and Sportiche 1982). Second, in order to have binding, c-command is required, and *jo* does not c-command *vo*. Thus the claim is that it is the CP clause that binds the variable, not the operator *jo*.

[5] Note that Srivastav maintains that the relative clause is a sister to N′ rather than NP, as proposed elsewhere (Bach and Cooper 1978). This analysis distinguishes restrictive relatives from non-restrictive relatives, which she claims attach at the NP level (1991a, Sections 3.2, 3.3). Also, an anonymous reviewer questions why the determiner *vo* is adjoined to NP, rather than be a sister to N′. Srivastav (1991a:62–66) analyses the pronominal form *vo* as a determiner that heads a Determiner Phrase (DP) which takes an NP complement. After proposing this analysis (Srivastav 1991a:65) she reverts to calling the topmost XP an NP, which results in the structure shown above.

[6] An anonymous reviewer asks how we in fact know that the *vo* occurring with left adjoined clauses is a variable and an argument, while the other *vo*'s are determiners. While Srivastav never addresses this question directly, she presents the following arguments for her distinction. Modifying Subbarao (1984), Srivastav (1991b:650) claims that the "restriction on the main clause NP in the left adjoined structures is stricter than definiteness; the NP must contain a demonstrative." No such restriction is found for embedded and right adjoined structures. She interprets this asymmetry to support her syntactic structures; for left adjoined structures "[t]he demonstrative requirement follows from the fact that a base-generated relative clause, being a quantifier, must bind a variable, and the demonstrative provides this variable", (Srivastav 1991b:655).

As for the determiner analysis of *vo* in the noun modifying structures, Srivastav adapts Postal (1966), where it is proposed that pronouns are determiners. She

2.2 Topicalization

2.2.1 What is Topicalization?

Hindi behaves like a free word order language. Below, the six logical possibilities of SOV word order are shown for the sentence 'The girl hit the boy'.[7]

(4) larkiiNE larkeKO maraa
girl-Erg boy-Acc hit-Pf.0
'The girl hit the boy.'

a. maraa larkiiNE larkeKO
b. larkeKO larkiiNE maraa
c. maraa larkeKO larkiiNE
d. larkiiNE maraa larkeKO
e. larkeKO maraa larkiiNE

It is difficult to distinguish the operation of topicalization from that of scrambling (see Saito 1985 and Mahajan 1990 for relevant discussion). Scrambling has been used as a cover term for word order permutations in languages different than English. Meanwhile the term "topicalization" has referred to movement of an element to the left periphery of a sentence, an operation familiar to English. This permutation is usually associated with some change in meaning, which is represented at Logical Form by invoking a topic-focus structure (see Partee 1991). It is unclear whether the same interpretation results from scrambling configurations. A pertinent difference in interpretation is

---

admits that this is intuitively appealing for Hindi, since the demonstrative may always function as a determiner or a pronoun (e.g., *vo ciiz* 'that thing', *vo* 's/he'). Not going into the details of her arguments (cf. Srivastav 1991a:59–66) she proposes that *vo* in right adjoined and embedded structures is base generated in Det, as in (i):

(i) $[_{DP}$ $[_{Det}$ vo] $[_{NP}$ $[_{N'}$ larkii$[_{CP}$ ...]]]]
that girl

The head noun may be a small pro, in which case it would appear that the *vo* is an argument.

Finally, another anonymous reviewer notes the following interesting fact which supports Srivastav's distinction: the right adjoined relative and the embedded relative both allow the distal and proximate demonstratives, *yeh* and *vo*. However, the demonstrative used with the left adjoined relative can only be *vo*. That reviewer concludes that perhaps the demonstrative associated with the left adjoined relative is in fact a real cataphoric correlate, and not a determiner.

[7]The following abbreviations are used in the gloss: M, masculine; F, feminine; 0, default agreement (which is isomorphic to 3psg. masc.); Erg, ergative; Pf, perfective; Compl, completive aspect; Dat, dative; Acc, accusative; REL, relative marker *jo*; DEM, demonstrative *vo*; Obl, oblique; Hon, honorific; Emph, emphatic marker; Fut, future; Imp, imperfective; Pst, past; Pres, present; Prog, progressive marker; 1/2/3p., first/second/third person; Pl, plural; Inf, infinitive; /N/ indicates nasalization on the preceding vowel; /D/ retroflex /d/ or flap.

described in Mohanan (1990:15–17), where she describes that if a (indefinite) direct object is scrambled leftward in a sentence, it assumes a definite reading.

At this point in time, I do not have a definitive description of the difference between topicalization and scrambling in Hindi. For the purposes of this paper, I assume that topicalization occurs across clause boundaries (cf. Srivastav 1991a, Mahajan 1990, but see Mohanan 1990), whereas scrambling is a clause internal phenomenon.

The type of word order change examined in this paper can be translated in English as 'About that question, the girl who asked it will be giving a speech.' A discourse context that would support such a sentence would be something like the following: Suppose that you are at a convention. There is a speaker at the podium answering questions from the audience. One person asks a really good question. So you and your friend start talking about it. Then later you say something like, or it occurs to you that, 'Right, speaking of that question, the girl who asked it will later give a speech.' This is like the Japanese use of *-wa* topics (Kuno 1973). The form of that sentence in Hindi (for the embedded relative) is 'That question, the girl who asked it will later give a speech'.

2.2.2 The Syntax of Topicalization

Topics in Hindi may be of any category — NP (subject or object), Adv, VP. As such, in this paper I examine topicalization of subjects, objects, Adverbs, and Verbs for each relative clause construction.

Topicalization in Hindi is standardly assumed to be an instance of wh-movement (Mahajan 1990, Srivastav 1991a). I assume that, in contrast to topicalization in general, (referential) NP-topicalization is an instance of Topic Dislocation. This construction is just like Left Dislocation, except that the resumptive pronoun is small pro. I assume that Topic Dislocation and Left Dislocation are non-movement relations. The topic is base generated in a Topic Phrase position that is adjoined to CP and co-indexed with a pronominal. Topicalization, on the other hand, is an instance of IP adjunction.[8] [9]

I show two brief arguments for the pronominal nature of the gap

[8] Cf. Lasnik and Saito (1992). Also, see Dwivedi (forthcoming, Chapters 1 and 2) for further discussion.

[9] This analysis predicts that only one element may be topic dislocated (left dislocated) in Spec TopP, whereas more than one may topicalize and adjoin to IP (as per the structures in (7) and (8)). This is indeed the case.

(i) Topicalization

?*laRkiiNE*$_i$	*laRkeKO*$_j$	hame	lagtaa	hai	ki	e$_i$	maraa
girl-Erg	boy-Acc	me-Dat	seems	is	that		hit-Pf.0

associated with referential NP topics. Below, the relation between the NP topic and its empty category is contrasted with that of the wh-element and its trace. First, in (5) I show that the NP topic may escape the (strong) Complex NP island, whereas wh-fronting may not (NB: topicalized XPs are italicized):

(5) a. *RajuKO*$_i$ mujhe lagtaa hai ki [$_{NP}$vo laRkii
Raju-Acc me-Dat seems is that DEM girl
[$_{CP}$jisNE $\mathbf{e}_i$ maraa]] sawaal puuch rahii hai
REL-Obl.Erg hit-Pf.M question ask Prog.F is
'It seems to me that [that girl [who hit *Raju*]] is asking a question.'

b. **kisKO*$_i$ tumhe lagtaa hai...
who-Acc you-Dat seems is...
*'Who does it seem to you that [that girl [who hit **e**]] is asking a question?'

In (5a) the name *Raju* is topicalized from the embedded relative position, where it is the object of *maraa* 'hit'. In (5b) a wh-word cannot be related to that same position. Next, example (6) shows that referential NP-topics do not show standard weak crossover effects:

(6) *RajuKO*$_i$/*kisKO$_i$ [uskii$_i$ bahinKO] lagtaa hai ki
Raju-Acc who-Acc his/her sister-Dat seems is that
Supriya $\mathbf{e}_i$ pyaar kartii hai
Supriya love do-Imp.F is
'It seems to his$_i$ sister that Supriya loves *Raju*$_i$/**who*$_i$'.

The lack of weak crossover effects in (6) for the topic shows that it does not enter the same relation held between the wh-word and its trace. If what I argue to be pro were instead a wh-trace, the reason why referential NP topics may escape strong islands and not show weak cross over effects would be unexplained. As a result, I claim that the gap in these constructions is a base generated null argument pro which co-refers with an NP-topic. Thus the configuration mirrors Left Dislocation, except that the pronoun is silent. In fact, the breakdown of

---

$\mathbf{e}_j$, tabhii to sab laRkiyaaN has rahiiN haiN
so Emph ll girl.Pl laugh Prog.F.Pl be-Pres.Pl
'It seems to me that it's the girl who hit the boy, and that's why all the girls are laughing.'

(ii) Topic Dislocation
**SudhaNE*$_i$, *kitaab*$_j$, Ali samajhte hai ki [vo
Sudha-Erg book-Nom Ali-Nom understand is that DEM
laRkii [jisse $\mathbf{e}_i$ $\mathbf{e}_j$ dii]] bahut sundar hai
girl REL.Obl.Dat give-Pf.0 very beautiful is.

constituents that can bind small pro in Topic Dislocation constructions vs. those that cannot corresponds to which types of constituents can pro-drop in a sentence.[10] The syntactic structures I assume for these constructions are exemplified below:[11]

(7) Topic Dislocation

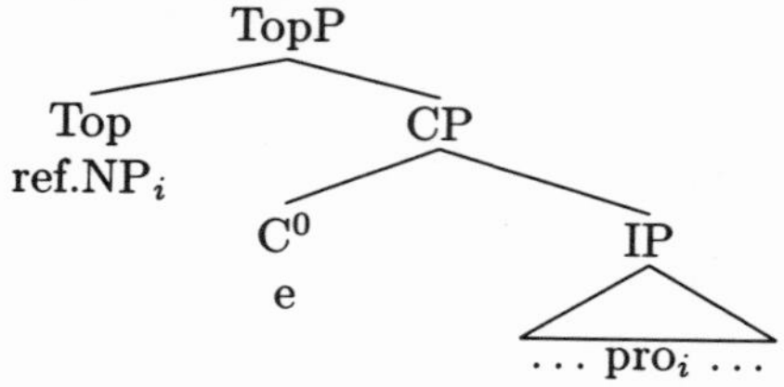

(8) Topicalization

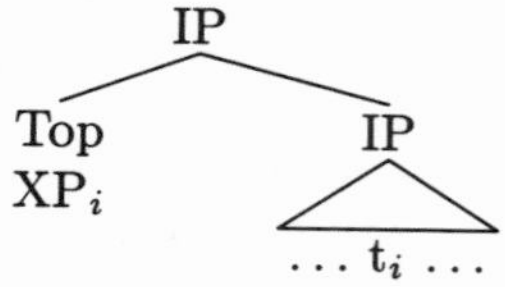

I will not go into detail beyond this. The generalization is that NPs that can refer when in topic position will bind a small pro; all other (non-referential) elements will bind a trace.[12]

Now that we have laid a foundation, we can examine the facts and give an analysis of them.

3 Trace Binding

3.1 Introduction

In this section, I examine topicalization of non-referential items as instances of trace binding. I will show that topicalization from the left adjoined construction (called 'L' in the table below) is always allowed, but embedded and right adjoined ('N' and 'R') constructions do not allow this long distance dependency. The facts are summarized below:

[10] See Dwivedi (forthcoming) for further elaboration.

[11] Left Dislocation in Hindi has the same structure as (7). The only difference between the two constructions is that there is an overt pronominal in Left Dislocation, and a null pronominal in Topic Dislocation.

[12] See Cinque (1990) and Postal (1992) for further discussion of the non-variable like behaviour of gaps in topicalization constructions.

Table 2: Trace binding possibilities for *jo*-relatives

	L	R	N
Adv	√	*	*
Verb	√	*	*
Non-ref. NPs	√	*	*

Below the sentences containing the topic gap are embedded in matrix sentences, *mujhe lagtaa hai ki...* 'it seems to me that...' or *usNE kahaa ki* 's/he said that...' in order to ensure that topicalization, and not scrambling is the phenomenon under study. The form of the data are as follows: the (a) sentence will be the non-topicalized version, and the (b) version will show the constituent under consideration as topicalized.

The topicalized element is italicized and its corresponding empty element is marked as a boldface **e**.

Left-adjoined relative

(9) a. mera khayaal hai [jo makaan tum khariidnaa
my.M feeling is REL house you buy-Inf
caahtii thii] [vo picle itvaarKO bik
want-Imp.F be-Pst.F DEM last Sunday-Acc sell
cukaa hai]
Compl.M is
'It seems to me that the house you wanted to buy was sold last Sunday.'
(Lit. 'It seems to me that which house you wanted to buy, that house was sold last Sunday.')
(adapted from Gambhir 1981, Ch.4, Ex. 141)

b. *khariidnaa* mera khayaal hai [jo makaan tum **e** caahtii thii] [vo picle itvaarKO bik cukaa hai]

In this example, the infinitival *khariidnaa* 'to buy' may topicalize from the left adjoined correlative. A discourse context that would support this word order would be a situation where two people are talking about buying things in general. A speaker would utter the above sentence in English as 'About buying, it seems to me that the house you wanted to buy was sold.' Below, the temporal adverb *kal*[13] 'yesterday' may also topicalize from the left correlative. Since the matrix sentence is

[13]Literally *kal* means 'one day away'. The tense of the verb in the sentence determines whether *kal* means 'tomorrow' or 'yesterday'. Hindi also has a term, *paDso* which means 'two days away'. Depending on the tense of the verb, it can take on past or future meaning.

in present tense, the adverb may not modify it; it is unambiguously modifying the relative *jo* clause.[14]

(10) a.

mujhe	lagtaa	hai	ki	[jis	kitaabKO	tum	kal
me-Dat	seems	is	that	REL-Obl	book-Acc	you	yest.
maaNg	rahe	the]	[vo	picle	itvaarKO		
ask	Prog.Pl	be-Pst.Pl	DEM	last	Sunday-Acc		
Mohan	maaNg	rahe	the]				
Mohan	ask	Prog.Pl	be-Pst.Pl				

'It seems to me that the book you were asking for yesterday was also asked for by Mohan.'
(Lit. 'It seems to me that which book you were asking for yesterday, that book Mohan was asking for last Sunday.')

b. *kal* mujhe lagtaa hai ki [jis kitaabKO tum e maaNg rahe the] [vo picle itvaarKO Mohan maaNg rahe the]

Next, the object NP *kuch kitaabeN* 'some books' may also topicalize from the left adjoined correlative:

(11) a.

mujhe	lagtaa	hai	ki	[jis	laRkiiNE	kuch
me-Dat	seems	is	that	REL-Obl	girl-Erg	some
kitaabeN	paDhiiN	hai]	[vo	baadme	bhaasar	
book-Pl	read-Pf.F.Pl	is	DEM	after	speech	
degii]						
give-Fut.F						

'It seems to me that the girl who is reading some books will later give a speech.'
(Lit. 'It seems to me which girl is reading some books, that one will later give a speech.')

b. *kuch kitaabeN* mujhe lagtaa hai ki [jis laRkiiNE e paDhiiN hai] [vo baadme bhaasar degii]

This apparent transparency with respect to topicalization is not found for the other types of relative clauses. In the sentences below, I show that for different constructions using the same sentences as above, top-

[14]Note that the 2nd person pronoun is grammatically plural, as is the honorific usage of any NP. Thus, there are two ways to say 'Amar is working', one in which the verbal agreement is masculine, as in (i), and one where the agreement is plural, as in (ii). The former agreement morphology indicates that Amar is a peer or junior to the speaker, whereas the latter indicates that he is senior (in position, age, rank) to the speaker.

(i)	Amar	kaam	kar	rahaa	hai
	Amar	work	do	Prog.M	be-Pres.3p.Sg.
(ii)	Amar	kaam	kar	rahe	haiN
	Amar	work	do	Prog.Pl	be-Pres.3p.Pl

icalization is illformed for verbs, adverbs and non-referential NPs from the right adjoined and embedded relative.[15]

Right adjoined relative

(12) a.

mera	khayaal	hai	ki	[vo	makaan	picle
my.M	feeling	is	that	DEM	house	last

itvaarKO	bik	cukaa	hai]	[jo	tum
Sunday-Acc	sell	Compl.M	is	REL	you

khariidnaa	caahtii	thii]
buy-Inf	want-Imp.F	be-Pst.F

Lit. 'My feeling is that that house got sold last Sunday which you wanted to buy.'

b. **khariidnaa* mera khayaal hai [vo makaan picle itvaarKO bik cukaa] [jo tum **e** caahtii thii]

(13) a.

mujhe	lagtaa	hai	ki	[vo	kitaab	picle
me-Dat	seems	is	that	DEM	book	last

itvaarKO	Mohan	maaNg	rahe	the]
Sunday-Acc	Mohan	ask-for	Prog.Pl	be-Pst.Pl

[jo	tumNE	kal	maaNgii]
REL	you-Erg	yest.	ask-for-Pf.F

Lit. 'It seems to me that that book that you were asking for yesterday was asked about last Sunday by Mohan.'

b. **Kal* mujhe lagtaa hai ki [vo kitaab Mohan picle itvaarKO maaNg rahe the] [jisKO tum **e** maaNg rahe the]

(14) a.

mujhe	lagtaa	hai	ki	[vo	laRkii	baadme	bhaasar
me-Dat	seems	is	that	DEM	girl	later	speech

degii]	[jisNE	kuch	kitaabeN	paDhiiN
give-Fut.F	REL-Obl.Erg	some	book-Pl	read-Pf.F.Pl

hai]
be-Pres.3p

Lit. 'It seems to me that the girl who read some books will later give a speech.'

b. **kuch kitaabeN* mujhe lagtaa hai ki [vo laRkii baadme bhaasar degii][jisNE **e** paDhiiN hai]

It is clear that the same constituents may not topicalize from the right adjoined constructions. Since I have assumed, following Srivastav (1991a,b), that the right adjoined relative is an extraposed clause, a plausible account of the facts above could appeal to the descriptive

[15]Since the sentences below are the other two ways that Hindi translates the English relative clause construction, only the literal meaning will be given.

theorem called the "Freezing Principle" (Wexler and Culicover 1980). The Freezing Principle says that once a constituent is moved, it cannot then have anything move from its non-base position. However, while this may serve as a good organising tool, it is not quite an adequate explanation. First, in Section 4 I show that even binding may not occur in that clause. This opacity would presumably need to be accounted for by something else. Second, I show below that the right adjoined clause patterns with the embedded clause with regards to topicalization of non-referential elements. A more elegant theory would explain what these two constructions have in common before using two separate theories to account for each construction (which would be entailed by a "Freezing Principle" account). Thus, below I show that the embedded relative is opaque for extraction:[16]

[16] I show in example (17) that while referential NPs (which include names) can escape embedded relatives, non-referential NPs, such as quantified NPs, cannot. This correlates with the fact that referential NPs may be dropped in a sentence, unlike quantified NPs, which may not. Argumenthood is not an issue here. As suggested by an anonymous reviewer, this is further shown by the fact that possessive NPs show exactly a similar pattern as above: whereas topicalising a possessive across a clause is possible from a left adjoined relative, it is completely impossible from the right adjoined and embedded constructions.

(i) *Left adjoined*

mujhe	lagtaa	hai	ki	jo	laRkii	mohan	kii
me-Dat	seem-Pf.0	is	that	REL	girl	Mohan	POSS

kitaab	paD	rahii	hai	vo	bahut	tez	hai
book	read	Prog-F	is	DEM	very	smart	is

'It seems to me that the girl who is reading Mohan's book is very smart.'
(Lit. 'It seems to me that which girl is reading Mohan's book, that girl is very smart.')

a. ?*mohan KII* mujhe lagtaa hai ki jo laRkii **e** kitaab paD rahi hai, vo bahut tez hai

(ii) *Right adjoined*

mujhe	lagtaa	hai	ki	vo	laRkii	bahut	tez
me-Dat	seem-Pf.0	is	that	DEM	girl	very	smart

hai	jo	mohan	KII	kitaab	paD	rahii	hai
is	REL	Mohan	POSS	book	read	Prog.F	is

a. **mohan KII* mujhe lagtaa hai ki vo laRkii bahut tez hai jo **e** kitaab paD rahii hai

(iii) *Embedded*
mujhe lagtaa hai ki vo laRkii jo mohanKII kitaab
paD rahii hai bahut tez hai

a. **mohanKII* mujhe lagtaa hai ki vo laRkii jo **e** kitaab paD rahii hai bahut tez hai

Embedded Relative

(15) a. usNE kahaa ki [vo makaan [jo tum
S/he-Erg say-Pf.0 that DEM house REL you
khariidnaa caahtii thii]] picle itvaarKO
buy-Inf want-Imp.F be-Pst.F last Sunday-Acc
bik cukaa hai
sell Compl.M is
Lit. 'S/he said that the house that you wanted to buy was sold last Sunday.'

b. **khariidnaa* usNE kahaa ki [vo makaan [jo tum **e** caahtii thii]] picle itvaarKO bik cukaa hai

(16) a. mujhe lagtaa hai ki [vo kitaab [jo tumNE
me-Dat seems is that DEM book REL you-Erg
kal maaNgii]] picle itvaarKO Mohan maaNg
yest. ask-for-Pf.F last Sunday-Acc Mohan ask-for
rahe the
Prog.Pl be-Pst.Pl
Lit. 'It seems to me that that book that you were asking for yesterday was asked about last Sunday by Mohan.'

b. **kal* mujhe lagtaa hai ki [vo kitaab[jo tumNE **e** maangii]] picle itvaarKO Mohan maaNg rahe the

(17) a. mujhe lagtaa hai ki [[vo laRkii [jisNE
me-Dat seems is that DEM girl REL-Obl.Erg
kuch kitaabeN paDhiiN hai]] baadme bhasar
some books read-Pf.F.Pl is after speech
degii]
give-Fut.F
'It seems to me that that girl who has read some books will give a speech later.'

b. * *kuch kitaabeN* mujhe lagtaa hai ki [[vo laRkii [jisNE **e** paDhii hai]] baadme bhasar degii]

Table 2 is repeated below in order to summarize the robust paradigm described above:

Table 2: Trace binding possibilities for *jo*-relatives

The facts are consistent with the fact that possessive NPs may not pro-drop in a sentence.

	L	R	N
Adv	√	*	*
Verb	√	*	*
Non-ref. NPs	√	*	*

Table 2 shows that the left adjoined *jo* clause is transparent for topicalization, whereas the right adjoined and embedded *jo* clauses are opaque to such a long distance dependency.

The above pattern looks strikingly similar to a set of facts discussed by Koster (1987).[17]

Although the exact constructions are not alike, I think that the fact that a similar array of data are found in a related language should not be ignored.

Like Koster, I propose to account for the pattern above using the notion of "directionaliy of government". Hindi is a head final language: the verb takes its complements to the the left. It is clear that the left adjoined relative is transparent with respect to topicalization, whereas the *right* adjoined and embedded relative (which occurs to the right of a head noun) are opaque. I propose that the first of these domains is a governed domain, and thus does not block extraction. The noun in the embedded relative is not a structural governor (see Koster 1987 and references therein) so the embedded *jo* clause is not governed.[18]

[17]Infinitival complements in Dutch may occur to the left, right and as "noun complements" according to Koster (1987, Chapter 3). He characterizes the three clauses in exactly the same way as Table 2: the left infinitival complement is "transparent" whereas the right (extraposed) infinitival complement and the noun complement are opaque. "It appears... that N-complements are opaque and behave like extraposed complements-and not like VR-complements [infinitivals to the left–VDD] in Dutch." (Koster 1987:140).

He accounts for the differences by adhering to a theory of directionality of government: verbs in Dutch may only govern to the left. When the infinitival complement is to the left of the verb, it is in a governed position. As such, it is transparent to government. When it is to the right of the verb, the clause is not governed. Also, nouns are not governors, so it is not governed there either.

"Extraposed complements are either opaque because they have a complementizer, or in principle transparent, but not affected by government from the matrix V, since this V governs only in the other direction. N-complements are not affected by government either, since Ns do not govern into complements in general. It is the notion of government, therefore, that ultimately explains the very complex distribution of facts..." (Koster 1987:141).

[18]Since I assume, following Koster (1987), that the noun is not a structural governor, it follows that the noun cannot assign case. The possibility of the noun being a potential case assigner was pointed out by an anonymous reviewer who proposed that the Freezing Principle account could be maintained on this assumption. It was proposed that CP relative clauses are base generated to the left of the nominal,

Since the right extraposed clause is to the right of the verb, it too is ungoverned.

There is a problem with the above account. The left adjoined *jo* clause is adjoined to IP and therefore not in a position where it could be governed by the verb, under the assumption that government requires sisterhood. Although it is on the correct "side" of V for government, at S-structure anyway, it is not in a position where it can be governed.

Elsewhere I have argued that verbs must move at S-structure to attach to aspect, and sometimes to Infl.[19] If the Verb is in Infl at S-structure, then it should be able to govern into the adjoined IP by (20). I show a partial tree structure for the sentence (11b), repeated here in (18):

(18) a.

mujhe	lagtaa	hai	ki	[jis	laRkiiNE	kuch
me-Dat	seems	is	that	REL-Obl	girl-Erg	some

kitaabeN	paDhiiN	hai]	[vo	baadme	bhaasar
book-Pl.Acc	read-Pf.F.Pl	is	DEM	after	speech

degii]
give-Fut.F

'It seems to me that the girl who is reading some books will later give a speech.'
(Lit. 'It seems to me which girl is reading some books, that one will later give a speech.')

b. *kuch kitaabeN* mujhe lagtaa hai ki [jis laRkiiNE e paDhiiN hai] [vo baadme bhaasar degii]

---

a potential case assigner. Due to the Case Resistance Principle of Stowell (1981), which disallows CPs from appearing in positions to which case is assigned, the CP relative would then right adjoin to NP. Since both the embedded and the right adjoined relatives are then assumed to be adjoined to NP and IP, respectively, a Freezing Principle type of account could work. However, this proposal rests on the assumption that the noun is a case assigner, which I assume to be untrue.

19 Dwivedi (1990), generals paper.

(19)

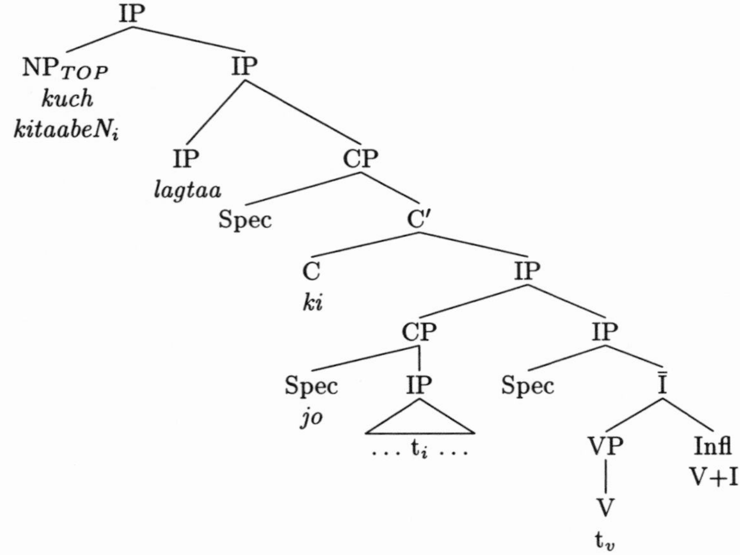

(20) Definition of government: α governs β if α does not dominate β and every γ (γ a maximal projection) that dominates α dominates β.

My claim is that from the position of I^0, the verb can govern[20] the CP *jo* clause. That is, in the adjunction structure above, Infl (=α) governs the CP (=β) since the maximal projection, γ that dominates α (IP) dominates β. This is only true if it is assumed that m-command does not distinguish between different segments of an adjunction structure. On that assumption, the left adjoined CP clause will indeed be governed. Though the right extraposed CP clause is adjoined to IP also, it remains ungoverned, since verbs in Hindi (like Dutch) do not govern to the right.

The above account is reminiscent of Huang's Condition on Extraction Domains, i.e., that they must be governed domains (Huang 1982:503).[21]

[20] See Chomsky 1986:8–9.

[21] Obviously I need to say something about *ki*-clauses which are to the right of the verb. *Ki*-clauses allow leftward scrambling of referential NPs (see Mahajan 1990, Srivastav 1991a). And in Dwivedi (forthcoming) it is demonstrated that verbs, adverbs, and non-referential NPs may also topicalize from there.

To account for this anomaly, I need to point out that *ki*-clauses are "potentially" arguments of the verb. Nonfinite clauses (which never have *ki*) occur to the left of the verb, unlike finite clauses which must occur to the right. Potentially then the *ki*-clause could be base generated as argument to V^0 and then extrapose (cf. Srivastav

4 Pro-binding

4.1 Introduction

In this section, I examine the topicalization of referential NPs only (Topic Dislocation facts). The hypothesis here is that when a referential NP is related to an empty position across an island, the empty position is a small pro, not a trace as was assumed above. Not unexpectedly, the facts for this type of construction are somewhat different from the trace binding type.

Table 3: pro-binding possibilities with respect to the different *jo* clauses

	L	R	N
subject	√	*	√
object	√	*	√

Hindi does not show subject-object asymmetries in general. It is clear that the difference between the different types of topicalization is that pro may be bound within a complex NP (embedded relative) construction, whereas a trace does not have this option.

Presumably this has to do with the fact that a trace can only be licensed in a governed domain. No such condition is found on potential anaphoric relations. That said, it is not clear why the right extraposed relative should not allow topicalization. I will present an analysis using Pesetsky's Path Containment Condition below.

First, let us examine the data.

Left adjoined relative

Subject

(21)	a.	mujhe	lagtaa	hai	ki	[jo	kissa	aapNE
		me-Dat	seems	is	that	REL	story	you.Hon-Erg
		abhii	sunaayaa]	[vo	Anu	pahle	bhii	sun
		just-now	tell-Pf.0	DEM	Anu	before	also	hear

1991a:47); or it could be linked to a pleonastic small pro argument of V^0. To make the account work, I would have to differentiate between adjuncts that are linked to arguments (as *ki*-clauses are) vs. adjuncts which are linked to non-arguments (as the right adjoined *jo*-clauses are). It seems that *ki*-clauses are able to be governed via the co-indexing relation that exists between its trace from movement or its co-referring pleonastic argument. See Dwivedi (forthcoming, Chapter 4), which avoids this problem altogether by offering a different syntactic analysis for *ki* clauses.

cukii hai]
Compl.F is
'The story which you told just now Anu has also heard that before.'
(Lit. 'It seems to me that which story you just told that story Anu has heard before.')
(adapted from Gambhir 1981, Ch. 4, Ex. 140)

b. *aapNE* mujhe lagtaa hai [jo kissa **e** abhii sunaayaa] [vo Anu pahle bhii sun cukii hai]

In the above example, the (ergative) subject pronoun of the left adjoined correlative is in the topic position and related to the empty category. It has a meaning like 'About you, the story that you just told, Anu has heard it before.' Below, the object of *puuchnaa* 'to ask' may also serve as a topic:[22]

Object

(22) a. mujhe lagtaa hai ki [jis laRkiiNE
me-Dat seems is that REL-Obl girl-Erg
sawaal puuchaa] [vo baadme bhaasar
question ask-Pf.M DEM after speech
degii]
give-Fut.F
'It seems to me that the girl who is asking a question will later give a speech.'
(Lit. 'It seems to me that which girl is asking a question that one will give a speech later.')

b. *yeh sawaal* mujhe lagtaa hai ki [jis laDkiiNE **e** puuchaa] [vo baadme bhaasar degii]

The discourse context of the sentence above is that Speaker A and B are talking about a certain question that was asked during some convention. Speaker A then says to B, 'By the way, about that question, the girl who asked it will later give a speech.' For the right adjoined construction below, we see that the same contrast holds as before: no long distance dependency may be held by this CP clause. It is completely opaque to any external syntactic dependency.[23]

[22]When NPs are topicalized, they must be unambiguously referential. This is marked by the determiner *yeh* 'this', or *voh* 'that'.

[23]Whereas there is some dialectical variability in terms of what can topicalize in general, I should mention that no matter what that variability might be for topicalising an element out of a left adjoined *jo* clause, topicalising out of the extraposed *jo* clause in the right adjoined (*vo-jo*) sentence is consistently illformed.

Right Adjoined relative

(23) a. mujhe lagtaa hai ki [vo kissa Anu
me-Dat seems is that DEM story Anu
pahle bhii sun cukii hai] [jo
before Emph hear Compl.F is REL
aapNE abhii sunaayaa thaa]
you.Hon-Erg now tell-Pf.0 be-Pst.M
Lit. 'It seems to me that that story that you just told, Anu has heard it before.'

b. **aapNE* mujhe lagtaa hai ki [vo kissa Anu pahle bhii sun cukii hai] [jo **e** abhii sunaayaa thaa]

(24) a. mujhe lagtaa hai ki [vo laRkii baadme
me-Dat seems is that DEM girl after
bhaasar degii] [jisNE sawaal
speech give-Fut.F REL-Obl.Erg question
puuchaa]
ask-Pf.0
Lit. 'It seems to me that that girl will give a speech later who is now asking a question.'

b. * *yeh sawaal* mujhe lagtaa hai ki [vo laRkii baadme bhasar degii] [jisNE **e** puuchaa]

It is clear that the same elements may not serve as topics when they are related to the *jo* clause that is right adjoined. Next I show that the embedded relative construction departs from its earlier role, where it patterned with the right adjoined relative. Now it patterns with the left adjoined relative. Topic Dislocation is possible from the embedded relative.

Embedded Relative

(25) a. mujhe lagtaa hai ki [$_{NP}$ vo kissa [$_{CP}$ jo
me-Dat seems is that DEM story REL
aapNE abhii sunaayaa thaa]] Anu
you.Hon-Erg now tell-Pf.0 be-Pst.M Anu
pahle bhii sun cukii hai
before Emph hear Compl.F is
Lit. 'It seems to me that that story which you just told now Anu has heard it before.'

b. *aapNE* mujhe lagtaa hai ki [vo kissa [jo **e** abhii sunaayaa thaa]] Anu pahle bhii sun cukii hai

This sentence has the same intuitive grammaticality as the corresponding left adjoined construction. The same is true below, for the object *yeh sawaal* 'this question'.

(26) a. mera khayaal hai ki [vo laDkii [jisNE
my feeling is that DEM girl REL-Erg
sawaal puuchaa]] baadme bhaasar degii
question ask-Pf.0 after speech give-Fut.F
Lit. 'My feeling is that that girl who asked a question will later give a speech.'

b. *yeh sawaal* mera khayaal hai ki [[vo laDkii [jisNE **e** puuchaa]] baadme bhaasar degii]

I repeat Table 3 below to summarize the data that I have presented above. Again, what is interesting to note is that the embedded relative now patterns with the left adjoined relative, and not the right adjoined relative. Further, given that I have analysed topicalization of referential NPs as an instance of Topic Dislocation, it is unclear why there should be any restrictions whatsoever.

Table 3: pro-binding possibilities with respect to the different *jo* clauses

	L	R	N
subject	√	*	√
object	√	*	√

I claim that the data can be accounted for in terms of the Path Containment Condition of Pesetsky (1982). His theory assumed that wh-traces are path creating, and essentially ignored small pro. Here I claim that A′ bound null pronouns are path creating also.

4.2 Review of Path Theory

In Chapter 3 of his dissertation, Pesetsky (1982) attempts to account for grammaticality contrasts that exist in sentences with multiple gaps associated with wh-movement. His theory relies on the notion of a *Path* that connects the gap with its antecedent. In the sentence below:

(27) Who did you see **e**?

(27) a.

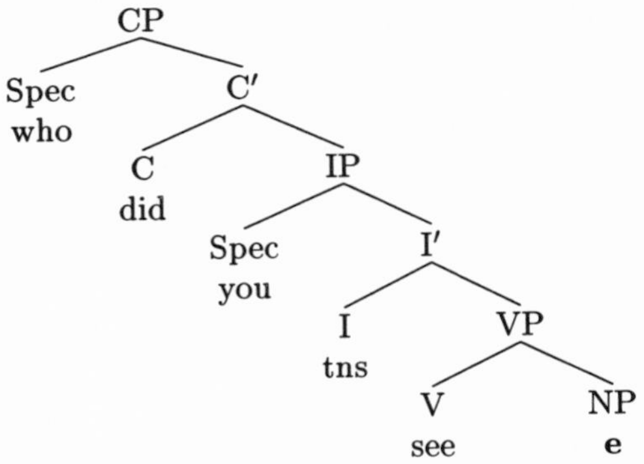

The path that connects the gap with its antecedent is {VP, I′, IP, C′, CP}. That is, the path consists of the first maximal projection dominating the gap to the first maximal projection dominating the antecedent. This is formally defined below:

(28) *Definition of Paths*
Suppose t is an empty category locally A′-bound by b. Then
(i) for α the first maximal projection dominating t
(ii) for β the first maximal projection dominating b
(iii) the *path between t and b* is the set of nodes P such that $P = \{x \mid (x{=}\alpha) \vee (x{=}\beta) \vee (x.\ \text{dom.}\ \alpha\ \&\ \neg\ \text{dom.}\ \beta)\}$ (Pesetsky 1982, 289).

Thus, "[a] path is essentially a line segment in a tree, which runs from the first maximal projection dominating a trace and the first maximal projection dominating its local A′ binder." (loc.cit.) Formally we might equally well conceive of paths as sets of line segments, i.e., as sets of *pairs* of nodes. That is, the path described above for (18) is formally {{VP, I′}, {I′, IP}, {IP, C′}, {C′, CP}}. Pesetsky does not differentiate between the two conceptions of paths, since it does not make any empirical difference to him (Pesetsky 1982:310). When there is more than one gap in a sentence, the following condition applies:[24]

(29) *Path Containment Condition*
If two paths overlap, one must contain the other.
(Pesetsky 1982:309)

That is, the intersection of paths is non-null.

[24]For the sets of nodes approach, this amounts to "If two paths have a non-null intersection, one must contain the other." (Pesetsky 1982:310)

4.3 The Path Containment Condition and Extraposed Relatives

In the appendix to Chapter 3, Pesetsky discusses expletive null pronouns that are co-indexed with their postverbal subject in Italian. He stipulates that these small pros do not create paths (Pesetsky 1982:486). The type of null pronoun under consideration here, in contrast, is referential. I suggest that Hindi A′ bound small pro is indeed path creating, perhaps due to its referential property. The path begins at the maximal projection that dominates pro and ends at the maximal projection that dominates the topic.

If we examine the schematic trees below, we see that connecting (subject) pro with its antecedent is rather straightfoward for the left adjoined and embedded relative constructions.

(30)

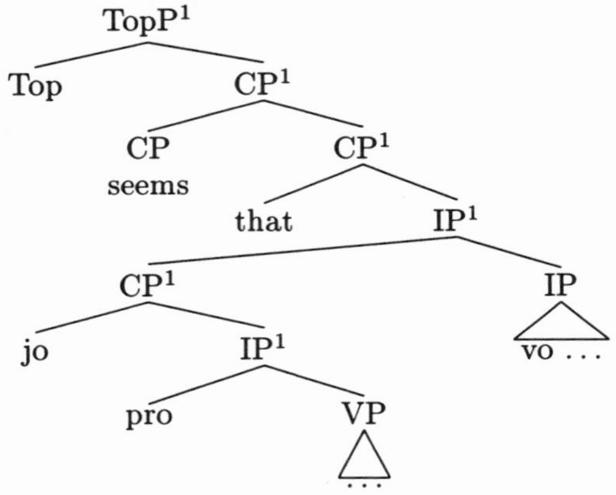

(31)

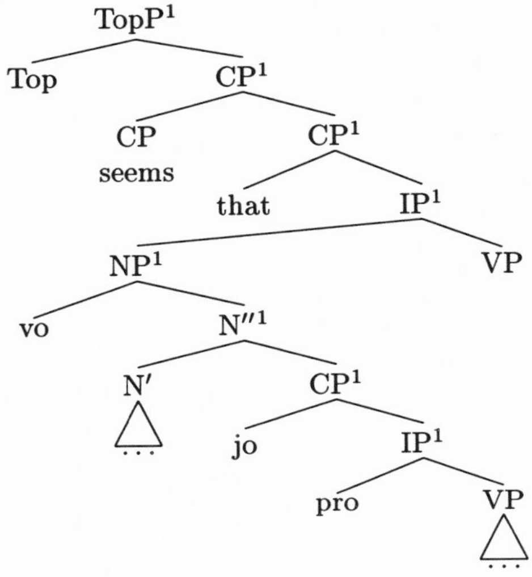

However, for the right adjoined clause, there are two gaps in the construction. One is the trace that marks the original position of the right extraposed CP *jo* clause. The other is pro in that clause.

If we draw the two paths below, we see that there is crossing between paths; that is, one path does not contain the other. The Path Containment Condition has been violated, and the ungrammaticality has been accounted for.

(32)

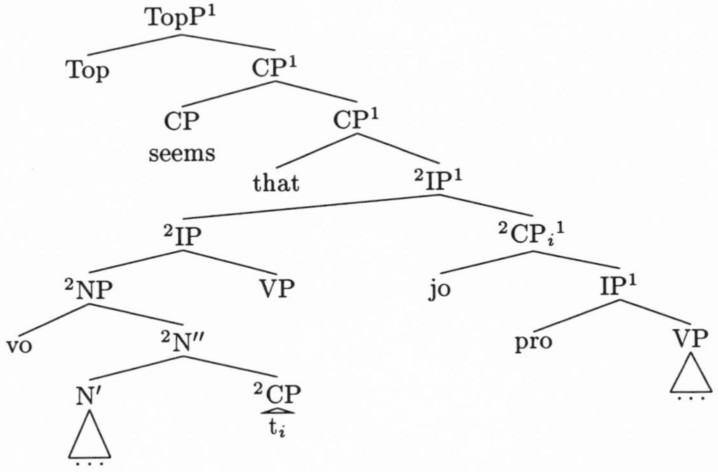

Thus the reason why small pro cannot occur in the right extraposed clause is because it is a gap that is path creating. Because the path that connects pro to its topic crosses the path between the moved CP and its trace, this construction is illformed.[25] The facts for object pro are exactly analogous; the only difference is that the path connecting pro with the topic is longer, since it starts at VP.

The extension of the PCC to pro raises interesting questions about the role of the PCC in the theory of grammar. It is clear from Pesetsky's discussion that the PCC is independent of other conditions in the grammar, such as the Empty Category Principle. And it is also clear that the PCC does not apply to overt pronouns. At a semantic level, it would be interesting to see whether the PCC corresponded to crossing different discourse domains at Discourse Representation Structure (Kamp 1981, Roberts 1987), at least in the Hindi cases discussed above. As the above account is a starting point, I leave these queries for further research.

5 Conclusion

In this paper I examined topicalization from the different types of relative clause constructions in Hindi. I showed that the left adjoined relative is transparent for topicalization of all types of constituents. The right adjoined relative is opaque for topicalization of any constituent. The embedded relative allows for topicalization of referential NPs only.

I accounted for the facts above by assuming two things; first, I assumed the structures proposed in Srivastav (1991a,b) for the relative constructions. Second, I assumed that "topicalization" in Hindi is an ambiguous construction: where the constituent has no referential properties (such as verbs, adverbs and quantified NPs), the topic binds a trace, and is an instance of adjunction. Where the constituent is referential, the topic binds a small pro. The latter construction I call 'Topic Dislocation', a non-movement relation. Given these assumptions, I re-

[25] Again, the *ki* clause proves to be a problem on this account. This is because under standard analyses, it is considered to be right extraposed from the complement of the matrix V^0. Since it is the case that *ki* clauses are transparent for extraction phenomena at S-structure, it seems that the proposed account assumes that traces need not be path creating, as one anonymous reviewer pointed out. Given this, I need to assume the following: the *ki* clause is in fact base generated to the right of the main clause. This is in fact what Bayer (1990) proposes for German. Since it is base generated, there is no trace created by movement with which it must create a potential path. Further, under an analysis that assumes that the base generated *ki* clause is related to a pleonastic pro in the complement of V^0 position, the assumption is that such small pros, which are not referential, are not path creating. In Dwivedi (forthcoming) I propose a different account for the opacity of the right adjoined relative, which avoids the above problem.

lied on a theory of directionality of government and of Path Theory to account for the topicalization paradigm.

The reason why the left adjoined relative is transparent for topicalization of all types of constituents is because it is generated to the left of V^0 and may be governed. Thus trace binding is allowed. Because a path may connect the small pro with its antecedent topic, pro-binding is also licensed.

The embedded relative is not governed; it is sister to N^0 which is not a governor. As such, trace binding may not occur there. However, a path connecting the small pro with its topic is well-formed in this construction. So only referential NPs may topicalize from this position.

The right adjoined relative is not governed either. It is adjoined to the right, where the verb may never govern. Further because it is extraposed, it is connected to its base position by a gap. This path crosses the path created by small pro and its topic. Thus neither trace binding, nor pro-binding is possible from this position.

In conclusion, a complicated array of facts has been accounted for by assuming a theory of Government (Chomsky 1986) and by assuming that null pronouns that are A′ bound are path creating, so that the Path Containment Condition could apply (Pesetsky 1982). Further, Srivastav's syntactic analyses have been fruitful in explicating the facts of topicalization with respect to the different relative clauses. It is to be contrasted with accounts that maintain that the left and right adjoined relatives are mirror images of each other (Hock 1989). Such (symmetrical) analyses do not immediately explain the strong contrast between left and right adjoined relatives with regards to topicalization constructions.

Acknowledgements

I have benefitted from the helpful comments and suggestions of Hagit Borer, Roger Higgins, Barbara Partee, Veneeta Srivastav, the audience at SALA XIV, three anonymous reviewers and especially Peggy Speas. I would also like to thank my tireless consultant, Harpreet Sawhney.

References

Bach, E. and R. Cooper. 1978. The NP-S Analysis of Relative Clauses and Compositional Semantics. *Linguistics and Philosophy* 2:145–150.

Bayer, J. 1990. *Directionality of Government and Logical Form: A Study of Focussing Particles and WH-Scope*. Doctoral dissertation, University of Konstanz.

Chomsky, N. 1986. *Barriers*. Cambridge MA: MIT Press.

Cinque, G. 1990. *Types of A′ Dependencies.* Cambridge MA: MIT Press.

Dwivedi, V. 1990. Negation as a Functional Projection in Hindi. Generals paper, University of Massachusetts at Amherst. (Condensed version in K. Hunt, T. Perry and V. Samiian (Eds.), *1991 Proceedings of the Western Conference on Linguistics* Vol. 4, 88–101, California State University-Fresno)

Dwivedi, V. (forthcoming). *Syntactic Dependencies and Relative Phrases in Hindi.* Doctoral dissertation, University of Massachusetts at Amherst.

Fiengo, R., C.-T. J. Huang, H. Lasnik, and T. Reinhart. 1988. The syntax of WH-in-situ. In H. Borer (Ed.), *Proceedings of the Seventh West Coast Conference on Formal Linguistics.*

Gambhir, V. 1981. *Syntactic Restrictions and Discourse Functions of Word Order in Standard Hindi.* Doctoral dissertation, University of Pennsylvania.

Huang, C.-T. J. 1982. *Logical Relations in Chinese and the Theory of Grammar*. Doctoral dissertation, MIT.

Hock, H. 1989. Conjoined we stand: theoretical implications of Sanskrit Relative Structures. *Studies in the Linguistic Sciences* 19(1): 93–126

Kachru, Y. 1973. Some Aspects of Pronominalization and Relative Clause Construction in Hindi-Urdu. *Studies in the Linguistic Sciences* 3:87–103.

Kachru, Y. 1978. On Relative Clause Formation in Hindi-Urdu. *Linguistics* 207:5–26.

Kamp, H. 1981. A Theory of Truth and Semantic Representation. In J. Groenendijk, T. Janssen and M. Stokhof (Eds.), *Formal Methods in the Study of Language* Vol. 1. Amsterdam: Mathematische Centrum.

Koopman, H., and D. Sportiche. 1982. Variables and the Bijection Principle. *The Linguistic Review* 2:139–160.

Koster, J. 1987. *Domains and Dynasties*. Dordrecht: Foris Publications.

Kuno, S. 1973. *The Structure of the Japanese Language*. Cambridge MA: MIT Press.

Lasnik, H., and M. Saito. 1992. *Move alpha*. Cambridge, MA: MIT Press.

Mahajan, A. 1990. *The A/A' Distinction and Movement Theory*. Doctoral dissertation, MIT.

Mohanan, T. 1990. *Arguments in Hindi*. Doctoral dissertation, Stanford University.

Partee, B. 1991. Topic, Focus and Quantification. In S. Moore and A. Wyner (Eds.), *Proceedings of the First Semantics and Linguistic Theory Conference*, 159–187. Cornell University Working Papers in Linguistics 10.

Pesetsky, D. 1982. *Paths and Categories*. Doctoral dissertation, MIT.

Pesetsky, D. 1987. Wh-in-situ: Movement and unselective binding. In Ter Meulen and Reuland (Eds.), *Representation of (In)definiteness*, 98–129. Cambridge, MA: MIT Press.

Postal, P. 1992. Overlooked Extraction Distinctions. Ms., T.J. Watson Research Center, IBM.

Rizzi, L. 1990. *Relativized Minimality*. Cambridge, MA: MIT Press.

Roberts, C. 1987. *Modal Subordination, Anaphora, and Distributivity*. Doctoral Dissertation, University of Massachusetts at Amherst.

Ross, J.R. 1967. *Constraints on variables in syntax*. Doctoral dissertation, MIT.

Saito, M. 1985. *Some Asymmetries in Japanese and their Theoretical Implications*. Doctoral dissertation, MIT.

Srivastav, V. 1989. Hindi WH and Pleonastic Operators. In J. Carter, R.-M. Dechaine, B. Philip and T. Sherer (Eds.), *Proceedings of the North Eastern Lingustics Society* 20:443–457. Amherst MA: GLSA.

Srivastav, V. 1991a. *WH Dependencies in Hindi and the Theory of Grammar*. Doctoral dissertation, Cornell University.

Srivastav, V. 1991b. The Syntax and Semantics of Correlatives. *Natural Language and Linguistic Theory* 9:637–686

Stowell, T. 1981. *Origins of Phrase Structure*. Doctoral dissertation, MIT.

Subbarao, K.V. 1984. *Complementation in Hindi Syntax*. Delhi: Academic Publications.

Verma, M.K. 1966. *The Noun Phrase in Hindi and English*. Delhi: Motilal.

Wexler, K., and P. Culicover. 1980. *Formal Principles of Language Acquisition*. Cambridge MA: MIT Press.

6

Afterthoughts, Antitopics, and Emphasis: The Syntacticization of Postverbal Position in Tamil

SUSAN C. HERRING

1 Introduction

1.1 Postposing in Verb-Final Languages

It is a well-known fact that even in the strictest of verb-final languages, elements occasionally appear to the right of the finite verb, as in 'A book (she-)wrote, Sita'. Functional treatments of this phenomenon tend to adopt one of two approaches. The first of these — what we might call the "unifunctional" approach — subsumes all rightward dislocation in a given language under a single functional label, with the meaning of the label so defined as to cover a broad assortment of phenomena. Examples of this approach include Kuno's (1978) use of the term "afterthoughts" to characterize right-dislocation in Japanese, and Erguvanlí's (1984) analysis of all types of postverbal elements as "backgrounding" in Turkish. Alternatively, the "taxonomic" approach identifies a set of seemingly disparate functions associated with postverbal position, without however proposing a unifying relationship among them. Thus Kim and Shin (1992) state that the functions of postposing in Korean include "corrections", "forced displacement", and "emphasis/confirmation", and Junghare's (1985) list of functions for Indo-Aryan includes "de-emphasis" and "emphasis", both distinct from "afterthoughts", which add on something that the speaker originally neglected to say. According to this latter analysis, a syntactic distinction comes into play as well: true afterthoughts are outside the clause, while pragmatically-motivated postposings (emphasis, de-

Theoretical Perspectives on Word Order in South Asian Languages
Miriam Butt, Tracy Holloway King, Gillian Ramchand (Eds.)

emphasis, etc.) are crucial components of the clause itself (Junghare 1985:250).

In this paper, I analyze the functions associated with the postverbal position in Tamil, an otherwise strict verb-final language. My analysis shows that postverbal position is *multifunctional* in ways that cannot be captured adequately by a global functional account. Rather, I identify three distinct functional types, each associated with a characteristic intonation pattern and characteristic syntactic behaviors. I further propose that each postverbal type occupies a different underlying postverbal position, depending on whether the relevant unit of analysis is taken to be the sentence, the utterance, or the "extended utterance" in natural speech production. Ultimately, despite the differences among them, the three postverbal types can be seen to be synchronically related along a continuum of syntacticization (Givón 1979) reflecting differing degrees of unity between the main proposition and the right-dislocated element. These claims, along with their implications for diachronic change, are developed with evidence from spoken and written narrative texts.

1.2 The Tamil Situation

As indicated above, Tamil (a Dravidian language with basic SOV word order) is, for all intents and purposes, strictly verb-final. Herring and Paolillo (in press) found that 94% of finite clauses in spoken Tamil, and 100% of finite clauses in normative, pedagogically-oriented written Tamil narrative texts, have the finite verb in absolute sentence-final position.[1] Main clauses follow dependent clauses, and verb-finality is observed in dependent clauses as well, as illustrated in example (1). (See appendix for a list of abbreviations in glosses.)

(1) ammā nāykuṭṭiy-ai vīṭṭu-kk-uḷḷē *ko-ṇṭu*
mother puppy-ACC house-DAT-inside take-CP
va-nta uṭanē, kumār at-aik koñcam pāl
come-P:AjP as.soon.as Kumar it-ACC little milk
koṭu-tt-ān.
give-P-3SG:MASC
'As soon as mother brought the puppy into the house, Kumar **gave** it a little milk'.

[1]The oral narratives analyzed by Herring and Paolillo include personal narration, folk tales, and performed epics. The written narrative sample includes first and second-grade level children's stories, and classical narratives rewritten in simplified modern Tamil for adult non-native learners.

When and why is strict verb-finality in Tamil violated? In this paper, I suggest that postposings in Tamil are essentially of three functional types: afterthought, backgrounding, and emphatic. *Afterthoughts* are elements that end up in postverbal position not as the result of deliberate planning, but rather by default, as a consequence of the speaker having decided after uttering the main proposition that something more needs to be added. Postverbal elements of this type may be of any category or phrase type, and fulfill a variety of after-the-fact modification functions. *Backgrounding* postposings, in contrast, are conventionalized, and vary systematically in function according to the grammatical category of what is postposed. Thus *antitopics* signal the secondary or transitional discourse-pragmatic status of (typically) nominal referents, while the conventionalized postposing of *adverbials* and *dependent clauses* functions to signal their lesser importance relative to constituents in preverbal positions. Finally, *emphatic* postposings involve the rightward movement of nominal referents for increased emphasis or saliency.

These three postposing types not only have different pragmatic functions, but they differ intonationally and syntactically as well. As a consequence, any attempt to subsume them under a unifunctional characterization seems destined to overlook the essential multifunctionality of postverbal position in Tamil, and would thus fail to provide an adequate description. The question then arises as to what relationship, if any, obtains among the various postposing types. Are they unrelated strategies which happen to have in common the same marked result, *viz.*/ that something construable (loosely or otherwise) as part of the same sentence appears to the right of the finite verb? Or are they related functionally or (more likely) structurally, by virtue of the fact that all employ a common structural device?

In what follows, I adduce evidence for a logical continuum of relatedness among the three postposing types with respect to degree of syntactization, or bondedness of postposing to main clause. Afterthoughts are characterized by a loose, communicatively-based association between original utterances and after-the-fact modification. For antitopics, the association is conventionalized via the pragmatic bond between the two components of the utterance. Emphatic postposing represents the most bonded or "syntacticized" postposing type, in that the postposed nominal is an argument of the main clause itself. In support of the continuum-like nature of this relationship, I present evidence that native speakers blur the boundaries between the individual types by mixing functional and intonational features to represent intermediate degrees of bondedness.

2 The Investigation

2.1 The Tamil Corpus

Postverbal constituents were analyzed in 3,773 finite clauses of spoken and written Tamil narrative text. The spoken corpus, made up of 19 oral narratives representing both traditional and contemporary storytelling genres, contains postposings in 144 out of 1787 finite clauses (8.1%). The written corpus, consisting of seven published short stories by well-known 20th century Tamil authors and one fifth-grade level children's story,[2] has postverbal elements in 141 out of 1986 (7.1%) of its finite clauses.[3] Each finite clause containing one or more postposed elements was identified, and postposings classified by grammatical category. The following information about each postposing in the context of the overall utterance was also noted:

Intonation, i.e., 1) whether the postposed element is part of the intonation contour of the main clause, or separate; 2) whether the postposed element is preceded by a pause (or in written texts, by a comma or elipses); and 3) the degree of stress, if any, accorded the postposed element.

Discourse-pragmatic status, i.e., 1) importance (could the postposed element have been omitted without sacrificing comprehensibility?); and, for nominal referents, 2) information status, i.e., whether the information expressed by the referent is given, accessible, or new;[4] 3)

---

[2]The short stories analyzed are "Kaṭavuḷum Kantasāmi Piḷḷaiyum" and "Poṉṉakaram", by Pudumai Pittan; "Guru Pīṭam" and "Enkō, Yārō, Yārukkākavō", by Jeyakandan; "Marumakaḷ Vākku", by Krisnan Nambi; "Ammā Mandapam", by Sujata; and "Kaliforniyā Kaṇṭa Kuttuviḷakku", by Indira Parttasarati. The children's story, by V. Govindan, is entitled Piḷḷaiyār Kōvilil Piccaikkāraṉ.

[3]The greater frequency of postposing here than that reported in Herring and Paolillo is due to two factors. First, with the exception of the children's story, the written texts analyzed in the present study are literary, rather than pedagogical. Erguvanlí's (1984: 67) observation that sentences with post-predicate elements in Turkish are "extremely rare ... in the more traditional or formal styles of writing", but "far more frequent" in the language of written literature is true for Tamil as well. Second, finite clauses in quoted dialogue were included in the present study, but not in that of Herring and Paolillo. Quoted dialogue often attempts to represent colloquial speech, and thus contains a higher concentration of postposings.

[4]The terms "given", "accessible", and "new" refer to the speaker's assessment of what is in the hearer's consciousness at a particular point in the discourse (Chafe 1976; 1987; ms.). "Given" information is that which has been recently mentioned, or which is "externally evoked" (Prince 1981) by some feature of the physical or psychological context, and is thus actively present in the hearer's consciousness. "Accessible" information is that which the speaker assumes the hearer is able to access (from a previous mention, experience, context, or shared knowledge), even if it is not currently uppermost in the hearer's thoughts. Finally, "new" information

subject/topic continuation, i.e., whether the referent is continued over from the immediate previous discourse context; and 4) persistence, i.e., whether the referent persists as subject/topic in the immediate following discourse context (cf. Givón, 1983).

The results of this analysis are discussed and illustrated below.

2.2 Grammatical Postposing Types

The overwhelming majority of all postposed constituents in Tamil are NPs in the role of grammatical subject (63%). These include NPs marked for dative (i.e., in dative experiencer constructions; 9%) as well as nominative case (54%). Other phrasal types that appear in postverbal position include NPs in other case roles (15%),[5] adverbs (9%), conjunctive participals (including direct quotes embedded by the quotative particle *eṉṟu*; 9%), and dependent (e.g., nominalized and infinitival) clauses (4%). Postverbal elements in Tamil invariably stand in the same case-marked relationship with respect to the verb as if they had appeared in their unmarked, preverbal position[6] Further, the main clause may, but need not, contain an element that is coreferential with the postverbal constituent, such as a pronoun or agreement marking on the verb. However, since Tamil is a zero anaphora language, it is not always apparent on the basis of sentences in isolation whether a postposed element is coreferential with a preverbal zero, or whether the postposed element is the argument itself, displaced over the finite verb (but cf. Section 2.3.3.)

An example of a postverbal subject (nominative) NP, a postverbal object (accusative) NP, a postverbal NP (locative) functioning as an adverbial, and a complex postverbal adverbial expression made up of a conjunctive participal and an adverb are given in (2)–(5) below.

---

is that which is introduced for the first time, and thus not accessible from any previous source.

[5]Tamil distinguishes eight morphological cases: nominative (zero), accusative, dative, genitive, sociative, instrumental, locative, and ablative.

[6]Lambrecht (1981:79), noting a similar tendency with respect to antitopics in Spoken French, proposes an explanation grounded in linear processing:

> At the time the verb is uttered, the case roles of all following NPs are already determined by the preverbal agreement markers, so that not marking the antitopic for its case would amount to ignoring syntactic information encoded more or less immediately before.

That is, since case information is derived from the verb, it is easily accessed after the main proposition has been uttered. In this respect, right-dislocations differ from left-dislocations or "fronting" operations, which do not preserve case distinctions in a number of languages.

(2) "un̠kaḷ kamiṣan̠..." en̠-r̠-ān̠ *nārman̠.*
your commision say-P-3SG:MASC Norman
'"Your commission," said *Norman*.'

(3) avan̠ "nān̠ ce-ñc-ēn̠-ē kaṇṇ-ai tor̠antu-kiṭṭu
he I do-P-1SG-REL eye-ACC open-hold:CP
ceyyi" appaṭi n̠n̠u coll-iṭ-ṭ-ān̠
do-IMP thus QUOT say-PFV-P-3SG:MASC
mantirivittaikkāran̠-ai.
magician-ACC
'"Keep your eyes open and do what I did", he told *the magician*.'

(4) lañcam perukiy-irunt-iru-kk-u *anta*
bribes be.great-PERF-PERF-PR-3SG:NEUT that
kālatt-iley-oē.
time-LOC-EMPH
'It seems that (taking) bribes was prevalent *at that time*.'

(5) "vara-ṭṭum-ē..." en̠-r̠-ēn̠ *avaḷ-aip pār-ttuc*
come-PERM-EMPH say-P-1SG she-ACC look-CP
ciritta-vār̠-ē.
laugh-ADV-EMPH
'"Let him come," I said *looking at her and laughing*.'

In Tamil, these sentences are pragmatically marked. However, since English does not have a strict verb-final constraint, the literal translations do not convey a marked pragmatic value (except in (2), where what is postposed is the grammatical subject).[7] What leads Tamil narrators to situate normally preverbal elements after the finite verb?

2.3 Functional Postposing Types

2.3.1 Afterthoughts

The first and most basic motivation for placing an element after the finite verb in Tamil is as an *afterthought* in unplanned speech. True afterthoughts function as modifications, i.e., to clarify or add to information that the speaker assesses to be insufficient as uttered. Hyman (1975), who claims that afterthoughts play an important role in word

[7] For the purposes of this paper, I have elected to translate Tamil postposed utterances into English rather literally, without attempting to capture the pragmatic effect of the original by more marked English constructions (such as clefting, alternative word orders, idioms, etc). A disadvantage of this method of translation is that the meaning of the Tamil sentences can only be fully appreciated through the accompanying discussion; the advantage, however, is that no additional complexities of interpretation inhering in the English structures are introduced.

order change in Niger-Congo languages, describes the motivation for afterthought "postposing" as follows:

> Once the speaker has put the verb down (in a strict SOV language), it is no longer possible to add anything. However the speaker may forget to say something in the course of an utterance; or he may find that it is necessary to add something, because his interlocutor has not understood; or he may realize that the sentence he just uttered is unclear or ambiguous. In all of these cases (and doubtless others), he may wish to add something after the verb-final utterance. (Hyman 1975:119–120).

The Tamil postverbal "afterthought" type fits this characterization well. Afterthoughts in the Tamil corpus function as additions, corrections, reformulations, and explanations, as illustrated in (6)–(8) below.

(6) tūṇ onṟu iru-kk-utu, *aḻakāṉa tūṇ.*
pillar one be-PR-3SG:NEUT beautiful pillar
'There's a pillar (there), *a beautiful pillar'.*

(7) enka father.. av- avar at-ile member, *theosophical society-le.*
our father h- he that-LOC member theosophical society-LOC
'My father, h- he was a member of that, *of the theosophical society.'*

(8) anta vīraṉ .. inta cāṭṭai .. va-ccu, oru iṭatt-ukku kūṭṭu-ṭṭu va-r-āru, *aṭi-kkiṟ-atu-kku .. aṭi vāṅk-a aṭi-kkiṟ-atu-kku.*
that soldier this whip put-CP one place-DAT take-CP come-PR-3RESP beat-PR-VN-DAT blow receive-INF beat-PR-VN-DAT
'The soldier takes this whip, and brings [Tenaliraman] to a place, *for the beating .. in order* [for Tenaliraman] *to receive the blows- for the beating.'*

In example (6), the speaker adds the supplementary information that the pillar is 'beautiful' after the first part of the utterance is already complete. The speaker in example (7)[8] — an elderly man — appears momentarily unable to recall the term 'theosophical society'; he marks its position and case role in the clause with the pronoun *at-ile* 'that (thing)-LOC' and later appends the full NP, also marked for locative

[8]Note that this sentence, which is equational, does not contain an overt copular verb. In such constructions, the predicate nominal normally occupies the position of the finite verb, that is, it appears in absolute sentence-final position.

case, as a correction of sorts. Finally, in explicating the purpose of the action of the main clause postverbally in (8), the speaker appears concerned to avoid any possible vagueness or confusion. Presumably, these and similar modifications appear after the finite verb because the speaker had not thought to include them when he formulated his original utterance.

True afterthoughts are typically associated with a prosodic contour which signals their after-the-fact nature. In (6)–(8), the postverbal material is set off from the main utterance by a pause, represented in the transcription system by a comma. In even more clear-cut cases, the speaker comes to a full stop before appending the afterthought material in an intonationally-separate utterance, as in (9) below.

(9) Appuṟam vantu, oru letter pōṭ-ṭ-ā. Anke
then TOP one letter send-P-3SG:FEM there
yār-ukkum paṭi-kka teriy-ātu. *Anta*
no.one-DAT read-INF know-NP:NEG:3SG:NEUT that
letter-ai.
letter-ACC
'And then, she sent a letter. No one there knew how to read (it). *The letter.*'

In this example, after completing her second utterance, the speaker apparently realizes that it is potentially ambiguous (taken out of context, the utterance can mean either 'No one there knows how to read' or 'No one there knows how to read (it)'). She then goes on to restrict the interpretation by adding the direct object 'the letter', marked for accusative case, in an intonationally separate unit. In all instances, the clause preceding the afterthought could stand alone; that is, it is intonationally independent, having final, falling intonation, a fact which further suggests that the afterthoughts in these examples were generated by the speaker after the clause was already complete.

Lambrecht (1981), following Hyman (1975), claims that true afterthoughts tend to receive prosodic stress. Most postverbal elements that serve a repair function and follow a break in timing in the Tamil corpus, however, show only very slight stress. This raises the question often discussed in connection with right-dislocation of the 'importance' of what appears after the finite verb. In principle, true afterthoughts could contain information that is essential for the overall communication, as in (7) above. Typically, however, competent speakers do not "forget" essential information very often. Rather, most of the afterthoughts in the Tamil corpus appear to have been added on "just in case" the speaker's intended meaning was not clear; they could have been left off without seriously compromising the success of the communication. The tendency to stress afterthought material only slightly, if at all, is in keeping with this observation. Further, afterthoughts in the corpus tend to favor given or accessible, rather than new information,[9] and thus rarely modify the clause in a way that is surprising or unpredictable. It is important to note, however, that these observations are tendencies, rather than structural or pragmatic constraints on afterthoughts, the production of which is in an important sense outside the conscious control of the speaker.

2.3.2 Conventionalized Postposing: Backgrounding

Not all elements that appear after the finite verb in Tamil are afterthoughts or *post facto* repairs; some, indeed the majority, are deliberate postposings. If nothing else, the fact that 141 orthographical sentences in the published written texts have postverbal elements provides evidence for this claim; given the editorial process, we would expect such elements, if indeed they were true afterthoughts, to have been edited out. What we find in written Tamil texts and in much of the spoken language as well are what have been referred to by Erguvanlí (1984) for Turkish as "backgrounding" postposings.[10] Moving constituents to the right of the finite verb in a verb-final language such as Turkish or Tamil serves the pragmatic function of assigning to such constituents a de-emphasized status in the discourse. The term "backgrounding" is somewhat problematic, however, in that in Tamil, a speaker/writer also has the option of "backgrounding" a referent by leaving out mention of it altogether, i.e., as a zero anaphor. More accurately, then, we might say that Tamil distinguishes three degrees of "ground": a salient "foreground" (associated with preverbal positions, especially sentence-initial and immediate preverbal positions); a "background" (associated with zero anaphora); and an "intermediate ground" (associated with postverbal position).

The notion of "intermediate ground" derives via implicature from the normal associations of true afterthoughts. As noted above, afterthoughts typically do not contain essential information, or they would not have been left out in the first place. Nor are they trivial, or the speaker would not have bothered to append them as afterthoughts. Their importance is intermediate between information uttered preverbally, and information left unsaid. "Intermediate ground" postposings, in their most general sense, can be seen to represent a conventional-

[9] Such is the case, at least, for postverbal NPs. Adverbial afterthoughts sometimes contain new information, albeit of a secondary or supplementary nature.

[10] Erguvanlí includes true afterthoughts under the label "backgrounding" as well.

ization of this intermediate status. Pragmatically, such postposings invariably contain given or accessible (i.e., predictable) information, and are prosodically unstressed. Unlike true afterthoughts, however, they are not deletable, for in addition to signalling relative importance, they fulfill more specific discourse-pragmatic functions. I distinguish two broad types of "intermediate ground" postposings for Tamil: *antitopicalization*, which involves argument NPs, and *adverbial* postposing, including subordinate clauses as well as lexical adverbs and NPs in locative case roles.

Antitopicalization

Antitopics (cf. Chafe 1976) are otherwise topical NPs that the speaker elects for discourse-pragmatic reasons to situate postverbally. Like preverbal topics, they tend to encode thematically important referents which are given, or at least potentially accessible, information prior to being antitopicalized, and which stand in a general "aboutness" relationship to the predicate of the main clause. Generally speaking, antitopicalization indicates that a referent has either been promoted or demoted to intermediate ground. According to the promotion strategy, postposing reactivates referents that were previously mentioned but which have since lapsed into accessible (i.e., background) information status. The demotion strategy, in contrast, deactivates referents that are currently given (active, i.e., foreground) information.

The first strategy is found in all of the written narratives, and in many oral narratives as well. Its primary function is to reintroduce thematic referents that were previously active but have since lapsed into semi-active or accessible information status (Chafe 1987, ms.), typically because another referent has taken over as topic in the interim. In the short story from which the following passage was excerpted, Murugesan's wife Ammalu has been introduced and described ten sentences earlier.

(10) aṉṟaikku murukēcaṉ-ukku kuṣi. avaṉ-um, avaṉ
that.day Murugesan-DAT joy he-and his
kutiraiy-um 'taṇṇi' pōṭṭu-viṭṭu rēs viṭ-ṭ-ārkaḷ.
horse-and water drink-PFV:CP race let-P-3PL
vaṇṭi 'tōkkar' aṭi-tt-atu. ērkkāl
cart pothole hit-P-3SG:NEUT shaft
oṭi-nt-atu. kutirai-kku palamāṉa kāyam.
break-P-3SG:NEUT horse-DAT strong wound
murukēcan-ukku ūmaiyaṭi. vīṭṭ-il koṇṭu vantu
Murugesan-DAT internal.injury house-LOC bring:CP

pōṭ-um	pol̲utu	pēccu	mūcc-illai.	nalla
put-F:AjP	time	speech	breath-NEG	good

kālam	kuṭitt-iru-nt-ān̲,	inta	mātiri	vali
time	drink-PERF-P-3SG:MASC	this	manner	pain

teriy-āl-āvatu	kiṭa-kka.	vīkkatt-ir̲ku
know-NEG:CP-at.least	lie-INF	swelling-DAT

en̲n̲att-aiy-ō	arai-ttu	pūc-in̲-āḷ	*ammāḷu.*
whatever-ACC	grind-CP	smear-P-3SG:FEM	Ammalu

appol̲utu	tān̲	car̲r̲up	pēc-in̲-ān̲.
then	EMPH	a.little	speak-P-3SG:M

'On that day, Murugesan was in a good mood. He and his horse got drunk and had a race. The cart hit a pothole. The shaft broke. The horse was grievously wounded. Murugesan (suffered) internal injuries. When (they) brought him into the house and set him down, he didn't have the breath to speak. Fortunately he'd been drinking, so he at least remained unaware of the pain. She ground something up and rubbed it on the swelling, *Ammalu.* Only then did he speak a little.'

In this example, the status of Ammalu as active, "given" information has lapsed in the 18 sentences since she was first mentioned, and hence, she must be reactivated. Her role in this mention is not foregrounded — indeed the sequence as a whole is about Murugesan —; rather, she is represented as an antitopic, on intermediate ground. To borrow a theatrical metaphor, she emerges from the wings for a brief appearance, but not to occupy center stage.

While far from categorical in the corpus overall, the strategy of postposing to reactivate previously-mentioned referents is highly systematic in a number of the written short stories. In the story from which the following excerpt was taken,[11] referents tend to appear postverbally whenever the subject has switched from that of the previous sentence. Antitopicalization here functions as a device for referent tracking, akin to retrospective or "backward-looking" switch reference systems in other languages.

(11)

nārman	avar-iṭam	aintu	pattu	rūpāy
Norman	he-LOC	five	ten	rupee

nōṭṭu-kkaḷ-ai	eṇṇ-ik	koṭu-tt-ān.	"itu
bill-PL-ACC	count-CP	give-P-3SG:MASC	this

[11] "Kaliforniyā Kaṇṭa Kuttuviḷakku", by Indira Parttasarati.

etu-kku?" eṉṟu kēṭ-ṭ-ār *paṭṭu.*
what-DAT QUOT ask-P-3RESP Pattu

avar-ukku nārman mītu ciṟitu kōpam
he-DAT Norman on little anger

ēṟpaṭ-ṭ-atu. "uṉkaḷ kamiṣaṉ..."
experience-P-3SG:NEUT your commision

eṉ-ṟ-āṉ *nārmaṉ.* "nalla kamiṣaṉ..."
say-P-3SG:MASC Norman good commision

eṉṟu colli-kko-ṇṭ-ē paṇatt-ai vāṅk-i
QUOT say-hold-CP-EMPH money-ACC receive-CP

itupp-il ceruki-kko-ṇṭ-ār *paṭṭu.*
waist-LOC insert-BEN-P-3SG:RESP Pattu

"cāppāṭṭ-ukku eṉṉa ēṟpāṭu ṉṉu kēḷ-uṉkō..."
food-DAT what plan QUOT ask-IMP:PL

eṉ-ṟ-āṉ *raṅku.*
say-P-3SG:MASC Rangu

'Norman counted out five ten rupee bills and gave (them) to him. "What's this for?" asked *Pattu* .
He felt a twinge of anger at Norman.
Your commission, said *Norman.*
Saying "Nice commission, took the money and tucked it into (the pouch at) his waist *Pattu.*
"Ask him what he plans to do for meals," said *Rangu.*'

In written narrative, "switch reference" postposing is especially common in reported dialogue to signal a change of speaker, as in the example above: fully 81% of postposed NPs follow a quote and a verb of saying, as compared with only 11% which follow a quote in the oral narratives.[12]

Further evidence for the switch-reference function of postposing is found in contexts where the postposed NP is ambiguous (i.e., could

---

[12]Interesting parallels can be noted in this respect between Tamil and English. In literary English, it is possible to invert subject and verb after a quote and a verb of saying, as in "[quote]", said Mary.' Inversion is excluded in other sentence types, however, except when Mary is presentationally-focused; thus: **The book read Mary* (meaning 'Mary read the book') and **Sat down Mary* are ungrammatical, although the presentational *Into the room strode Mary* is possible. What is the basis for the correlation between subject postposing and quotes? I suggest that it arises out of a need to track participants during conversational exchanges, while at the same time preventing this necessity from detracting from the impact of the quoted dialogue. Postposing effectively backgrounds the speaker while unambiguously signalling her identity. It is not clear to me, however, why this strategy should be employed more in writing than in speaking, other than that it has become conventional to do so in both English and Tamil.

refer to more than one locally-accessible referent). In such instances, the fact of postposing alone may signal that a switch in topic/subject has taken place. This is illustrated in the oral example in (12).

(12) avan̲-uṭaiya māman̲ cakun̲i anku varu-kin̲r̲-ān̲.
he-GEN uncle Cakuni there come-PR-3SG:MASC
(...) appaṭi kaiy-ai va-cc-ān̲. tirumpi
thus hand-ACC place-P-3SG:MASC turn-CP
pār-kkir̲-ān̲ *avan̲*.
look-PR-3SG:MASC he
'His uncle Cakuni comes there. (...) (He) placed
his hand (on his shoulder). Turns around and looks *he*.'

In this passage, both uncle Cakuni and his nephew are third person singular masculine referents, as indicated by the agreement marker *-ān̲* on the finite verbs. Although the personal subject pronoun *avan̲* he could refer equally well to either, the fact that it is postposed in the final utterance effectively shifts the reference from the subject of the previous utterance (Cakuni) to the other participant; that is, it is the *nephew* who turns around and looks.

Antitopics where the subject/topic switches from that of the immediately preceding utterance account for 78% of all antitopics in the written narratives, and 60% of those in the oral narratives. Of these, those in the oral texts continue as topical in the subsequent discourse in a slight majority (59%) of uses, while those in written texts are followed by another shift in topic 79% of the time that is, they typically represent an entity that is only topical for the duration of one sentence.[13]

The second antitopicalization strategy, which is in some respects the mirror image of that described above, is attested exclusively in oral narration. According to this strategy, a topic/subject in active "given" status is demoted or deactivated to intermediate status via postposing (that is, it is moved from center stage to a less prominent position on the stage). No switch from the previous subject/topic is involved; rather the topical status of a continuous referent is modified. Examples of this type are given in (13)–(15) below.

(13) rājāv-ai pākk-aiy-ile kāvalar-kaḷ varicaiy-ā
king-ACC see-VN-LOC guard-PL row-ADV
ni-pp-ānka. rājā anke iru-nt-ār ṇṇā ..
stand-F-3PL king there be-P-3RESP COND

[13]These and related correlations are summarized in Tables 1 and 2 at the end of this section.

mūṉu vācal-le kāvalar-kaḷ ni-pp-ānka. reṇṭu
three gate-LOC guard-PL stand-F-3PL two
reṇṭu pēr-ā reṇṭu reṇṭu pēr-ā.
two people-ADV two two people-ADV
appa uḷḷa viṭa-māṭṭ-ēṉ-ṭ-ānka *kāvalar-kaḷ*.
then inside let-F:NEG-1SG-(say)-PFV:P-3PL guard-PL
appa tāṉ teṉālirāmaṉ colliy-iru-kk-āṉ.
then EMPH Tenaliraman say-PERF-PR-3SG:MASC
'When (he goes) to see the king, **guards** are standing in rows. If the king was there, **guards** would stand at the three gates. Two by two. And wouldn't let (him) inside *the guards* (i.e., the guards wouldn't let him inside).
So then Tenaliraman speaks, it seems.'

(14) Avaṉ kañcā vēṟa aṉṉaikki
he ganja moreover that.day
kuṭicc-iru-kk-āṉ. Kañcā ellām
smoke-PERF-PR-3SG:MASC ganja all
pōṭu-v-āṉ *avaṉ*. appuṟam vantu, anta
put-F-3SG:MASC *he* afterwards TOP that
kutirai mēle ēṟ-i,
horse top climb-CP
'**He**'d smoked ganja too that day. Did ganja and everything *he*. Afterwards, (he) climbed on the horse, and ...'

(15) nāṉ tāṉ, āmā, anta patil-ellām nāṉ tāṉ
I EMPH yes that answer-all I EMPH
eḻut-iṉ-ēṉ. oru nāl-añcu letter eḻut-iṉ-ēṉ *nāṉ*.
write-P-1SG one four-five letter write-P-1SG I
at-ile mu-kkāl vāci eṉṉa eḻutu-v-ōm?
that-LOC three-quarter time what write-F-1PL
'**I**, yeah, I wrote all the replies. Wrote about four or five letters *I*. (You know) what we wrote most of the time? ...'

A question which immediately arises regarding examples of this type is the following: if the function of postposing a same subject/topic referent is to demote it to a lesser status, and if there is no competing intervening subject/topic with which it could be confused, why mention it at all? Why not simply "background" it by encoding it as an anaphoric zero?

The key to understanding the presence of such mentions can be found in the utterances which immediately *follow* antitopics of this type. In each case, there is a shift to a new topic after the clause containing the postposing: in (13), from the guards to Tenaliraman; in (14), from the ganja-smoking of the protagonist to his accident on horseback (not directly related to smoking ganja, but rather to the wildness of the horse); and in (15), from the speakers agency in letter-writing, to the content of the letters themselves. In the switch-reference examples considered previously, different-subject antitopics *retrospectively* mark a shift from one topical entity to the next. Same-subject antitopics, in contrast, mark a topic shift *prospectively* (i.e., they signal that a shift is about to occur).

Further compelling evidence of the prospective-switching function is found in examples such as the following, where a zeroed topic is *re*-introduced as an antitopic immediately prior to a switch to a new topic, for no apparent reason other than to highlight the switch. In the text preceding example (16), Kovalan — the errant husband of the faithful Kannaki — has been the topic of four consecutive utterances, in the first of which he is referred to by a full NP, in the second and third by a pronoun *avaṉ* 'he', and in the last utterance, by an anaphoric zero (i.e., only via subject agreement on the finite verb). He is thus a well-established thematic referent at this point in the narration.

(16) anta vēciy-iṉ-uṭaiya vīṭ-ley-ē
that prostitute-INC-GEN house-LOC-EMPH
iru-kk-āṉ. [zero]
be-PR-3SG:MASC
mātavi vīṭ-ley-ē iru-kk-āṉ *avaṉ*.
Matavi house-LOC-EMPH be-PR-3SG:MASC he
[postposed pronoun]
kaṇṇaki .. avaḷ vīṭ-le iru-kk-ā.
Kannaki her house-LOC be-PR-3SG:FEM
[preverbal NP — new topic]

'(He)'s staying only at the prostitute's house.
(He')s staying only at Madavi's house *he*.
Kannaki .. is at her (own) house.'

The pronoun *avaṉ* is reintroduced in postverbal position in the clause immediately preceding the shift in topic to Kannaki. As such, it both closes off the topic of the husband and signals that a different topic is to follow.

Finally, the prospective-switching function also accounts for some otherwise anomalous instances in colloquial speech where an NP — typically a pronoun — is mentioned both preverbally and postverbally in the same utterance. In such cases, the speaker apparently decides to change topic in the following utterance after having already encoded an overt subject in clause-initial subject position. He modifies his utterance to signal the upcoming topic shift by (redundantly) postposing a subject pronoun, as in (17).

(17) uṭaṉē **avaṉ** .. caṭṭaiy-ai eṭu-ttu aṭi eṭṭu aṭi
then he whip-ACC take-CP blow eight blow
aṭicc-iṭ-ṭ-āṉ *avaṉ*. tirupp-i aṭutta itu-kku
hit-PFV-P-3SG:MASC he turn-CP next thing-DAT
vā-ṟ-ār.
come-PR-3RESP
'Then **he** [the soldier] took the whip
and struck eight blows *he*. He [Tenaliraman] turns and comes to the next thing.'

There is a correlation between antitopics that continue the same topic as that of the previous clause, and an immediately following shift in topic: 69% of all instances of the phenomenon are followed by a topic shift. In the spoken language, the two antitopicalization strategies are complementary in distribution and function, with different-subject antitopics typically continuing as topics in what follows, and same-subject antitopics followed by an immediate shift in topic. In the written texts, in contrast, both same-subject and different-subject antitopics are followed by a shift in topic the majority of the time (77%). The correlation between antitopicalization, previous topic, and following topic is summarized in Table 1 (for written Tamil) and Table 2 (for spoken Tamil).

	following topic same	following topic different	Total:
previous topic same	32% N=9	68% N=19	100% N=28 (22%)
previous topic different	21% N=21	79% N=81	100% N=102 (78%)
Total:	23% N=30	77% N=100	100% N=130 (100%)

Table 1: *Antitopicalization and topic continuity in Written Tamil*

	following topic same	following topic different	Total:
previous topic same	31% N=10	69% N=22	100% N=32 (40%)
previous topic different	59% N=29	41% N=20	100% N=49 (60%)
Total:	48% N=39	52% N=42	100% N=81 (100%)

Table 2: *Antitopicalization and topic continuity in Spoken Tamil*

In all, 93% (N=121) of antitopics in the written texts and 88% (N=71) of antitopics in the spoken texts correspond to a topic switch in one direction or the other, as compared with only 6% (N=9) of the written texts and 12% (N=10) of the spoken texts where the topic remains the same throughout. Antitopicalization in Tamil thus generally functions to indicate topics that are *transitional* in the discourse.

In addition to their discourse-pragmatic characteristics, antitopic constructions have prosodic characteristics that further distinguish them from true afterthoughts. While true afterthoughts are typically separated from the finite verb by a break in timing, antitopics are incorporated along with the finite verb as part of a unified intonation contour.[14] Moreover, while the postverbal element in an afterthought construction may receive some degree of stress, antitopics are invariably unstressed, that is, uttered with lowered pitch and volume, and often with increased tempo. In both constructions, the main stress in the utterance, if there is one, falls on or before the finite verb.[15] The two resulting prosodic contours are illustrated for the minimal pair in (18), based on the sequence *veḷiyē pōṉāṉ kaṇṇaṉ,* lit. 'outside go-P-3SG:MASC Kannan'.

(18) a.

veḷiyē pōṉāṉ, kaṇṇaṉ. Went outside, Kannan. (i.e., He went outside, Kannan, that is.) ['Kannan' is an afterthought]

b.

veḷiyē pōṉāṉ kaṇṇaṉ. Went outside Kannan. ['Kannan' is an antitopic]

[14] Correspondingly, in the written examples, no comma appears between an antitopic and its main clause (see examples (10) and (11)).

[15] The issue of whether Tamil has predictable stress (or "accent") has been the subject of some debate (Andronov 1975; Asher 1985; Christdas 1988). In the present corpus, stress appears to be primarily emphatic, and hence variable from utterance to utterance.

The existence of prosodic differences of this sort suggests that there is a closer unity between antitopics and their immediately preceding clauses than between afterthoughts and the clauses they follow.

Adverbial and dependent clause postposing

The second major sub-type of intermediate ground postposing involves adverbials and dependent clause constructions. Such postposings specify additional modification (manner, time, location, purpose, etc.) to the main predicate of the utterance, and as such would appear to be of secondary or intermediate importance by definition, even though the information they contain is often strictly speaking not recoverable from context. In general, postposed adverbials and clauses are best analyzed as conventionalized afterthoughts, without further pragmatic specialization. One possible motive for appending them after the finite verb, especially in unplanned speech, is as a means of stating the important information (i.e., subject and predicate) first, without the clutter of adverbial detail, a strategy which Aske (1991), following Dik (1989), calls "uncluttering the pre-field", and which Kim and Shin (1992) characterize as "forced displacement". A motive of this sort may be discerned in examples such as the following.

(19)	appuṟam	rompa	nāḷ	kaḻi-ccu,	letter
	then	many	day	pass-CP	letter

	vant-iru-cc-u,	*anta*	*poṇṇu kkiṭṭa iruntu.*
	come-PERF-P-3SG:NEUT	that	girl-ABL

'Then many days later, the letter arrived, *from the girl.*'

(20)	vāḷ-ai	eṭu-kkiṟ-āṉ	*veṭ-r-atu-kkāka*	*vēṇṭi.*
	sword-ACC	take-PR-3SG:MASC	cut-PR-VN-BEN	PURP

'He takes up the sword *in order to cut.'*

In these examples, the speakers state the information that advances the narrative story line first (the letter arrived; he takes up the sword), followed by adverbial modification (source; purpose) in postverbal position. The principle of reserving preverbal positions for important information could also account for the tendency for subject NPs to be postposed after quotes.[16]

Evidence of the status of postposed adverbials relative to other

[16] A more marked variant of the "most important information first" strategy allows the finite verb to appear in sentence-initial position, followed by its arguments and modifiers. This is illustrated in the following dialogue, from the short story "Ammā Mandapam".

A:	"vint-i	vint-i	naṭa-nt-āṉ-ā?"
	limp-CP	limp-CP	walk-P-3SG:MASC-Q

postposing types can be adduced from examples in the corpus where two constituents appear postposed to the right of the finite verb (N=23). In 9 instances (39%) all of them following a quote both an antitopic and a backgrounding adverbial are postposed.[17] In all of the instances, the order is antitopic+adverbial, as in the oral example in (21) and the literary example in (22) below.

(21) "avan̲-ai kīl̲e taḷḷi-ṭṭ-ān̲-ē.. en̲
he-ACC down push-PFV:P-3SG:MASC-EMPH my
makan̲" appaṭi n̲n̲u, al̲a-r̲-ān̲.. *anta rājā*
son thus QUOT weep-PR-3SG:MASC that king
uṭkā-ntu.
sit-CP
'Having said "Knocked him down .. my son (did)", wept .. *the king sitting down.*'

(22) "avaḷ-ā? avaḷ-ai jeyi-kka yār-āl
she-Q she-ACC win-INF who-INST
muṭiy-um?" en̲-p-ārkaḷ *ūr peṇ-kaḷ, oru vita*
be.able-F:3SG:NEUT say-F-3PL town girl-PL one kind
acūyaiy-uṭan̲.
envy-with
'"Her? Who can beat her?" say *the women of the town, with a sort of envy.*'

The consistent relative ordering of adverbial after antitopic suggests a looser syntactic bond between postposed adverbials and their preceding clauses than that for antitopics and their preceding clauses.

Intonationally, adverbials tend *not* to be incorporated into the contour of the main clause, except in the case of high-frequency adverbs such as 'here', 'now', 'yet', 'a lot', 'a little', etc.

B: "ōṭ-in̲-ān̲ *rompa vēkamā ... paya-ntu koṇṭ-ē.*"
run-P-3SG:MASC very fast fear-CP hold:CP-EMPH

A: "Did (he) walk with a limp?"
B: "(He) *ran, really fast ... (like he) was scared.*"

What appears to motivate this example is not so much a need to postpose the adverbials, as it is to *pre*pose the verb, i.e., to emphasize the verbal action and contrast it with the verb of the preceding utterance.

[17]The other combinations attested are antitopic + afterthought (26%), afterthought + afterthought (22%), adverbial + adverbial (9%), and antitopic + antitopic (4%). No combinations of three or more postverbal elements were found in the corpus.

(23) kār-iṉ mītu veyil vil̲u-nt-atu *ippōtu.*
car-GEN top sunlight fall-P-3SG:NEUT now
'The sun was shining on the car *now*.'

(24) at-ai nī il̲a-kkav-illai *iṉṉum*. at-ai vai-ttu
that-ACC you lose-NF:NEG yet that-ACC place-CP
āṭu.
play-IMP
[in a gambling game] 'THAT you haven't lost *yet*. Bet
that and play.'

Otherwise, longer and more complex adverbials are typically appended after a pause, as in (19) and (22), a further indication of their more peripheral relationship to the proposition of the main clause. Similarly, postposed subordinate clauses are separated intonationally from the main clause in speaking (example (25) below), and set off by a comma in written texts (example (26) below).

(25) rompa vēkam-ā ōṭu-ṟ-atu,... *pāl-ai*
very speed-ADV run-PR-3SG:NEUT milk-ACC
pār-tta uṭaṉē.
see-P:AjP as.soon.as
'It runs really fast, ... *as soon as it sees the milk.*'

(26) Atu tān añku 'meyiṉ' rastā. Kaikōtta nāṉku
that EMPH there main street. hand.hold-P:AjP four
pēr varicai tārāḷamāka pōk-alām, *etirē vaṇṭi-kaḷ*
people row freely go-POSS opposite vehicle-PL
var-āviṭṭ-āl.
come-NEG-COND
'That is the 'main' street there. Four people holding
hands in a row can go along freely, *if no vehicles
come from the other direction.*

Given the tendency to pause between main clause and adverbial postposing, and the generally supplementary nature of its content, it is often difficult to determine whether a postverbal adverbial in speech is conventionalized or a true afterthought. The distinction (from the point of view of the linguist) may reside in little more than the slight stress typical of afterthoughts vs. the absence of stress in conventionalized postposing, and even this criterion is not without exception, as noted in Section 3.2.

2.3.3 Emphatic Postposing

We come now to the third function of postposing in Tamil: emphasis. This type is considerably more restricted in occurrence than the afterthought or backgrounding functions described above,[18] appearing primarily in traditional oral narrative genres such as Villu Pāṭṭu ('Bow Song') or Kathākālakshēpam performances. Postposings of this type involve the presentation of new and/or emphasized nominal referents. Unlike the other postverbal types, emphatic postposed referents are intonationally highly stressed. Moreover, each is the unique focus of assertion of the sentence in which it appears, and thus must be considered to occupy a position within, rather than outside, the clause.

The principal pragmatic function of emphatic postposing is the presentation of new referents into the discourse; the referent is then treated as given information and elaborated upon in the clauses that follow. Examples of new referent presentation are given in (27) and (28).[19,20]

(27)

ēḻu	pēr-un	tāṉ	mūṉki	mūṉki
7	people-and	EMPH	immerse:CP	immerse:CP

nīr-āṭa-ṟ-āḷ-ē. ...	Uṭaṉē	pār-tt-āḷ
water-play-PR-3SG:FEM-TAG	suddenly	see-P-3SG:FEM

at-ilē	*orutti!*	"aṭiyē!	nām	vantu
that-LOC	one:female	FEM-VOC	we	TOP

evvaḷavu	nēram	ā-kiṟ-atu!"
how.much	time	become-PR-3SG:NEUT

'All seven of them are immersing themselves and playing in the water, right? Suddenly looked up *one of them*! (i.e., one of them looked up!) "Hey! It's getting late!" (she said)'

(28)

Nappācai	uṇṭ-ākki-ṉ-āṉ.	It-aik
false.desire	exist-cause to be-P-3SG:MASC	This-ACC

kēṭ-ṭ-āṉ	*vituran.*	avaṉ	nallavaṉ	cittappā.
hear-P-3SG:MASC	Viduran	he	good-MASC	uncle

"eṉṉa,	nāṭṭ-ai	vaittu	āṭu-v-at-ā?	vēṇṭ-ām,
what	country-ACC	place-CP	play-F-VN-Q	must-neg

[18] Just under 10% of the postposings in the oral corpus are of this type, including hybrid uses such as that illustrated in example (35).

[19] Both of these examples are from performances in the Villu Pāṭṭu tradition.

[20] Note that (28) contains, in addition to the emphatic postposing *vituran*, an antitopic *avaoṉ* 'he' (here signaling a prospective topic switch) and an afterthought elaboration, *cittappoā* 'uncle'.

vēṇṭ-ām" ṉṉu coṉ-ṉ-āṉ avaṉ.
must-NEG QUOT say-P-3SG:MASC he
'[Cakuni] instilled [in Dharman] the desire (to gamble further). Heard this *Viduran* (i.e., Vituran heard this). He was a good man, (their) uncle. "What, wager the country?
No, no!" said he.'

In these examples, neither *Vituran* nor the referent of *atilē orutti* 'one of them' has been mentioned before, nor are they otherwise recoverable from context. Indeed, *Vituran* is highly *un*predictable information, since without explicit mention of him, the listener would almost certainly interpret the subject of the verb *kēṭṭāṉ* 'heard' to be one of the two other masculine referents, Cakuni or Dharman. These postposings, rather than being semantically "redundant", "supplementary", or "deletable" as has been claimed for afterthoughts and background-type postposings (cf. Kuno 1978), are crucial to the intended interpretation of the sentence.

Other uses of emphatic postposing highlight a referent regardless of whether or not it is a new mention. This is illustrated in (29).

(29) "kaṭumaiyāṇa cāpatt-aik koṭu-kkiṟ-ēṉ pār!
cruel curse-ACC give-PR-1SG see-IMP
piṭi *cāpatt-ai!* cāk-āta cuṭalaiy-ile
take-IMP curse-ACC die-NEG:AjP burning.ground-LOC
nī cāmpal-āka pō!" eṉṟu
you ash-ADV go-IMP QUOT
capittu-viṭ-ār.
curse-PFV-P-3RESP
'"I'm going to give you a cruel curse, see! Receive *the curse!* You will turn to ashes at the eternal burning ground!", thus he cursed (him).'

In (29) as well as in the two previous examples, the postposed referent has a cataphoric function: it points ahead in the discourse to where it receives further elaboration.

Corresponding to their emphatic function, postposings of this type have emphatic intonation as well. In (27)–(29), the sentences containing the postposing are pronounced with sharply rising (utterance non-final) intonation on the verb, and heavy falling stress on the postverbal constituent.[21] This pattern contrasts strikingly with both the "afterthought" and the "antitopic" patterns, in which the intonation on

[21] It was presumably this emphatic intonation that led the native speaker transcriber of examples (27) and (29) (whose transcription I have retained here) to punctuate the sentences with an exclamation point.

the verb falls, rather than rises, and the postposed constituent receives little or no stress. Applying this intonation pattern to the sample sentence in (18a–b) produces the following utterance, in which the postposed NP 'Kaṇṇaṉ' is emphasized, i.e., as a focus of immediate subsequent interest in the discourse.

(18) c.

veḷiyē pōṉāṉ kaṇṇaṉ!	Went outside Kannan! ['Kannan' is emphasized]

The fact that the heaviest stress falls not on the verb but rather on the postverbal NP provides strong evidence that postverbal position in emphatic constructions of this type is clause-internal.

There is independent syntactic evidence for this view as well. To begin with, an overt subject pronoun cannot be added to the beginning of (18c) above, a fact which suggests that the postposed NP is itself the subject of the clause, rather than a co-referential copy of an anaphoric zero in preverbal position.

(18) c′.

*avaṉ veḷiyē pōṉāṉ kaṇṇaṉ!	He went outside Kannan! ['Kannan' is emphasized]

In contrast, the same sentence with Kannan as an antitopic is acceptable (although somewhat odd pragmatically; cf. example (17) above), and with Kannan as an afterthought, is both acceptable and perfectly normal.

(18) b′.

?avaṉ veḷiyē pōṉāṉ kaṇṇaṉ.	He went outside Kannan. ['Kannan' is an antitopic]

a′.

avaṉ veḷiyē pōṉāṉ, kaṇṇaṉ.	He went outside, Kannan (that is). ['Kannan' is an afterthought]

Second, while it is marginally possible to follow an emphatic postposing with an antitopic,[22] the reverse order is not possible (at least, not if emphatic intonation and function is intended).

[22]This observation is based on elicited data. The constraint against sequences of emphatic postposing + antitopic appears to be pragmatic, rather than syntactic. It is somehow odd to focus one referent and antitopicalize another (e.g., for purposes of switch reference) in the same utterance; presentational focus, when it occurs, appears to take precedence over all other word-order related pragmatic operations. It follows from this that sequences of emphatic + antitopic + afterthought are also odd, although the combined relative ordering of emphatic + antitopic and antitopic + afterthought leads us to expect that if the three postposing types did co-occur, they would occur in this order.

(30)

Uṭaṉē pār-tt-āḷ *at-ilē orutti!*
suddenly see-P-3SG:FEM that-LOC one:female

anta paittiyakkāraṉ-ai.
that crazy-MASC-ACC
'Suddenly looked up *one of them, at the crazy man.*'
(i.e., 'Suddenly one of them looked up at the crazy man.')

(31)

* Uṭaṉē pār-tt-āḷ *anta paittiyakkāraṉ-ai*
suddenly see-P-3SG:FEM that crazy-MASC-ACC

at-ilē orutti!
that-LOC one:female
'Suddenly looked up, *at the crazy man. One of them.*'

Further, there can be only one emphatic postposing per sentence, although sentences with more than one backgrounding postposing are possible.[23]

Finally, emphatic postposing is precluded if another constituent in the sentence is in focus. Unlike antitopics (A-TOP) or afterthoughts, emphatic focus cannot co-occur with questions or negation, as shown by (32)–(34).

(32) a.

*It-aik kēṭ-ṭ-ān-ā *vituran?*
this-ACC hear-P-3SG:MASC-Q Vituran
'Heard this Vituran?!' [Vituran is emphasized]

b.

It-aik kēṭ-ṭ-ān-ā *vituran?*
this-ACC hear-P-3SG:MASC-Q Vituran
'Heard this(,) Vituran? [V. is A-TOP or afterthought]

(33) a.

*eṉṉa kēṭ-ṭ-āṉ *vituran?*
what hear-P-3SG:MASC Vituran
'What heard Vituran?!' [Vituran is emphasized]

b.

eṉṉa kēṭ-ṭ-āṉ *vituran?*
what hear-P-3:SG:MASC Vituran
'What heard(,) Vituran?' [V. is A-TOP or afterthought]

[23]See Fn. 17.

(34) a.

*It-aik kēṭ-kav-illai *vituran!*
this-ACC hear-NF-NEG Vituran
'Didn't hear it Vituran!' [Vituran is emphasized]

b.

It-aik kēṭ-kav-illai *vituran.*
This-ACC hear-NF-NEG Vituran
'Didn't hear it(,) Vituran.' [V. is A-TOP or afterthought]

These restrictions fall out from the fact that focus in Tamil is syntactically unique that is, there can be one and only one constituent in focus per clause. The incompatibility of emphatic postposing with focusing operations such as question formation and negation supports the view that emphatic postposing is itself focused.

3 Summary and Discussion

I have presented functional, intonational, and syntactic evidence in support of the view that postverbal elements in Tamil are of three distinct types. To the extent that this view is correct, it should be apparent that the question of how and why strict verb-finality is violated cannot be answered by a single generalization on either formal or functional grounds. Indeed, it may not be going too far to state that the only feature all instances of postverbal word order in Tamil have in common is postverbal word order.

Having said that, I would like to go further and suggest that even such an apparently tautological statement is incorrect, if by "postverbal word order" we mean that all elements that appear to the right of the finite verb occupy the same underlying position and are the result of the same formal process (e.g., "right-dislocation"). Rather, the evidence suggests that there are three underlying postverbal positions, each of which operates according to different principles within a different linguistic domain.

3.1 Postverbal Positions and Linguistic Domains

The most general domain evoked here is that of *speech production.* The production domain includes not only (more or less) complete grammatical utterances, but afterthoughts which repair or modify the communication in a variety of ways. Afterthoughts are in a loose syntactic and pragmatic relationship to the assertion in the main clause, and may be separated from it prosodically by separate intonation contours and pauses, and syntactically by other post-clausal elements such as antitopics. It makes little sense to say that afterthoughts are "right-dislocated" in a transformational sense; rather they end up after the finite verb by default, as a consequence of the linear nature of speech production.

Antitopics, in turn, occupy a position that is closer to and intonationally unified with the main clause. This position is systematically associated with pragmatic functions related to information status, thematicity, topicality, grounding, etc., and thus the domain within which the position operates may be termed the *pragmatic* domain. If both an antitopic and an afterthought appear, the former precedes the latter, and thus can be considered to form a tighter syntactic bond with the main clause, although the unity can be interrupted by an emphatic postverbal element.[24] Because of the intentional nature of such postposings, they can be considered to "move" rightward, or rather, a copy of the referent moves, leaving a coreferential pronoun or zero in preverbal position.

Finally, emphatic focus postposings occupy a position inside the clause, immediately after the finite verb. They are syntactically focused, pragmatically salient, and intonationally stressed. The position is further subject to a variety of formal co-occurrence constraints to which the other positions are not, and thus is defined, at least in part, within the *syntactic* or clause-level domain. Postposings of this type represent the clearest cases of movement, since it is the argument itself that appears postverbally (i.e., no copy or trace remains in preverbal position).

Figure 1 schematically represents the relationships among the three postverbal positions and their respective domains. Note that for each post-clausal position, there is an analogous preclausal position and a function associated with it. Afterthoughts mirror false starts, prefatory comments, etc. that may occur in natural speech production before the speaker embarks on the utterance proper. The unit containing these production-based elements constitutes an *extended utterance*. On the *utterance* level, antitopics are paired with presentential topics, i.e., those of the marked or shifted variety, as in the English expression 'as for X, ...' and the Tamil expression 'X vantu, ...' or 'X eṉṟāl ....' Finally, within the *sentence* itself, initial (subject) position is preferred for non-shifted topics, and this function is mirrored by sentence-final 'focus' position, represented in the diagram as F.[25]

[24]Backgrounding adverbials should probably be included in the pragmatic domain as well, although it is difficult to draw a principled distinction between them and true afterthoughts.

[25]I include F in the diagram as part of a maximally differentiated system, e.g., that

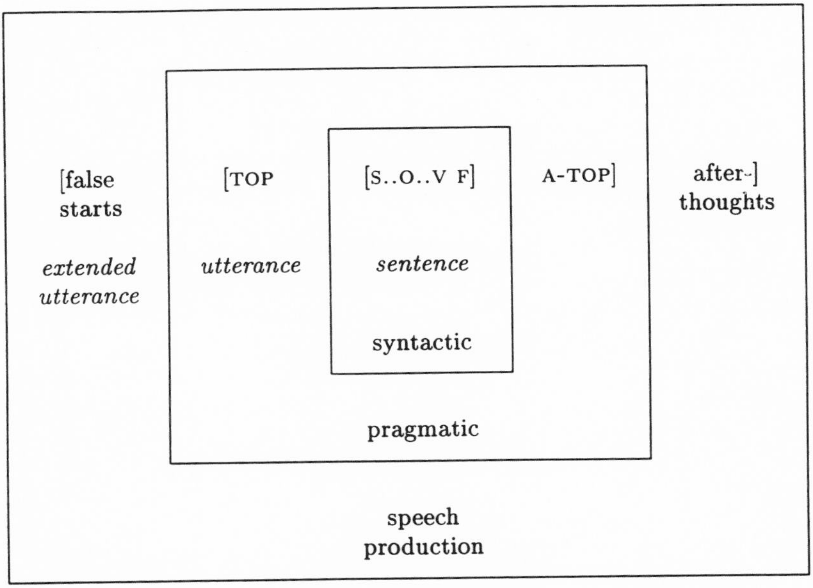

Figure 1: *Functional positions in three domains in Tamil*

As figure 1 suggests, the three postverbal positions are situated along a continuum of increasing closeness of bond between postverbal element and finite clause, proceeding inward from speech production in contexts of use to the pragmatic and ultimately to the syntactic or sentence-level domain. That is, the three types pattern synchronically according to a model that was originally intended by Givón (1979:222) to describe a diachronic process, that of syntacticization, whereby "[tightly bound] constructions arise diachronically ... from looser, conjoined, paratactic constructions."[26] The question then arises as to whether the model implies a necessary diachronic relationship among the three postposing types in Tamil.

employed by narrators in traditional oral performance genres. In other discourse genres, the clause-internal position represented by F may not be available.

[26]Cf. also Lehmann (1985) and Traugott (1993).

3.2 Diachronic Considerations

Unfortunately, few studies to date have addressed the history of word order in Tamil, and none systematically. Lacking diachronic data, I can only speculate as to which of the postposing types came first, and whether or not there is a direct historical relationship among them. For the purposes of this discussion, I will assume (along with Givón) a path of diachronic development that mirrors the syntacticization continuum.[27] The problem is then to account for two links: that between afterthoughts and backgrounding, and that between backgrounding and emphasis.

It is implicit in a number of studies (Lambrecht 1981, Erguvanlí 1984) that antitopics and other conventionalized backgrounding postposings have their genesis in true afterthoughts. Indeed such a development is consistent with general principles of grammaticalization as articulated by Hopper (1991); specifically, the tendency for an emerging grammatical structure to be more restricted in function and distribution than its source, and the tendency for older and newer functions to coexist in a "layered" synchronic relationship. A diachronic development from afterthoughts to backgrounding postposings, with the latter representing a conventionalization and a specialization of the functions of the former, is highly plausible according to these criteria.

The relationship between backgrounding and emphasis is more controversial. On the one hand, a relatively high frequency of backgrounding postposings could have at some point licensed a weakening of the strict verb-final constraint, thereby opening the door for postposings of other (i.e., non-backgrounding) functional types. Such a view can be reinforced by appealing to the notion of sentence-final focus position as a pragmatic (or language type-relative) universal (cf. Firbas 1964; Halliday 1967; Herring 1990; Herring and Paolillo in press; Hetzron 1975).[28] On the other hand, a shift in function from backgrounding (de-emphasis) to emphasis is not widely attested in languages for which diachronic evidence is available, nor is there direct evidence to support such an interpretation for Tamil. On the contrary, the fact that emphatic postposing is limited to traditional oral performance genres suggests that the strategy, rather than being innovating, may be archaic, a relic of a time when word order in Tamil was less strict.[29] In

[27] A different developmental order is, of course, theoretically possible.

[28] Independent evidence of a tendency towards final focus position in Tamil can be adduced from the order of elements in cleft constructions (Lehmann 1989:368) and verbless presentational constructions (Herring and Paolillo in press).

[29] Cf. Andronov (1991). Native speakers of Modern Tamil feel that emphatic postposing sounds "poetic", which further suggests an archaic status.

light of these considerations, and until such time as historical research establishes a direct link, we cannot assume any necessary diachronic relationship between backgrounding postposing and emphatic postposing.

Does this then mean that the continuum model is flawed as a description of the facts of postposing in Tamil? Not at all. It is valid in two important respects. First, the properties of each postposing type are amenable to being arranged in a particular linear order, that order being the same regardless of whether the criterion is syntactic bondedness, intonation, or motivatedness of function; this is presumably not a random coincidence, but rather reflects a principled relationship. Second, the actual attested data represent a gradient of uses. Thus in addition to the "core" cases presented as examples of each type above, there are "mixed" or "hybrid" uses, where features of one type are combined with features of another. For example, much of the difficulty in distinguishing afterthought adverbials and conventionalized adverbial postposings in speech is that both sometimes follow an intonational break (normally a feature of afterthoughts alone); cf. the variation in examples (19) and (20) above. This represents an area where the two postposing types are not separated by a very great functional distance. Moreover, antitopics as well are sometimes accompanied by true afterthought intonation, i.e., delivered as if they were afterthoughts when they clearly fulfill a specific pragmatic function, a fact which suggests that the notion of the afterthought is available in some sense even in conventionalized uses.[30] The antitopic 'king' in (21) could be considered an example of this type, although antitopics following an even more pronounced intonation break can be identified in the corpus.[31] More surprising perhaps are uses which blur the distinction between antitopicalization and emphasis, two functions which might at first glance appear to be mutually exclusive. In traditional oral epic narration, referents that otherwise function as antitopics e.g., for purposes of switch reference are sometimes intonationally emphasized, as in the following example.

[30] A possible link preserved between the two is whatever stylistic connotations speech containing true afterthoughts may possess informality, spontaneity, colloquiality, etc. These observations are not surprising, of course, if true afterthoughts and backgrounding postposings are diachronically related, the latter arising out of the former as "conventionalizations" of the afterthought strategy.

[31] There are also postposings that appear to function as true afterthoughts which do not follow an intonational break, e.g. 'uncle' in example (28).

(35) [the immediately preceding discourse topic is 'Duryodhana's brothers']

oru	nāḷ	ivan̠	anta ..	anantappuratt-ilē	tann-uṭaiya
one	day	he	that	A.-LOC	self-GEN

ar̠aiy-ilē	amar-ntu	iru-kkin̠r̠-ān̠	*turiyōtanan!*
room-LOC	sit-CP	be-PR-3SG:MASC	Duryodhana

'One day he was sitting in his room in Anandapuram *Duryodhana!*'
(i.e., Duryodhana was sitting in his room in Anandapuram)

'Duryodhana' in this example is an antitopic in that the referent is thematic, given information and represents a retrospective shift in topic. At the same time it is emphasized intonationally in the manner characteristic of new mention postposings. The functional motivation for mixing the two strategies appears to be to signal simultaneously a shift to a new topic and to underscore the *re*introduction of Duryodhana, the protagonist of the narrative. The existence of hybrid uses of this sort suggests that there is an overlap or at least a perceived relationship between the functions of antitopicalization and emphasis in the minds of speakers. A continuum model is thus necessary to characterize postposing as it is manifested in its full range of uses.[32]

To sum up, the three postposing types in Tamil afterthought, backgrounding, and emphatic are related along a continuum of syntacticization, here defined as a type of linear organization in terms of tightness of syntactic bond between component elements. The syntacticization model is not only descriptively adequate, but would appear to have psychological reality for Tamil speakers, who relate the three postposing types in the same linear order, as manifested through hybrid uses. These observations are essentially synchronic; that is, they do not depend on there being an analogous diachronic relationship among the Tamil postposing types, although such a relationship is not of course ruled out. More generally, the evidence that speakers effectively reconstruct a syntacticization continuum independent of historical relatedness provides support for the motivated nature of syntacticization as a diachronic process.

[32] The nature of such a continuum is aptly characterized by Traugott (1993:1) as "a [unidirectional] path ... from less to more compressed, ... with 'way-stations' where prototype constructions cluster along the way; in other words, not a slippery slope but a stairway with landings".

3.3 Conclusion

In concluding, I return to the problem of postposing in verb-final languages more generally. Despite differences in terminology and descriptive approach, the studies cited at the outset agree remarkably in terms of what constitutes the overall functional character of postverbal position. Kuno (1978) uses the term "afterthoughts" to characterize what in our terms would be both afterthoughts and backgrounding in Japanese (cf. also Fujii 1991), and Erguvanlí (1984) labels as "backgrounding" a similarly diverse set of phenomena in Turkish. The same three functions, more or less, as are found in Tamil are attributed by Kim and Shin (1992) to Korean and by Junghare (1985) to Indo-Aryan: afterthoughts ("corrections"), de-emphasis, and emphasis. All languages, presumably, make use of afterthoughts as a repair mechanism in unplanned speech. Further, it would seem that this strategy regularly becomes conventionalized in a backgrounding or de-emphatic function. Emphatic postposing, in contrast, is considerably more restricted in its occurrence crosslinguistically and within any given language (it is the least frequently attested type in both Korean and Indo-Aryan). Presumably, this is due to the fact that postverbal emphatics, as focusing devices, form a closer syntactic bond with the main clause, and thus constitute a potential threat to basic word order in ways that more loosely conjoined afterthoughts, antitopics, etc. do not. Thus the continuum model, in addition to accounting for the facts of Modern Tamil, has implications for the analysis of postposing more generally.

Acknowledgements

The author acknowledges, with thanks, insightful criticism by Wallace Chafe, James Gair, Talmy Givón, Alan Kim, Knud Lambrecht, and John Paolillo of an earlier version of this paper.

APPENDIX: Abbreviations

ABL	ablative	NF	non-future
ACC	accusative	NP	non-past
ADV	adverbializer	P	past
AjP	adjectival participle	PERF	perfect
BEN	benefactive	PERM	permissive
COND	conditional	PFV	perfective
CP	conjunctive participle	PL	plural
DAT	dative	POSS	possibilitative
EMPH	emphatic	PR	present
F	future	PURP	purpose
FEM	feminine	Q	yes-no question
GEN	genitive	QUOT	quotative
IMP	imperative	REL	relativizer
INC	increment	RESP	respective
INF	infinitive	SG	singular
INST	instrumental	TAG	tag question
LOC	locative	TOP	topic
MASC	masculine	VN	verbal noun
NEUT	neuter	VOC	vocative
NEG	negative		

1	first person
2	second person
3	third person

References

Andronov, M.S. 1975. Observations on accent in Tamil. In H. Schiffman, and C. Eastman (Eds.), *Dravidian Phonological Systems*. Seattle: University of Washington.

Andronov, M.S. 1991. Word order: causality and relations. In B. Lakshmi Bai and B. Ramakrishna Reddy (Eds.), *Studies in Dravidian and General Linguistics*. Hyderabad: Osmania University.

Asher, R.E. 1985. *Tamil*. Croom Helm Descriptive Grammar Series. London: Routledge.

Aske, J. 1991. Explaining clause-level constituent order. Ms., University of California, Berkeley.

Chafe, W. L. 1976. Givenness, contrastiveness, definiteness, subjects and topics. In C.N. Li, (Ed.), *Subject and Topic*. New York: Academic Press.

Chafe, W. L. 1987. Cognitive constraints on information flow. In R. Tomlin (Ed.), *Coherence and Grounding in Discourse*. Amsterdam: Benjamins.

Chafe, W. L. Unpublished ms. Discourse, Consciousness, and Time: The Flow and Displacement of Conscious Experience in Speaking and Writing.

Christdas, P. 1988. *The phonology and morphology of Tamil.* Unpublished PhD dissertation, Cornell University.

Dik, S. 1989. *The Theory of Functional Grammar*. Part I: *The Structure of the Clause*. Dordrecht: Foris.

Erguvanlí, E. 1984. *The Function of Word Order in Turkish Grammar*. Berkeley: University of California Press.

Firbas, J. 1964. On defining the theme in functional sentence analysis. *Travaux Linguistiques de Prague* 1:225–240.

Fujii, Y. 1991. Reversed word order in Japanese A discourse-pragmatic analysis. *Gengo Kenkyu* 99:58–81.

Givón, T. 1979. *On Understanding Grammar*. New York: Academic Press.

Givón, T. (Ed). 1983. *Topic Continuity in Discourse: Quantitative Cross-Language Studies*. Amsterdam: Benjamins.

Halliday, M.A.K. 1967. Notes on transitivity and theme in English: Part 2. *Journal of Linguistics* 3:199–244.

Herring, S. C. 1990. Topic and focus position as a function of word order type. In *Proceedings of the 16th Annual Meeting of the Berkeley Linguistics Society*, 163–174.

Herring, S. C. and J. C. Paolillo. In press. Focus position in SOV languages. To appear in P. Downing and M. Noonan (Eds.), *Word Order in Discourse*. Amsterdam: John Benjamins.

Hetzron, R. 1975. The presentative movement, or why the ideal word order is V.S.O.P. In C.N. Li (Ed.), *Word Order and Word Order Change*, 347–388. Austin: University of Texas.

Hopper, P. J. 1991. On some principles of grammaticization. In E. Traugott and B. Heine (Eds.), *Approaches to Grammaticalization*, Vol. 1, 17–35. Amsterdam: Benjamins.

Hyman, L. M. 1975. On the change from SOV to SVO: Evidence from Niger-Congo. In C.N. Li (Ed.), *Word Order and Word Order Change*. Austin: University of Texas.

Junghare, I. Y. 1985. The functions of word order variants in Indo-Aryan. In E. Bashir, M. Deshpande, and P. Hook (Eds.), *Select Papers from SALA-7: South Asian Languages Analysis*

Roundtable Conference, 236–253. Bloomington: Indiana University Linguistics Club.

Kim, A. 1988. Preverbal focusing and type XXIII languages. In M. Hammond, E. Moravcsik, and J. Wirth (Eds.), *Studies in Syntactic Typology*, 147–169. Amsterdam: Benjamins.

Kim, A. and H. Shin. 1992. Postposing in Korean. Paper presented at the XVth International Congress of Linguists, Québec, August 9–14, 1992.

Kuno, S. 1978. Japanese: A characteristic OV language. In W.P. Lehmann (Ed.), *Syntactic Typology: Studies in the Phenomenology of Language,*. Austin: University of Texas.

Lambrecht, K. 1981. *Topic, Antitopic, and Verb Agreement in Non-Standard French*. Amsterdam: Benjamins.

Lehmann, C. 1985. Grammaticalization: Synchronic variation and diachronic change. *Lingua e Stile* 20:303–18.

Lehmann, T. 1989. *A Grammar of Modern Tamil*. Pondicherry: Pondicherry Institute of Linguistics and Culture.

Prince, E. 1981. Toward a taxonomy of given-new information. In P. Cole (Ed.), *Radical Pragmatics*. New York: Academic Press.

Traugott, E. C. 1993. The development of English that-comple-ments revisited. Paper presented at the Annual meeting of the Linguistic Society of America, Los Angeles, January 1993.

7

Issues in Word Order in South Asian Languages: Enriched Phrase Structure or Multidimensionality?

K. P. Mohanan & T. Mohanan

There are a number of intriguing word order phenomena in South Asian languages which challenge existing ideas in syntactic theory about the representation of word order, and the formal mechanisms for capturing word order freedom. In this paper, we will examine some of these phenomena and indicate how they impinge upon theoretical assumptions. Our goal is not to defend any particular theory of word order or a framework for analysing word order phenomena. Rather, we will spell out some of the consequences of word order phenomena to theoretical assumptions in current treatments of word order, and outline a conception of linguistic structure that makes possible a particular line of analysis. As the title indicates, the paper is to be taken as a set of issues surrounding multidimensionality in relation to word order, and a statement of some interesting problems for research, rather than as a set of solutions.

The mechanism of co-indexed traces in current syntactic theory allows us to express two different kinds of information within the same level of representation. Thus, in a passive construction, the chain of an NP and its trace is simultaneously a grammatical subject and a "logical object", the logical objecthood being signalled by the trace. In a sentence like *John, Mary said Bill likes,* the chain of a *wh-* and its trace is simultaneously the topic of the sentence and the grammatical object of the embedded verb, the grammatical objecthood being signalled by the trace. Thus, traces allow us to copy information from one level of representation to another. Compared with phrase structure repre-

Theoretical Perspectives on Word Order in South Asian Languages
Miriam Butt, Tracy Holloway King, Gillian Ramchand (Eds.)

sentations of the *Aspects* type, then, its descendents are considerably more enriched. The enrichment of phrase structure is taken still further by the introduction of functional categories which express inflectional features, grammatical functions, and discourse functions in terms of labels on phrase structure nodes. Phrase structure representations enriched by traces and functional categories have been claimed to provide a useful analytical tool to solve the problems of word order in South Asian syntax (Gurtu 1985, Madhavan 1987, Speas 1990, Mahajan 1990, Srivastav 1991, among others).

Rather than enriching a single level of representation with different types of information, T. Mohanan (1990, 1992, forthcoming, and this volume) factors out the different types of information along different simultaneous dimensions of representation, the representation in each dimension being severely impoverished. The Principles and Parameters program in the GB theories is highly modular in its design of the *principles* that hold on linguistic representations. The program of multidimensional representations takes a further step in proposing highly modular *representations* that interact in interesting ways. The central thrust of this paper is the demonstration that ENRICHED PHRASE STRUCTURE REPRESENTATIONS do not yield adequate descriptions of word order phenomena in South Asian language, and that the conception of MULTIDIMENSIONAL REPRESENTATIONS promises a viable alternative worth exploring.

This paper is organised as follows. Section 1 outlines some of the assumptions implicit in the use of phrase structure representations to analyse word order phenomena. Sections 2–5 outline four phenomena that challenge these assumptions, namely, non-clausebounded free word order, freezing effects, noncanonical order, and multiple focus. We indicate how the facts can be analysed in terms of multidimensional representations, without providing the details of the analysis or extensive justification. Within an enriched unidimensional approach, these phenomena have no analysis. Section 6 summarizes the conclusions.

1 Enriched Phrase Structure Representations

1.1 Phrase Structure Representations and Word Order

In Chomsky (1957, 1965), *phrase structure representations* were constructed exclusively out of grammatical categories. These representations encoded both *dominance* and *precedence* relations. The precedence relations expressed word order. As a consequence, an assumption implicit in this framework was:

(1) Requirements on word order are stated in terms of grammatical categories.

The introduction of functional categories into phrase structure representations led to the implicit abandonment of (1).[1] The birth of functional categories had two sources. One was the development of X-bar theory with the constructs SPEC, HEAD, and COMPLEMENT (Chomsky 1971). The other was the proposal for COMP as a node label in phrase structure representations that can be filled by any inherent category, such as NP, PP, or even $\bar{S}$, and denotes a position fulfilling a syntactic function (Bresnan 1972).

Extending this enrichment of phrase structure representations, current work in the GB tradition represents the grammatical functions subject and object as SPEC of AGR-S and SPEC of AGR-O, and the discourse functions topic and focus as SPEC of TOPIC and SPEC of FOCUS. We use the term ENRICHED PHRASE STRUCTURE REPRESENTATIONS to refer to these enriched representations, in which nodes in a single tree structure carry information about grammatical categories, grammatical functions, inflectional features, and discourse functions. Since word order information is expressed by such enriched PS representations, the claim in (1) is no longer tenable: it must be restated as:

(2) Requirements on word order are stated in terms of node labels in a single tree structure.

Abandoning the requirement that all statements of word order be made in terms of grammatical categories opens up other avenues for the statement of regularities in word order. One possibility is to state precedence relations in terms of grammatical functions, as in (3a) and (3b). Another is to state them in terms of discourse functions, as in (3c):

(3) a. The subject precedes the non-subject functions.
b. The predicate precedes the non-subject functions.
c. Topic occurs at the left edge.

These options are indirectly available in any theory that uses enriched PS representations.

---

[1]By grammatical categories, we refer to a *classification* of the words/morphemes or larger units of the language. Functional categories (e.g. AGR-O, AGR-S, CP, etc.) in the descendents of GB theory do not encode information about a classification of units, but the function of a unit in relation to the structure in which it occurs. Thus, the term COMP, unlike the term PP, does not refer to a part of speech or its projection, but to a *position* associated with a set of syntactic properties.

Other possibilities include word order restrictions in terms of argument structure or theta roles as in (4a), grammatical features such as case as in (4b), and phonological units as in (4c):

(4) a. Arguments higher on the theta role scale precede the ones lower on the scale.
b. Two arguments with the same case cannot be adjacent.
c. For a secondary object to precede a primary object, the latter must have at least two phonological words.

Uszkoreit (1985), Webelhuth (1989) and T. Mohanan (1992) have argued for the statement of word order restrictions in terms of argument structure. T. Mohanan (this volume) argues for the statement of word order restrictions in terms of case formatives. Zec and Inkelas (1990) have argued for word order restrictions stated in terms of phonological units.

Given this discussion, two questions immediately arise. First, what are the units on which requirements on word order are stated? That is, in statements of the form "x precedes y", "x is adjacent to y", "x is final/initial", what are x and y? Second, can these units be formally expressed in terms of labels in enriched PS representations? We will examine these issues in Sections 2–5.

1.2 Word Order Freedom as Optional Transformations of a Basic Order

In frameworks that employ transformational rules, word order at a more abstract level of representation can be manipulated by transformational rules to yield the surface word order. This strategy lends itself to the expression of basic or canonical order as the "d(eep) structure" order (as required by PS rules or their equivalents), and the nonbasic or noncanonical orders as deviations from the basic pattern. Thus, in a "free word order" language, given the possible word orders SOV, OSV, SVO, OSV, VSO, and VOS, one could assume SOV to be the basic word order, and the other word orders to be the result of optional scrambling transformations.

The rule of scrambling has been abandoned in recent versions of transformational frameworks. However, the idea of expressing word order freedom in terms of optional transformations remains. Thus, within the tradition initiated by Saito and Hoji (1983) and followed in Gurtu (1986), Madhavan (1987), Gair and Wali (1989), Speas (1990), Mahajan (1990), Jayaseelan (1991), Srivastav (1991), among others, the basic word order in free word order languages like Japanese and Hindi is SOV, as in (5a). The remaining word orders are the results of the optional application of "move alpha", as illustrated in the OSV order in (5b).

(5) a.

b.

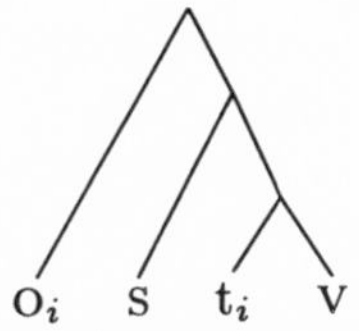

The enriched PS representation in (5b) expresses information about grammatical functions in terms of traces, and information about word order in terms of their overt antecedents.

Recent proposals in the Minimalist Program (Chomsky 1989, 1992) raise serious questions about this treatment of free word order. One of the fundamental ideas in the Minimalist Program is the "Last Resort" principle, which in effect requires that a movement transformation take place *only if driven* by some independent requirement. By this principle, "a step in a derivation is legitimate only if it is necessary for convergence had the step not been taken, the derivation would not have converged. NP-raising, for example, is driven by the Case Filter (now assumed to apply only at LF): if the Case feature of NP has already been checked, NP may not raise." (Chomsky 1992:46).

The Last Resort principle holds that if the requirements of the grammar permit two derivations, one longer than the other, then the longer derivation is disallowed (Chomsky 1992:43). This principle disallows the derivation in (5b), since it is not *driven* by anything in the grammar: the derivation converges even without the adjunction.

Faced with this problem, here are the options available to us:

A. Find driving factors that force the derivations which yield all the possible orders in free word order languages;
B. Abandon the Last Resort principle;
C. Abandon movement as a device for the formal expression of word order freedom.

Our hunch is that a search for driving factors will be fruitless. We take it that the Last Resort principle is an integral component of the Minimality Program, and abandoning it is not a viable option either. If so, the Minimality Program is forced to abandon the movement analysis of free word order, and look for alternative ways of expressing free word order. Needless to say, the alternative would be to make the more radical move and abandon the Last Resort Principle.

In the light of this discussion, we may raise the following questions:

Is it possible/desirable to account for the freedom of word order in terms of the formal device of movement? Is it possible to express the intuition of canonical and noncanonononical word order in a movement analysis? With these questions in mind, let us examine some word order phenomena in South Asian languages.

2 Non-clausebounded Free Word Order

2.1 Free Word Order

It is well-known that freedom of word order and its absence are relative terms. A "fixed" word order language like English exhibits a certain degree of freedom of word order, and a "free" word order language like Warlpiri exhibits certain restrictions on word order. Yet, most of us share the intuition that word order in languages like Warlpiri, Japanese, Korean, and Malayalam is qualitatively different from word order in languages like English, Mandarin, and Irish. To point out the obvious, when we exchange the positions of the two noun phrases in the English sentence in (6), there is a corresponding switch in the interpretation of theta roles:

(6) a. John pinched Bill.
b. Bill pinched John.

In (6a), John is the agent and Bill the undergoer of pinching; in (6b), Bill is the agent and John the undergoer. The same exchange in position in Malayalam in (7) does not cause a corresponding switch in the interpretation of theta roles:[2]

(7) a. jooṇ billine n̲uḷḷi.
John-N Bill-A pinched
John pinched Bill.
b. billine jooṇ n̲uḷḷi.
Bill-A John-N pinched
John pinched Bill.

Though the positions of the two noun phrases in (7a) are reversed in (7b), John is the agent in both, and Bill the undergoer. In order to avoid the analytical claims implicit in terms like "non-configurationality" and "scrambling", we will use the term FREE WORD ORDER to refer to

[2]The abbreviations used in this paper are:

N	: nominative	E	: ergative
A	: accusative	D	: dative
C	: commitative	I	: instrumental
INF	: infinitive	PERF	: perfective
CAUS	: causative		

the phenomenon illustrated in Malayalam in (7), contrasting with the fixed word order illustrated in English in (6).

2.2 Free Word Order across Clauses

Most descriptions and analyses in the literature have taken it for granted that unlike languages like Warlpiri, free word order in South Asian languages is clause bounded (K.P. Mohanan 1982, Gurtu 1985, Madhavan 1987, Mahajan 1990). However, the dependents of an embedded nonfinite predicate can be interspersed with the dependents of the matrix predicate. Let us first consider nonfinite clauses which are arguments of the matrix predicate. Interspersing the dependents of the matrix predicate and the embedded predicate in (8a) yields grammatical sentences in Hindi, with no change in their theta role interpretations (8b–e):

(8)	a.	aaj	mãã ne	bacce se	*kitaab*	*paḍ^{h}ne ko*	kahaa.
		today	mother-E	child-A	book-N	read-INF	told
		Today the mother told the child to read the book.					
	b.	aaj	*kitaab*	mãã ne	bacce se	*paḍ^{h}ne ko*	kahaa.
		today	book-N	mother-E	child-A	read-INF	told
	c.	aaj	bacce se	*kitaab*	mãã ne	*paḍ^{h}ne ko*	kahaa.
		today	child-A	book-N	mother-E	read-INF	told
	d.	bacce se	*kitaab*	mãã ne	*paḍ^{h}ne ko*	aaj	kahaa.
		child-A	book-N	mother-E	read-INF	today	told
	e.	mãã ne	*kitaab*	aaj	bacce se	*paḍ^{h}ne ko*	kahaa.
		mother-E	book-N	today	child-A	read-INF	told

Such interspersing is permitted in nonfinite adjunct clauses as well:

(9)	a.	aaj	bacce ne	*mãã ko*	*p^{h}uul*	*de kar*
		today	child-E	mother-D	flower-N	give-INF.comp
		apnaa kaam	kiyaa.			
		self's work	did			
		Today, after giving the flower to the mother, the child did self's work.				
	b.	aaj	*mãã ko*	bacce ne	*p^{h}uul*	*de kar*
		today	mother-D	child-E	flower-N	give-INF.COMP
		apnaa	kaam	kiyaa.		
		self's	work	did		
	c.	aaj	*p^{h}uul*	bacce ne	*mãã ko*	*de kar*
		today	flower -N	child-E	mother-D	give-INF.COMP
		apnaa	kaam	kiyaa.		
		self's	work	did		

d. aaj *mãã ko* *pʰuul* bacce ne *de kar*
today mother-D flower -N child-E give-INF.COMP
apnaa kaam kiyaa.
self's work did

The sentences in (8b–e) and (9b–d) require marked intonation patterns to provide cues for parsing. It is reasonably easy for Hindi speakers to intersperse dependents across clauses as illustrated above.

K.P. Mohanan (1982) shows that, in Malayalam, scrambling out of an NP or an embedded clause inside a PP is ungrammatical:

(10) a. inn̲ə amma *kuṭṭiye* *cir̄ippikkaan weeṇṭi* or̄ə paaṭṭə
today mother-N child-A make laugh-INF-for one song-N
paaṭi.
sang
Today the mother sang a song to make the child laugh.

b. *inn̲ə *kuṭṭiye* amma *cir̄ippikkaan weeṇṭi*
today child-A mother-N make laugh-INF-for
or̄ə paaṭṭə paaṭi.
one song-N sang

c. *inn̲ə amma *kuṭṭiye* or̄ə paaṭṭə
today mother-N child-A one song-N
cir̄ippikkaan weeṇṭi paaṭi.
make laugh-INF-for sang

The generalization in examples like (10) is that scrambling across the non-clausal dependents of a predicate is not permitted. On the basis of this generalization, it was concluded that non-clausebounded scrambling is not possible in Malayalam. However, the Malayalam sentences in (11), show that this conclusion is incorrect:

(11) a. inn̲ə amma kuṭṭiyooṭə *accʰanə* *pust̲akam*
today mother-N child-C father-D book-N
koṭukkaan paraññu.
give-INF told
Today the mother asked the child to give the book to the father.

b. inn̲ə *accʰanə* *pust̲akam* amma *kuṭṭiyooṭə*
today father-D book-N mother-N child-C
koṭukkaan paraññu.
give-INF told

c. inn̲ə kuṭṭiyooṭə *accʰanə* *pust̲akam* amma
today child-C father-D book-N mother-N

koṭukkaan parañ̃ñu.
give-INF told

Although the Malayalam examples in (11b,c) are somewhat artificial or forced compared to the Hindi examples in (8), the sharp contrast between the ungrammatical examples in (10b,c) and the grammatical ones in (11b,c) is quite robust.

Thus, both Hindi and Malayalam exhibit non-clausebounded free word order. All grammars of Hindi and Malayalam must recognize the conclusion in (12a). In addition, any analysis of non-clausebounded free word order must be able to express (12b):

(12) a. Evidence from phenomena such as passive, disjoint reference, and reflexive binding indicate that the syntactic representation of the sentences in (8)–(11) have two CLAUSAL UNITS each.
b. The dependents of the predicate in a nonfinite clause are not required to be ADJACENT. They can be interspersed with the dependents of the matrix predicate.

We now turn to a possible analysis of these facts.

2.3 Unidimensional and Multidimensional Representations

Consider the following sentence in Hindi:

(13) pʰuul mãã ko bacce ne diyaa.
flower-N mother-D child-E gave
The child gave the flower to mother.

Any analysis of (13) must express the idea that 'child' is the grammatical subject in (13), and 'flower' and 'mother' are the primary and secondary object respectively. Let us assume the following commonly adopted convention for representing grammatical functions:

(14)
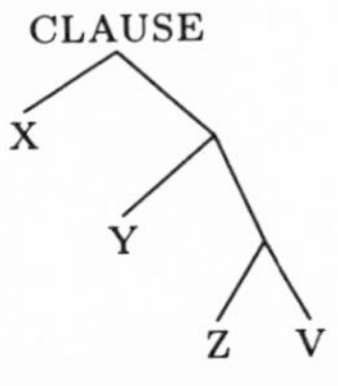

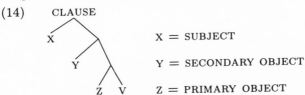

X = SUBJECT
Y = SECONDARY OBJECT
Z = PRIMARY OBJECT

The representation of the grammatical functions in (13) is given in (15).

(15) *Representation of Grammatical Functions*

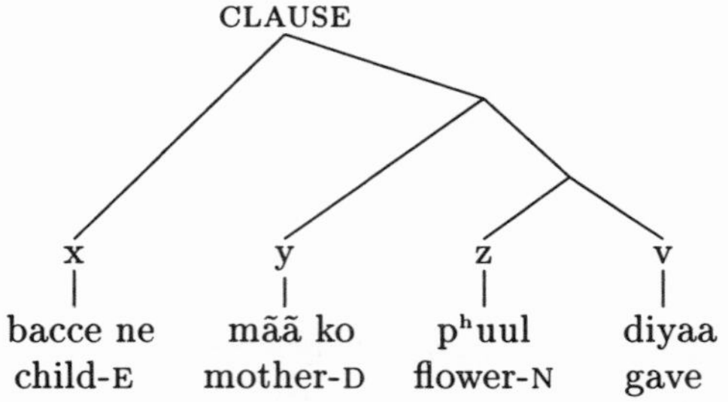

Any analysis of (13) must also express the information about word order given in (16), where "x < y" means "x precedes y".

(16) *Representation of Word Order*

p^huul <	mãã ko <	bacce ne <	diyaa
flower-N	mother-D	child-E	gave

The representation in (15) does not express this information. How are the pieces of information in (15) and (16) put together? One way is to represent them along different dimensions of representation, which are "linked" or "associated" with each other, following the approach taken in Chomsky (1981:127–135), K.P. Mohanan (1982, 1983), Hale (1983), T. Mohanan (1990), Simpson (1991) and others. The "bi-dimensional" representation of (13) given in (17) illustrates this approach:

(17) *Bi-dimensional Representation*

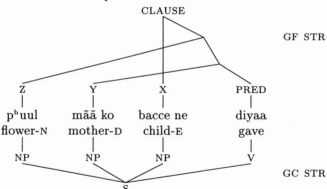

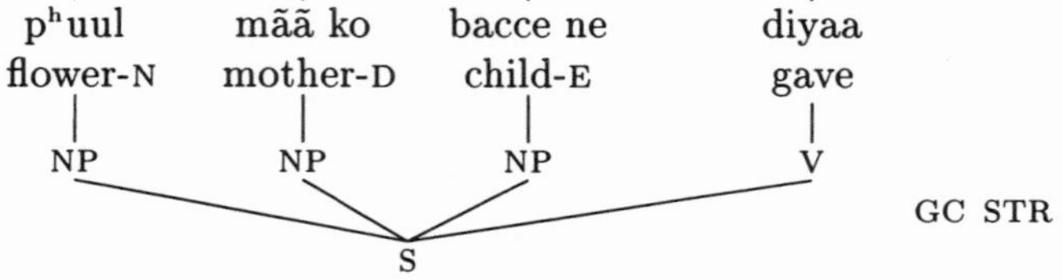

The tree above the sentence expresses the grammatical function structure (GF STR). It contains internal hierarchical structure but no precedence relations. The tree below the sentence expresses the grammatical category structure (GC STR). It encodes precedence relations but no internal hierarchical structure of the NP's inside an S.[3] Given this dual representation, the association between the two can be stated as (18):

(18) *The mapping function*

Given a verb α and its sister β at GC STR, associate β with x, y, z ... at GF STR. (subject to the independent requirements of case, subcategorization ...)

The absence of internal hierarchical structure in (17) is not crucial to the point we are making. Even though redundant, one can revise it to have a binary branching structure, as illustrated in (19):

(19) *Bi-dimensional Representation*

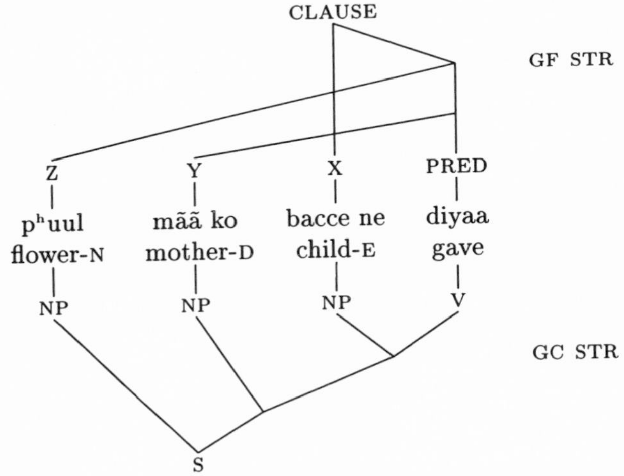

What is important is that the binary branching structure at the bottom signals word order, but not grammatical functions.

The solution adopted in (17) is to separate the information about grammatical functions and word order into two different *dimensions* of structure. An alternative is to separate them into two different *stages in the derivation*, as was done in pre-trace theoretic versions of transformational grammar, where a rule of scrambling converted the representation in (15) to (17) or (19). Yet another alternative is to separate them into two different *layers* of structure in a single dimension of representation, which is the approach taken in Saito and Hoji (1983), Gurtu (1985), Mahajan (1990), and so on. In this approach, the as-

[3]Since GF STR does not encode precedence relations, the branches in (17) do not 'cross', even though the left-to-right order forced by the picture on paper gives the illusion of crossing.

sociation between the two layers of structure is expressed in terms of co-indexed traces, as illustrated in (20):

(20) *Unidimensional Representation*

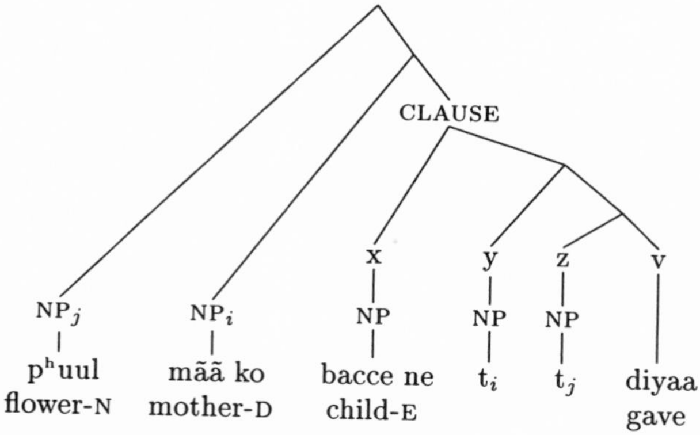

The inner layer of structure, which contains the traces, does not tell us anything about word order: it expresses the grammatical function information in (15). The outer layer of structure, which contains the antecedents of the traces, does not tell us anything about grammatical functions: it expresses the actual order of words in (16).

The representation in (20) is the result of *folding* into a single level of representation, the word order information in GC STR and the grammatical function information in GF STR in (19). If we ignore the specification of precedence in the representation of grammatical functions, and of hierarchical structure in the representation of word order, (17) and (20) are equivalent at an abstract conceptual level.[4] They both code grammatical functions and word order, and both allow simultaneous access to the two types of information. The mapping function in (18) is a concretisation of the proposal for "assume GF" in Chomsky (1981:127–135), which is a variant of "move alpha" that derives (20) from (15). The association between dimensions in (19) is governed by constraints which are equivalent to the constraints that hold on the association between different layers in (20).

As we see it, the fundamental difference between the two approaches is that one uses a *multidimensional* approach to representations where each representation is considerably *impoverished* ((17)), while the other uses a *unidimensional* approach by using an *enriched* representation ((20)). Given the substantial overlap between the two approaches, it

[4]See Yatabe (1993) for a proposal that combines the hierarchical and flat structure representations of word order without the use of traces.

is not easy to compare the relative descriptive or explanatory merits of these two approaches to the analysis of free word order on an empirical basis. However, empirical problems arise when we combine the unidimensional approach with the cluster of assumptions within which current unidimensional representations of transformational grammar are embedded. For example, as we pointed out earlier, the trace theoretic derivational approach conflicts with the Last Resort principle in Chomsky's Minimalist Program, and hence cannot be used in an analysis within this theory.

Furthermore, it is unclear how the *mechanism* of move alpha devised for the clause internal free word order can be extended to cover the phenomenon of non-clausebounded free word order. Let us take the Hindi sentences in (8). In order to express clausal constituency of these sentences ((12a)), any analysis will need a variant of the representation illustrated in (21).

(21) *Representation of Clausality*

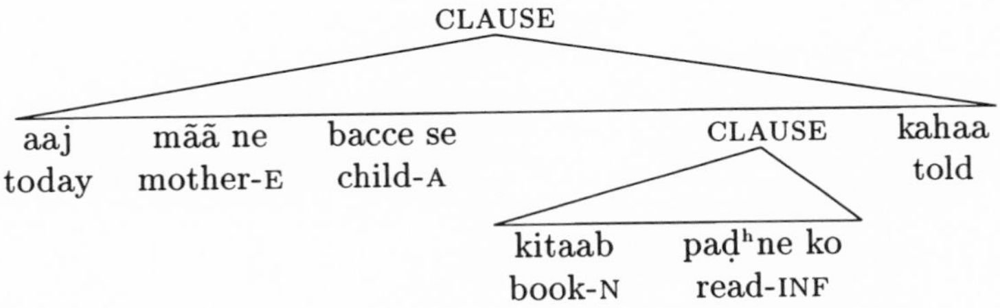

In addition, we also need a representation of the actual order of words, as in (22a) and (22b):

(22) *Representation of Word Order*

a. aaj < kitaab < mãã ne < bacce se <
   today book-N mother-E child-A
   paḍ^{h}ne ko < kahaa.
   read-INF told

b. aaj < bacce se < kitaab < mãã ne <
   today child-A book-N mother-E
   paḍ^{h}ne ko < kahaa.
   read-INF told

Our task is to put together the representation of clausehood in (21) and the representation of word order in (22), either in two levels of representation or in a single level of representation. Within the multidimensional approach, we will have the representation in (23) for the sentence in (8a):

(23)

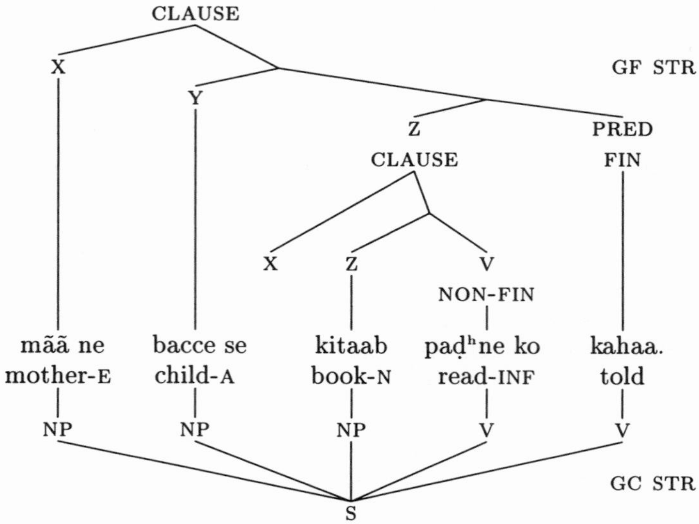

The PS rules that yields the GC STR in (23) can be given as (24):

(24) S $\longrightarrow$ X* , V (where X $\neq$ finite verb)

(24) allows an S to have two verbs as its daughters, as long as only one of them is finite. Since the rule does not stipulate any particular word order, it automatically provides for free word order. The question is, how is the GC STR in (23) mapped onto the GF STR? In order to answer this question, we revise the mapping principle in (18) as (25) and (26):

(25) *Conditions on* GF STR

a. A CLAUSE has one and only one PRED, and a PRED belongs to one and only one CLAUSE.
b. Every CLAUSE has a SUBJECT.
c. No CLAUSE contains more than one instance of the same GF.

(26) *Linking between* GC STR *and* GF STR

a. Every verb in an S in GC STR is associated with a PRED in GF STR.
b. Every daughter of S in GC STR is associated with a GF in GF STR. (subject to the requirements of case, subcategorization, and so on)
c. A NONFIN CLAUSE is a GF of some other clause.

The GF STR for (8b–e) will be identical to the one for (8a) in (23). The GC STR will be different for different sentences, but they will differ only in the precedence relations, not in the hierarchical structure.

In order to have a corresponding analysis of non-clausebounded free word order in a movement approach, one will have to allow movement from an embedded nonfinite clause to free adjunction positions in the matrix clause. No such proposals exist yet, and therefore it is impossible to evaluate movement analyses of non-clausebounded free word order. To the best of our knowledge, the effect of non-clauseboundedness of movement in current transformational grammar is achieved by moving from some unique position (such as SPEC of CP or I) to another. What would be the effects of allowing movement from multiple free adjunction positions in an embedded clause to similar positions in the matrix clause? How can this movement be restricted to nonfinite clauses? Until such questions are answered, the facts of non-clausebounded free word order constitute a serious challenge to the movement approach to free word order.

2.4 Free Word Order and Clefting

Another problem for the enriched phrase structure account of free word order is the correlation between clefting and word order freedom in Malayalam. In Malayalam, all and only those units which can be clefted can be scrambled (K.P. Mohanan 1982). In the cleft construction in Malayalam, a focus marker (*aaṇə* 'is' or *alla* 'is not') is attached to the focussed element, and the nominalising particle *at̠ə* 'it', which signals the scope of focus, is attached to the finite verb. An example is given in (27):

(27) a. kuṭṭi aanaye n̠uḷḷi.
child-N elephant-A pinched
The child pinched the elephant.

b. kuṭṭiyaaṇə aanaye n̠uḷḷiyat̠ə.
child-N-be elephant-A pinched-it
It was the child who pinched the elephant.

c. kuṭṭi aanayeyaaṇə n̠uḷḷiyat̠ə.
child-N elephant-A-be pinched-it
It was the elephant that the child pinched.

The freedom of word order is unaffected by clefting: each of the clefted constructions in (27b,c) allows the other five word orders.

The correlation between free word order and clefting holds in sentences with embedded nonfinite clauses as well. Thus, when a focus marker is attached to the matrix predicate in (11), the dependents of the embedded predicate can be clefted, as shown in (28):

(28) a. in̲n̲ə amma kuṭṭiyooṭə *jooṇin***aaṇə** *pust̲akam*
today mother-N child-C John-D-IS book-N
koṭ̲ukkaan paraññat̲ə.
give-INF told-it
It was to John that the mother asked the child to give the book today.

b. in̲n̲ə amma kuṭṭiyooṭə *jooṇinn̲ə* *pust̲akam***aaṇə**
today mother-N child-C John-D book-N-IS
koṭukkaan paraññat̲ə.
give-INF told
It was the book that the mother asked the child to give to John today.

In contrast, the dependents of a clause inside a PP ((10)) cannot be clefted, as (29) shows:

(29) *in̲n̲ə amma *kuṭṭiyey***aaṇə** *cir̃ippikkaan weeṇṭi* or̃ə
today mother-N child-A-IS makelaugh-INF-FOR one
paaṭṭə paaṭiyat̲ə
song-N sang-it
[Intended meaning: It was the child such that mother sang a song today to make him/her laugh.]

Within the analysis in (23)–(26), no special machinery is required to account for these facts. They follow from the condition that an S should have one and only one finite verb as a daughter. The categorial effect of attaching the cleft marker *aa* 'be' clefting in Malayalam is to make the clefted constituent into a final verbal unit. The effect of attaching *at̲ə* 'it' to the the finite verb is to make it into a nominal. Since *at̲ə* can be attached only to finite verbs, the condition of one and only one finite verb in an S correctly predicts both the scrambling facts and the clefting facts. (See K.P. Mohanan 1982 for details of the machinery.) If clefting is taken care of by LF movement, it is unclear how the correlation between the overt movement in scrambling and the LF movement in clefting will be taken care of.[5] Even if clefting is accounted for in terms of overt movement, following Madhavan (1987), the problem of accounting for the correlation remains.

[5] An anonymous reviewer claims that LF movement of in situ focus constructions of the type developed in Huang (1982) will provide a unified account of scrambling and clefting. We do not see how this can be done. Restrictions of space prevent us from a detailed discussion.

3 Definiteness Effects

3.1 Definiteness and Word Order

It is well-known that word order changes in free word order languages can affect meanings associated with discourse structure (see, for example, Gambhir 1981). A telling example is the interaction between definiteness and word order (Masica 1982, T. Mohanan 1992). In what follows, we briefly illustrate how definiteness effects in Hindi are relevant for the choice of representations.

Consider the following examples from Hindi.

(30) a. sunaar aaj haar laaegaa.
goldsmith-N tomorrow necklace-N bring-FUT
Tomorrow the/?a goldsmith will bring the/a necklace.

b. aaj sunaar haar laaegaa.
tomorrow goldsmith-N necklace-N bring-FUT
Tomorrow the/***a** goldsmith will bring the/a necklace.

In (30a), where the subject precedes the adjunct, it can be interpreted either as definite or indefinite. In (30b), where the subject follows the adjunct, it can be interpreted only as definite.

We assume that the NP's that exhibit definiteness effects of this kind are the topic that carry shared information. The question that we must ask is: what signals this kind of topichood in Hindi? Consider some more examples:

(31) a. sunaar ne laḍkii ko haar b^hejaa.
goldsmith-E girl-D necklace-N send-PERF
The/?a goldsmith sent the/a necklace to the/a girl.

b. sunaar ne haar laḍkii ko b^hejaa.
goldsmith-E necklace-N girl-D send-PERF
The/?a goldsmith sent the/***a** necklace to the/***a** girl.

c. haar sunaar ne laḍkii ko b^hejaa.
necklace-N goldsmith-E girl-D send-PERF
The/***a** goldsmith sent the/***a** necklace to the/***a** girl.

Speakers of Hindi intuitively recognize (30a) and (31a) to be in the "basic"/"canonical"/"unmarked" word order. (30b) and (31b, c) contain noncanonical sequences. A close examination reveals that a nominal in a noncanonical sequence is interpreted as definite. A noncanonical sequence is a sequence of elements that violates canonical word order.

(32)

sunaar ne	haar	laḍkii ko	b^{h}ejaa.	(=(31b))
goldsmith-E	necklace-N	girl-D	send-PERF	
	Noncanonical Sequence (=TOPIC)			

Having defined noncanonical sequence in terms of canonical word order, we are now required to provide a characterization of canonical order. How should canonical order be characterized? We investigate this question in the following section.

3.2 Canonical Order and Noncanonical Sequence

Examples of the asymmetry between canonical and noncanonical order discussed so far are consistent with the characterization of canonical order in terms of either the hierarchy of grammatical functions ((33))[6] or that of thematic roles ((34)):

(33) *Grammatical Function Hierarchy*
SUBJ < OBJ < SEC.OBJ < OBL < ADJUNCT

(34) *Thematic Hierarchy*
agent < beneficiary < experiencer < instrument < theme < location

Assuming in GF STR a "functional VP" that contains the predicate and all its dependents except the grammatical subject, the characterisation of canonical order in terms of (33) would be as follows: (i) the subject precedes the functional VP; (ii) the predicate occurs at the right edge; and (iii) within the functional VP, the higher of any two GF's in the hierarchy is closer to the predicate. The only difference between the fixed word order in English and canonical word order in Hindi would then be that in English, unlike Hindi, the predicate occurs at the left edge of the functional VP. The characterisation of canonical order in terms of (34) would be that the canonical order mirrors the order in the thematic hierarchy, with adjuncts occurring after the logical subject.

In order to choose between the two alternatives, we need to examine further data. Consider the examples in (35):

(35) a.

sunaarse	aaj	haar	banaayaa
goldsmith-I	today	necklace-N	become-CAUS-PERF
gayaa.			
go-PERF			

The/a necklace was made by the/?a goldsmith today.

[6]This statement yields the order in (i) for SVO languages, and the order in (ii) for SOV languages:

(i) subject < predicate < object < secondary object < adjunct
(ii) subject < adjunct < secondary object < object < predicate

b. sunaarse haar aaj banaayaa
goldsmith-I necklace-N today become-CAUS-PERF
gayaa.
go-PERF
The/***a** necklace was made by the/?a goldsmith today.

(35a,b) are passive constructions corresponding to the active constructions in (31a–c). As can be seen from the definiteness effects, (31a) and (35a) are in canonical order. In (31a), the agent-SUBJ precedes theme-OBJ. In (35a), the agent-ADJUNCT precedes theme-SUBJ. The characterization of canonical word order in terms of (33) incorrectly predicts that (35a) is noncanonical, while (35b) is canonical. The characterization in terms of (34) makes the right predictions in both cases. Hence we conclude that canonical word order in Hindi is best characterized in terms of theta roles, not grammatical functions. (Also see Uszkoreit 1985 for canonical order in German.)

This conclusion is further reinforced by the contrast between the canonical orders in (36a) and (36b). The locative-OBL in (36b) is closer to the verb than the theme-OBJ: if canonical order were determined by grammatical functions, we would expect the object to be adjacent to the verb:

(36) a. ilaa ne anuu ko ek haar b^hejaa.
Ila-E Anu-D a necklace-N send-PERF
Ila sent a necklace to Anu.

b. ilaa ne anuu ko ek šahar b^hejaa.
Ila-E Anu-A a city-L send-PERF
Ila sent Anu to a city.

The canonical word order in Hindi is therefore stated as follows:

(37) *Linking between Argument Structure and Word Order*
a. Arguments lower on the hierarchy are closer to the verb.
b. The adjunct immediately follows the logical subject.
c. The predicate is final.

As stated earlier, noncanonical word order is a deviation from canonical word order. If canonical order requires a set of elements {a,b,c,d,e} to be ordered as *abcde,* then *dc* is a noncanonical sequence in *abdce,* and *ecdb* is a noncanonical sequence in *aecdb*. One way of conceptualizing noncanonical sequence is as elements that participate in the crossing of association lines between the canonically required order and the actual order.

(38) *Noncanonical Sequence* (NCS): crossing association lines

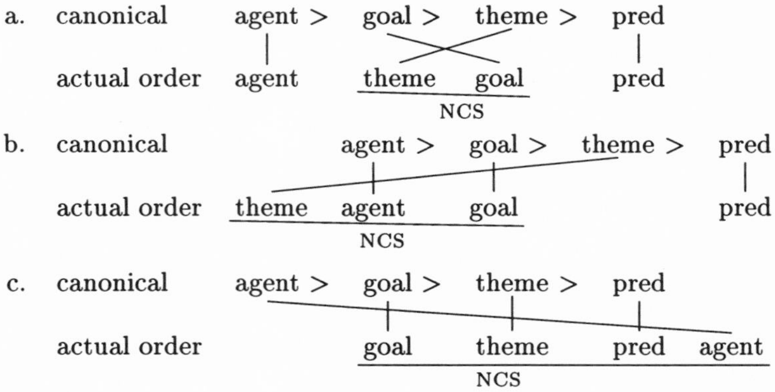

The contrast between (38a) and (38b) shows that a topic in these examples cannot be represented as a single unit of a phrase structure configuration. It is also hard to see how topichood can be related to a set of positions in a tree structure, or as a set of elements which have moved away from some prior positions in a tree structure. Therefore, we need to develop non-phrase structural accounts of canonical order and noncanonical sequence.

Given the uncontroversial assumption that linguistic regularities apply not to arbitrary *strings*, but to *units* of linguistic structure, we are forced to assume that *ncs* is a unit of linguistic representation. We have identified this unit as *topic*, and have argued that it does not form a phrase structure *constituent*.[7] It is natural to conclude therefore, that *topic* is a unit of linguistic description along a different dimension, say, that of discourse structure.

3.3 Representation of Topichood

In Section 2, we argued that the representation of grammatical functions and grammatical categories must be factored out into two dimensions of linguistic representation. The effect of the analysis in Section 3 is to add a third dimension of representation, namely, that of dis-

[7] A few words of explanation may be in order here. The word topic has been used in the literature to refer to a large number of related constructs. One of them is the topic of discourse that a sentence shares with the preceding sentences (old topic); the other is the entity that the speaker announces as the new topic of discourse (new topic). The topic we are concerned with here is the old topic. For reasons of space, it is impossible for us to spell out why it is necessary to regard the noncanonical sequence as a particular kind of topic. These reasons are discussed in T. Mohanan (1992).

course functions, to express the construct topic. Given in (39) is the representation of (31b) to illustrate this point:

(39)

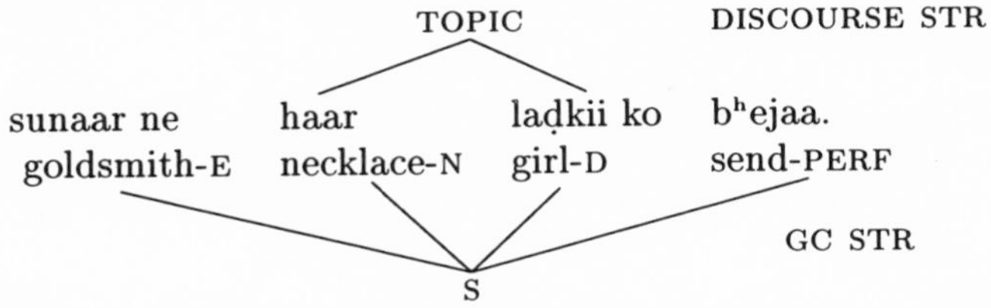

What we said about canonical order and noncanonical sequence in (38) may be thought of as statements on linking between DISCOURSE STR, ARG STR, and word order.

In order to avoid the practical problem of drawing a three dimensional representation on paper, the representation of GF STR has been left out in (39). The reader is requested to view (39) as a set of planes intersecting along an axis of the words of the sentence, each plane containing the representation of the structure of the sentence along that plane. (See T. Mohanan this volume.) This kind of representation was originally proposed for phonological structure in Halle and Vergnaud (1980), and is currently employed in the representation of segment structure in feature geometry (Clements 1985). In order to help the visualization, the reader may think of the words in a sentence as the rings that hold together a ring bound book, and the different dimensions as the pages in the open book, with structures on each page that take the rings as their terminal nodes:[8]

[8]For an account of multidimensional syntax, see T. Mohanan (1990) and this volume.

(40)

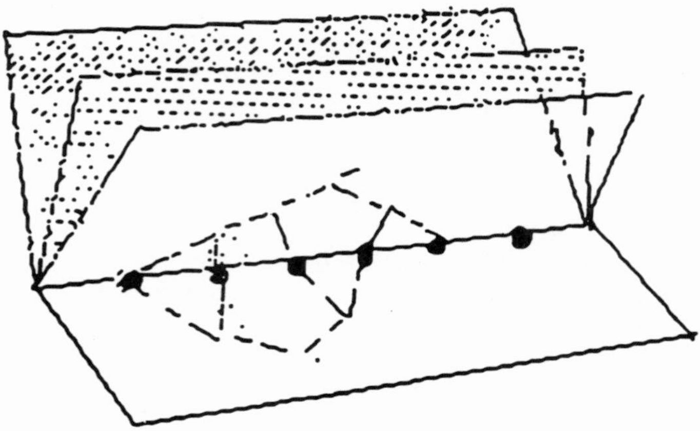

Under the conception in (40), the status of topic would be analogous to that of phonological units like phonological word and phonological phrase in phonological theory, in that they are not phrase structure constituents. (See Kanerva (1990) for a similar proposal for focus phrase.)

The different dimensions of structure in (40) are "co-present" in the sense that a principle of the grammar can access information from more than one dimension simultaneously. For example, a phonological principle can refer simultaneously to morphological structure and syllable structure, and a principle of word order can refer simultaneously to semantic structure, category structure, and grammatical function structure. These different structures are multidimensional, not linear, in that they do not entail any linear relation between them.

4 Freezing Effects

In a "free word order" language, we have said, word order does not signal grammatical functions. Now, it is not uncommon to find fixed word order constructions in free word order languages. The loss of the word order freedom of grammatical functions can be referred to as *freezing* (T. Mohanan 1992). The following examples show how the order of the subject and the object becomes frozen in Hindi when the subject is a theme and the object is an experiencer:

(41) a. anuu ko niinaa apnii bastii mẽ dik^{h}ii.
Anu-D Nina-N self-G neighbourhood-L appear-PERF
Anu$_i$saw Nina$_j$ in self's$_{i/*j}$ neighbourhood.

b. anuu ko niinaa uskii bastii mẽ dikʰii.
Anu-D Nina-N pron-G neighbourhood-L appear-PERF
Anu$_i$ saw Nina$_j$ in her$_{j/*i}$ neighbourhood.

c. niinaa apnii bastii mẽ dikʰii anuu ko.
Nina-N self-G neighbourhood-L appear-PERF Anu-D
Anu$_i$saw Nina$_j$ in self's$_{i/?*j}$ neighbourhood.

d. niinaa uskii bastii mẽ dikʰii anuu ko.
Nina-N pron-G neighbourhood-L appear-PERF Anu-D
Anu$_i$ saw Nina$_j$ in her$_{j/*i}$ neighbourhood.

e. niinaa anuu ko apnii bastii mẽ dikʰii.
Nina-N Anu-D self-G neighbourhood-L appear-PERF
Anu$_i$ saw Nina$_j$ in self's$_{i/j}$ neighbourhood.

f. niinaa anuu ko uskii bastii mẽ dikʰii.
Nina-N Anu-D pron-G neighbourhood-L appear-PERF
Anu$_i$ saw Nina$_j$ in her$_{i/*j}$ neighbourhood.

The reflexive in Hindi takes either the grammatical subject or the logical subject as its antecedent. The pronoun in Hindi cannot take the grammatical subject of its clause as its antecedent. Given the general principles governing the interpretation of reflexives and pronouns in Hindi, it follows that in (41a–d), Anu is the grammatical subject; in (41e,f), Nina is the grammatical subject.

In a clause with a theme-SUBJ and an experiencer-OBJ, word order in Hindi is fixed as SOV (41e,f). If the subject is the experiencer, all word orders except theme < experiencer < verb are possible. The facts of the passive of triadic predicates parallel the facts of diadic predicates illustrated in (41), where grammatical subjecthood is governed by the word order (T. Mohanan 1992). These facts can be accounted for by assuming the universal canonical word order restrictions in (42), with SOV languages choosing the right edge option in (42b.ii):

(42) *Linking between* GF STR *and Word Order*
a. The subject precedes the functional VP.
b. In the functional VP,
(i) functions higher on the hierarchy are closer to the predicate.
(ii) The predicate is at the right/left edge.

Given the default grammatical function statements in (42), what we need to say about (41) is that the word order in terms of grammatical functions becomes frozen (=rigid) in a predicate with theme-SUBJ and experiencer-OBJ. The unmarked association between theta roles and grammatical functions matches the relative prominence relations of theta roles and grammatical functions: experiencer-SUBJ and theme-

OBJ. Freezing happens when the prominence relations are reversed as theme-SUBJ and experiencer-OBJ.

Recall that the requirements on canonical word order in (37) are formulated in terms of theta roles/argument structure. The requirements of fixed word order in (42) are formulated in terms of grammatical functions. If this analysis is correct, then we must conclude that the formal statements on word order can be made in terms of categories, grammatical functions, theta roles or a combination of these.

In a movement analysis, free word order is the result of the choice of free adjunction to S (or its equivalent such as AGR-SUBJ) and the head movement of the verb. Fixed word order is the absence of these choices. In order to account for the freezing effect in (41) in a movement analysis, it will be necessary to prohibit both free adjunction and verb movement if the theme is the SPEC of AGR-SUBJ and the experiencer is the SPEC of AGR-OBJ. Furthermore, it will also be necessary to prohibit the free adjunction that yields the surface order theme < experiencer < verb if the experiencer is SPEC of AGR-SUBJ. Current versions of movement have no mechanism to ensure these results.

5 Multiple Focus

5.1 Contrastive Focus

We now turn to our last word order puzzle. We saw earlier that the linguisic unit that we identified as *topic* in Hindi is a noncanonical sequence which did not constitute a unit in phrase structure representations, enriched or otherwise. A parallel conclusion emerges when we examine the unit *focus* in Malayalam. The central point we wish to make is that the focus marker in Malayalam allows the focussing of a set of elements which do not constitute a single unit in phrase structure representations. In order to make this point, we will first discuss the contrastive focus construction which gives us a diagnostic for the focussed element.

As mentioned earlier, the focus or cleft construction in Malayalam has the verbal particle *aaṇə* 'is' or *alla* 'is not' on the focussed element, and the nominalizing particle *aṯə* 'it' on the verb ((27)–(28)). The cleft construction can be followed by a tag which expresses contrastive focus, illustrated in (43b) and (43c):

(43) a. kuṭṭi ammak'k'ə pennə koṭuṯṯu.
child-N mother-D pen-N gave
The child gave a pen to the mother.

b. *kuṭṭiy***aaṇə** ammak'k'ə pennə koṭuṯṯaṯə, joo̩ṇ**alla**.
child-N-is mother-D pen-N gave-it John-N-is-not
It was the child who gave a pen to the mother, not John.

c. kuṭṭi *ammak'k'***aaṇə** pennə koṭuṯṯaṯə, jooṇin**alla**.
child-N mother-D-is pen-N gave-it John-D-is-not
It was to the mother that the child gave the pen to, not to John.

In (43b) and (43c), the focussed elements are italicized. The parti-cle*alla* 'is-not' attached to the NP at the end is the negative focus marker. It can appear in independent cleft constructions as well:

(44) *kuṭṭiy***alla** ammak'k'ə pennə koṭuṯṯaṯə, jooṇ**aaṇə**.
child-N-is-not mother-D pen-N gave-it John-N-is
It was not the child who gave a pen to the mother, but John.

The tag yields a test to identify the focussed elements in a construction with multiple focus. Before discussing multiple focus, let me state the generalizations that will facilitate the discussion. First, as pointed out earlier, focussed elements exhibit the same word order freedom that the unfocussed elements do. Thus, (45a) and (45b) are variants of (43b) and (43c):

(45) a. ammak'k'ə *kuṭṭiy***aaṇə** pennə koṭuṯṯaṯə, jooṇ**alla**.
mother-D child-N-is pen-N gave-it John-N-is-not
It was the child who gave the pen to the mother, not John.

b. *ammak'k'***aaṇə** kuṭṭi pennə koṭuṯṯaṯə, jooṇ**alla**.
mother-D-is child-N pen-N gave-it John-D-is-not
It was to the mother that the child gave the pen, not to John.

Second, the focussed units must have identical grammatical functions:[9]

(46) a. **kuṭṭiy***aaṇə** ammak'k'ə pennə koṭuṯṯaṯə, jooṇin**alla**.
child-N-is mother-D pen-N gave-it John-D-is-not
It was the child who gave a pen to the mother, not to John.

b. *kuṭṭi *ammak'k'***aaṇə** pennə koṭuṯṯaṯə, jooṇ**alla**.
child-N mother-D-is pen-N gave-it John-N-not
It was to the mother that the child gave the pen to, not John.

With these preliminaries, we turn to the multiple focus construction.

[9]In these and all the other examples, the clefts are equally good without a tag. The tags are given only as a diagnostic for what is being focussed.

5.2 Multiple Focus

An interesting property of the focus construction in Malayalam is that the constituents that occur to the left of the constitutent carrying the focus can also be included in the scope of clefting, as illustrated in (47).

(47) a. *kuṭṭi* *ammak'k'***aaṇə** pennə koṭuṯṯaṯə, accʰan
child-N mother-D-IS pen-N gave-it father-N
jooṇin**alla.**
John-D-IS-NOT
The CHILD gave the pen to the MOTHER, not the FATHER to JOHN.

b. **kuṭṭi* *ammak'k'***aaṇə** pennə koṭuṯṯaṯə, jooṇ**alla**.
child-N mother-D-is pen-N gave-it John-N-is-not
The CHILD gave the pen to the MOTHER, not JOHN.

c. **kuṭṭiya***aaṇə** ammak'k'ə pennə koṭuṯṯaṯə, accʰan
child-N-IS mother-D pen-N gave-it father-N
jooṇin**alla.**
John-D-IS-NOT
The CHILD gave the pen to the mother, not the FATHER to JOHN.

The literal meaning of (47a) is as follows: It was the child who gave the pen and it was to the mother that the child gave it, not the father, and not to John. Such sentence glosses being rather cumbersome, we will simply use upper case letters to indicate focus in the glosses.

The focus marker is attached only to 'mother' in (47a); but, as shown by the contrastive focus tag, both 'child' and 'mother' are focussed. As shown by the ungrammaticality of (47b, c), the contrastive focus constructions with multiple focus must have the same number of focussed elements in the body and the tag. Further examples of the multiple focus construction are given in (48):

(48) a. *ammak'k'ə* *kuṭṭiya***aaṇə** pennə koṭuṯṯaṯə, jooṇinə
mother-D child-N-IS pen-N gave-it John-D
accʰan**alla.**
father-N-IS-NOT
(Meaning: same as in (47a))

b. *kuṭṭi* *ammak'k'***aaṇə** pennə koṭuṯṯaṯə, jooṇ
child-N mother-D-IS pen-N gave-it John-N
accʰan**alla.**
father-D-IS-NOT
The CHILD gave the pen to the MOTHER, not JOHN to the FATHER.

c. kuṭṭi *ammak'k'ə* *penn***aaṇə** koṭuṯṯaṯə, jooṇinə
child-N mother-D pen-N-IS gave-it John-D
pensil**alla.**
pencil-N-IS-NOT
The child gave a PEN to the MOTHER, not a PENCIL to JOHN.

d. *kuṭṭi* *ammak'k'ə* *penn***aaṇə** koṭuṯṯaṯə, acc^{h}an
child-N mother-D pen-N-IS gave-it father-N
jooṇinə pensil**alla.**
John-D pencil-N-IS-NOT
The CHILD gave a PEN to the MOTHER, not FATHER a PENCIL to JOHN.

e. **kuṭṭi* ammak'k'ə *penn***aaṇə** koṭuṯṯaṯə,
child-N mother-D pen-N-is gave-it
acc^{h}an pensil**alla**.
father-N pencil-N-is-not

The ungrammaticality of (48e) shows that the focussed elements in a multiple focus construction must be contiguous. The examples in (49) show that while the word order of the focussed elements in terms of grammatical functions within the body is free, the word order of the tag must agree with that of the body:

(49) a. *ammak'k'ə* *kuṭṭi* *penn***aaṇə** koṭuṯṯaṯə, jooṇinə
mother-D child-N pen-N-IS gave-it John-D
acc^{h}an pensil**alla.**
father-N pencil-N-IS-NOT
The CHILD gave a PEN to the MOTHER, not the FATHER a PENCIL to JOHN.

b. **ammak'k'ə* *kuṭṭi* *penn***aaṇə** koṭuṯṯaṯə, acc^{h}an
mother-D child-N pen-N-is gave-it father-N
jooṇinə pensil**alla**.
John-D pencil-N-is-not

In the light of the above discussion, we conclude that the following principles govern focus and contrastive focus in Malayalam:

(50) *Linking between Discourse Str and Word Order*

a. The FOCUS consists of a set of contiguous elements immediately to the left of the focus marker.
b. The two FOCI of a contrastive focus construction must carry the same number of elements.
c. The elements within the two FOCI in a contrastive focus construction must be parallel in their grammatical functions and their relative order.

The propositions in (50) are principles of association between discourse structure and other dimensions of linguistic structure. (50b) and (50c) perhaps apply to other languages as well. Following the widely held assumption that principles of the grammar hold on units of linguistic representation, not on arbitrary strings, we assume that the FOCUS sequence is a single linguistic unit. This proposal is reinforced by the observation that a focus sequence has a single intonation contour: breaking the unity of the intonation contour results in ungrammaticality.

Now, as the examples given above demonstrate, any contiguous clausal constituents to the left of the focus marker can form a focus unit in Malayalam. Some of the possible sequences are graphically illustrated in (51) by underlining the elements that can be focussed:

(51)

a.	subject	sec.object	object	predicate
b.	subject	sec.object	object	predicate
c.	subject	sec.object	object	predicate
d.	object	subject	sec.object	predicate
e.	object	subject	sec.object	predicate
f.	sec.object	object	subject	predicate
g.	sec.object	object	subject	predicate
h.	subject	object	sec.object	predicate
i.	subject	object	sec.object	predicate

As far as we know, none of the existing proposals for phrase structure representations, however enriched, can represent multiple focus in Malayalam as a single unit. The alternative would be to represent focus as a unit along the dimension of discourse structure. This possibility is illustrated in the following representation of the body of (48a) (without the tag). We omit the representation of grammatical functions for diagrammatic ease:

(52)

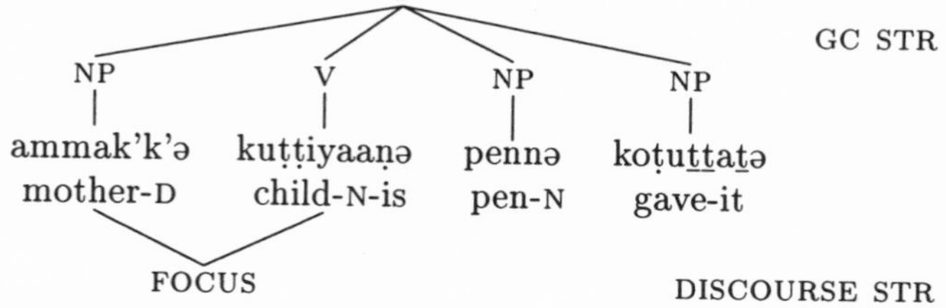

As stated earlier, the mapping between the representation of focus and other dimensions of representation (GC STR, GF STR, and so on) is governed by the linking principles in (50). The reader may think of these as being analogous to the linking principles that state the association between syntactic structure and units of phonological structure such as phonological word and phonological phrase. For a proposal in the same spirit, see Kanerva (1990) on the representation of focus for phonological purposes.

The requirements of contiguity and grammatical function parallelism in (50) apply not only to the cleft construction, but also to coordinate constructions in Malayalam. We will not discuss this construction here, but refer the reader to the discussion in K.P. Mohanan (1984).

6 Concluding Remarks

To summarize, in early syntactic frameworks of generative grammar, phrase structure representations coded information about grammatical categories and their mother-daughter relations. Restrictions on word order were stated in these and subsequent transformational frameworks in terms of a combination of PS rules and transformational rules that applied to PS representations.

Recent developments in most syntactic frameworks acknowledge the need to represent information other than that of grammatical categories. Within the tradition of the Revised Extended Standard Theory (GB, Barriers, Minimalist Theories), the formal devices of coindexed traces and functional categories have led to enriched phrase structure representations. Such representations code, in a single dimension of structure, information about grammatical categories, argument structure (logical subject, logical object), grammatical functions (grammatical subject, grammatical object), and discourse functions (topic, focus).

An alternative way of coding these types of information is in multidimensional representations, where different types of information coexist as linked structures along different dimensions. This approach is essentially an extension of the modular approach to linguistic structure already available in various theories such as GB, LFG, Lexical Phonology, Feature Geometry, and Prosodic Phonology. The Principles and Parameters program in GB is concerned with the modularity of the *principles* of the grammar. So is the distinction between the lexical module and the phrasal module in LFG and Lexical Phonology. The distinction between c-structure and f-structure in LFG, on the other hand, is concerned with the modularity of grammatical *representations*. So is the distinction between syntactic representations and phonological representations in Prosodic Phonology. The program of multidimensional representations is a logical extension of representational modularity to cover linguistic structuring in general.

Both modular and non-modular approaches to linguistic representation acknowledge the need for simultaneous access to different types of information. However, there is a crucial difference between them. The unidimensional enriched representations code different kinds of information on successive layers of tree structure, each layer being directly associated with the layers immediately above and below it. Thus, the layer expressing discourse functions (above the layer of AGR-SUBJ-PHRASE) is not directly linked to the layer expressing argument structure (internal to the VP). These two layers are associated only through the mediation of the layer of grammatical functions. In contrast, the different dimensions of structure in the multidimensional approach have direct association with one another.[10]

Using examples from Hindi and Malayalam, the preceding sections presented an outline of four types of word order phenomena in South Asian languages, namely, non-clausebounded free word order, definiteness effects, freezing effects, and multiple focus. We have tried to indicate how these phenomena can be handled in terms of a multidimensional approach to the architecture of linguistic representations. Mechanisms to deal with these phenomena are not yet available within frameworks that employ enriched phrase structure representations. Therefore, they constitute a serious challenge to the unidimensional approach to linguistic structure.

References

Bresnan, J. 1972. *Theory of Complementation in English Syntax.* Doctoral dissertation, MIT. Published 1979. New York: Garland Press.

Chomsky, N. 1957. *Syntactic Structures*. The Hague, Mouton.

Chomsky, N. 1965. *Aspects of the Theory of Syntax*. Cambridge, MA: The MIT Press.

Chomsky, N. 1971. Remarks on Nominalization. In R. Jacobs and P. Rosenbaum (Eds.), *Readings in English Transformational Grammar*. The Hague, Mouton.

Chomsky, N. 1981. *Lectures on Government and Binding*. Dordrecht: Foris.

Chomsky, N. 1989. Some Notes on Economy of Derivation and Rep-

[10]One of the reviewers has taken this statement to mean that we are making a proposal for level ordered syntax. We would like to warn the reader that nowhere in this article do we suggest the view that there is a linear relation (with or without order) in the different dimensions of representation in (40). Any two dimensions x and y are adjacent in the multidimensional conception.

resentation. In I. Laka and A. K. Mahajan (Eds.), *MIT Working Papers in Linguistics* 10:43–74.

Chomsky, N. 1992. A Minimalist Program for Linguistic Theory. *MIT Occasional Papers in Linguistics* 1.

Clements, G. N. 1985. The Geometry of Phonological Features. *Phonology Yearbook* 2:225–252.

Gair, J. W., and K. Wali. 1989. Hindi Agreement as Anaphor. *Linguistics* 27:45–70.

Gambhir, V. 1981. *Syntactic Restrictions and Discourse Functions of Word Order in Standard Hindi*. Doctoral Dissertation, University of Pennsylvania.

Gurtu, M. 1985. *Anaphoric Relations in Hindi and English*. Doctoral dissertation. CIEFL, Hyderabad, India.

Hale, K. 1983. Warlpiri and the Grammar of Non-configurational Languages. *Natural Language and Linguistic Theory* 1:5–48.

Halle, M. and J-R. Vergnaud. 1980. Three Dimensional Phonology. *Journal of Linguistic Research* 1:87–105.

Huang, C.-T. J. 1982. *Logical Relations in Chinese and the Theory of Grammar*. Doctoral Dissertation, MIT.

Jayaseelan, K. A. 1991. The Pronominal System of Malayalam. *CIEFL Occasional Papers in Linguistics* 3:68-107. CIEFL, Hyderabad, India

Kanerva, J. 1990. *Focus and Phrasing in Chichewa Phonology.* Doctoral Dissertation, Stanford University.

Madhavan, P. 1987. *Clefts and Pseudoclefts in English and Malayalam: A Study in Comparative Syntax*. Doctoral dissertation, CIEFL, Hyderabad, India.

Mahajan, A. K. 1990. *The A/A-bar Distinction and Movement Theory.* Doctoral Dissertation, MIT.

Masica, C. 1982. Identified Object Marking in Hindi and Other Languages. In O. N. Koul (Ed.), *Topics in Hindi Linguistics* Vol. 2. New Delhi, India: Bahri Publications.

Mohanan, K. P. 1982. Grammatical Relations and Clause Structure in Malayalam. In J. Bresnan (Ed.), *The Mental Representation of Grammatical Relations.* Cambridge, MA: The MIT Press.

Mohanan, K. P. 1983. Lexical and Configurational Structures. *The Linguistic Review* 3:113–139.

Mohanan, K. P. 1984. Operator Binding and the Path Containment Condition. *Natural Language and Linguistic Theory* 2:357–396.

Mohanan, T. 1990. *Arguments in Hindi.* Doctoral Dissertation, Stanford University.

Mohanan, T. 1992. Constraints on Word Order in Hindi. Paper presented at the Syntax Workshop, Stanford University.

Mohanan, T. 1993. Case OCP: A Constraint on Word Order in Hindi. In M. Butt, T. H. King, and G. Ramchand (Eds.), *Theoretical Perspectives on Word Order Issues in South Asian Languages.* Stanford, CA: CSLI.

Mohanan, T. Forthcoming. Wordhood and Lexicality: Noun Incorporation in Hindi. *Natural Language and Linguistic Theory*.

Saito, M., and H. Hoji. 1983. Weak Crossover and Move Alpha in Japanese. *Natural Language and Linguistic Theory* 1:245–259.

Simpson, J. 1991. *Warlpiri Morphosyntax: A Lexicalist Approach.* Dordrecht: Kluwer.

Speas, M. 1990. *Phrase Structure in Natural Language*. Dordrecht: Kluwer.

Srivastav, V. 1991. *WH Dependencies in Hindi and the Theory of Grammar*. Doctoral dissertation, Cornell University.

Uszkoreit, H. 1985. *Constraints on Order*. CSLI publications, Stanford University.

Webelhuth, G. 1989. *Syntactic Saturation Phenomena and the Modern Germanic Languages.* Doctoral dissertation, University of Massachusetts at Amherst.

Yatabe, S. 1993. *Scrambling and Japanese Phrase Structure.* Doctoral dissertation, Stanford University.

Zec, D., and S. Inkelas. 1990. Prosodically Constrained Syntax. In S. Inkelas and D. Zec (Eds.), *The Phonology-Syntax Connection.* Chicago: The University of Chicago Press.

8

Case OCP: A Constraint on Word Order in Hindi

TARA MOHANAN

1 Introduction

As is well-known, Hindi is a free word order language, in that word order does not usually signal grammatical functions in the language. It is also well-known that this ordering freedom is curtailed by a number of interacting principles. In this paper, I demonstrate the workings of one particular word order constraint in Hindi, namely, a constraint that disfavours adjacent nouns with identical case endings.

Two theoretical conclusions emerge from the analysis of this word order constraint in Hindi. First, formal statements on word order cannot be restricted to grammatical categories, but must be allowed to refer to other types of linguistic information such as grammatical features, semantic structure and phonological structure, not all of which can be coded in a phrase structure representation. Second, statements on word order must be allowed to refer simultaneously to these different types of information. The analysis argues for an interactive conception of multidimensional linguistic representation, in which a principle of grammar can simultaneously refer to more than one dimension of structure.

Prohibitions against adjacent identical entities are viewed in phonology as an effect of the *Obligatory Contour Principle* (Leben 1973). I suggest that the constraint against adjacent nouns with identical case endings in Hindi is another manifestation of this general principle. A consequence of accepting this proposal is that recurrent prohibitions against identical elements in phonology, morphology, and syntax become unified as a single universal principle of linguistic organization.

Theoretical Perspectives on Word Order in South Asian Languages
Miriam Butt, Tracy Holloway King, Gillian Ramchand (Eds.)

In order to account for the variability of the pattern across phenomena and across languages, grammars should have the provision to make language particular stipulations on the elements subject to the constraint and their environment, and the domain in which the constraint holds.

The paper takes the following course. Section 2 introduces the reader to the phenomenon the paper deals with. Section 3 sketches the theoretical conception that underlies the analysis of the phenomenon in section 4. Section 5 shows how a construction that appears to fall under the scope of the constraint against adjacency is in fact entirely orthogonal to it. Section 6 generalizes the Obligatory Contour Principle to cover the analysis proposed in Section 4.

2 The Phenomenon: A Constraint against Adjacency

Consider the sentences in (1):[1]

(1) a. raam k^hat lik^{h}egaa.
Ram-N letter-N write-FUT
Ram will write a letter.

b. raam-ne baccõ-ko samhaalaa.
Ram-E children-A take care of-PERF
Ram took care of the children.

The verbs in (1a,b) take either an ergative (ERG) or a nominative (NOM) subject. However, when a modal of obligation is superimposed on (1), the modal induces dative (DAT) case on that subject, as in (2a,b):

(2) a. raam-ko k^hat lik^{h}naa paḍaa.
Ram-D letter-N write-NF fall-PERF
Ram had to write a letter.

b. ??**raam-ko baccõ-ko** samhaalnaa paḍaa.
Ram-D children-A take care of-NF fall-PERF
Ram had to take care of the children.

In contrast to (2a), (2b) is either partially or completely unacceptable to many speakers of Hindi. What causes this asymmetry? Notice that the object (OBJ) in (2a) is NOM, while the OBJ in (2b) is accusative (ACC). Now, the DAT case ending and the acc case ending in Hindi are identical: they are both *-ko*. Thus, in (2b), we have two nominals, the DAT subject (SUBJ) and the ACC OBJ, marked with the same case

[1]In the word glosses, N=nominative, E=ergative, A=accusative, I=instrumental, G=genitive, D=dative, NF=nonfinite, PR=present, PA=past, PERF=perfective, FUT=future, HAB=habitual.

ending *-ko*: I will show that the unacceptability is the result of identical case endings on two adjacent nouns.[2]

Consider the contrast between (2b) and (3)–(5). The sentences in (3)–(5) are all versions of (2b) with added material:

(3) **raam-ko** kal **baccõ-ko** samhaalnaa paḍaa.
Ram-D yesterday children-A take care-NF fall-PERF
Ram had to take care of the children yesterday.

(4) **raam-ko** apnii bahin-ke **baccõ-ko** samhaalnaa paḍaa.
Ram-D self's sister-G children-A take care-NF fall-PERF
Ram had to take care of his sister's children.

(5) **raam-ko** [pause] **baccõ-ko** samhaalnaa paḍaa.
Ram-D children-A take care-NF fall-PERF
Ram [pause] had to take care of the children.

In these sentences, the two *-ko* ending nouns are separated from each other, in (3) by an adjunct, in (4) by the modifier of the second noun, and in (5) by a pause.

For some speakers, (2b) is unacceptable. For others, including myself, (2b) is only marginally acceptable. There are also speakers who find (2b) to be acceptable. However, even for those speakers, (2b) is less acceptable than (3)–(5). In other words, for all speakers, there is a clear asymmetry between (2b) and (3)–(5).[3] We must assume, there-

[2] I systematically use the term "unacceptable" to mean partially or completely unacceptable.

[3] The phenomenon of which the unacceptability of (2b) is an example is not restricted to a small set of speakers. One reviewer, clearly a non-native speaker of Hindi/Urdu, points out that one encounters the problem within a few months of starting to learn Hindi/Urdu.

As is to be expected with a phenomenon where judgements exhibit variability, another reviewer disagrees with the data, and suggests that (2b) "*considerably improves* when presented in appropriate discourses" (emphasis mine). Given below is (2b), placed in an appropriate context:

raam-ne pahle kab^{h}ii g^{h}ar-kaa kaam nahĩĩ kiyaa. par kal
Ram-D before ever house-G work-N not do-PERF But yesterday

uskii patnii biimaar t^{h}ii, to akele-hii **raam-ko baccõ-ko**
pron-G wife-N ill be-PA so alone-emph Ram-D children-A

samhaalnaa paḍaa, aur g^{h}ar-kaa saaraa kaam b^{h}ii karnaa paḍaa.
take care-NF fall-PERF and house-G all work-N also do-NF fall-PERF

'Ram has never done housework before. But yesterday, his wife was ill, so Ram had to take care of the children as well as do all the housework all by himself.'

While my judgement coincides with that of the reviewer, the point still holds that there is an aymmetry between a DAT SUBJ *raam-ko* and an ERG SUBJ *raam-ne* even in the above context. The reviewer's remark that the sentence "considerably improves" indicates the reviewer's own perception of the asymmetry. I should mention here that informant judgements on examples given in this paper were fore, that there is some constraint that renders (2b) unacceptable. The constraint is relatively weak for some speakers and extremely strong for others. It is not an absolute constraint; rather, it should be viewed as a 'preference condition' (Jackendoff 1986). This is the constraint I investigate in this paper.

The constraint is not restricted to the case clitic *-ko*. Take the instrumental case clitic *-se* in Hindi: it exhibits effects similar to those of *-ko* in (2b). Consider the sentences in (6):

(6) a. ram-ne ravii-ko **c^{h}aḍii-se** piiṭaa.
Ram-E Ravi-A cane-I beat-PERF
Ram beat Ravi with a cane.

b. **raam-se** ravii **c^{h}aḍii-se** piiṭaa gayaa.
Ram-I Ravi-N cane-I beat-PERF go-PERF
Ravi was beaten with a cane by Ram.

c. ravii **c^{h}aḍii-se** piiṭaa gayaa.
Ravi-N cane-I beat-PERF go-PERF
Ravi was beaten with a cane.

The case ending *-se* in Hindi indicates instruments, sources, paths, demoted subjects of passives and causatives, and so on. (6a) contains a *-se* marked instrument. In (6b), the passive of (6a), both the demoted agent and the instrument bear the clitic *-se*. In the passive in (6c), the demoted agent is unexpressed. Now consider (6d,e):

(6) d. ??ravii **raam-se** **c^{h}aḍii-se** piiṭaa gayaa.
Ravi-N Ram-I cane-I beat-PERF go-PERF
Ravi was beaten with a cane by Ram.

e. ravii **raam-se** bahut baar **c^{h}aḍii-se** piiṭaa
Ravi-N Ram-I many times cane-I beat-PERF
gayaa.
go-PERF
Ravi was beaten many times by Ram with a cane.

In (6d), the word order of (6b) is altered so that the two nouns with identical case endings are adjacent. (6d), like (2b), is only marginally acceptable. In (6e), the two nouns with identical case endings are separated by other material, as in (3) and (4). (6e) is acceptable.

Clearly, then, the unacceptability of (6d) is caused by the adjacent nouns with identical case endings. The effect of the constraint is not restricted to passives, as (7) shows:

checked within detailed and appropriate contexts; the contexts are omitted for lack of space.

(7) a.

raam-ne	**c^{h}aḍii-se**	cuuhe-ko	**kamre-se**
Ram-E	cane-I	mouse-A/D	room-I

b^{h}agaayaa.
run-CAUS-PERF
Ram drove the mouse out of the room with a cane.

b. **c^{h}aḍii-se** raam-ne cuuhe-ko **kamre-se** b^{h}agaayaa.
c. **kamre-se** raam-ne cuuhe-ko **c^{h}aḍii-se** b^{h}agaayaa.
d. raam-ne **kamre-se** cuuhe-ko **c^{h}aḍii-se** b^{h}agaayaa.
e. ??raam-ne **kamre-se c^{h}aḍii-se** cuuhe-ko b^{h}agaayaa.
f. ??raam-ne **c^{h}aḍii-se kamre-se** cuuhe-ko b^{h}agaayaa.

In (7a), the instrument and the locational source are both marked with *-se*. The relative order of the five constituents in (7a) is free: samples of the various possible orders are given in (7b–f). In (7e) and (7f), the two *-se* marked nouns are adjacent. Precisely those instances are unacceptable. The same effects are found in (8a), in contrast to (8b):

(8) a.

??mohan	**dillii-se**	**plen-se**	aayaa.
Mohan-N	Delhi-from	plane-I	come-PERF

Mohan came from Delhi by plane.

b.

dillii-se	mohan	**plen-se**	aayaa.
Delhi-from	Mohan-N	plane-I	come-PERF

Mohan came from Delhi by plane.

In short, there appears to be a resistence in Hindi to two nouns with identical case endings occurring adjacent to each other.[4]

3 Representation of Linguistic Structure: Layers vs. Dimensions

3.1

Central to the analysis of word order in this paper are two ideas. First, the *requirements* of word order can be stated not only in terms of the representation of grammatical categories, but also in terms of the representation of grammatically relevant meanings, argument structure, grammatical functions, discourse functions, and phonological structure. Second, the *representation* of word order is factored out of these other types of structural information.

---

[4]In (i) below, the subject bears the case ending *-ko*, and the unsuffixed NOM object also ends in *ko*.

(i)

raam-ko	limko	piinaa	paḍaa.
Ram-D	Limco-N	drink-NF	fall-PERF

Ram had to drink Limco.

The acceptability of (i) shows that phonological identity of the end of the noun is not sufficient: the identical entities must be case endings.

Thus, the observed word order is the result of an interaction of requirements imposed by different types of information. This presupposes a conception of linguistic organization in which different types of information are represented on different planes of structure, which converge on an axis of intersection. Word order information is represented along this axis of intersection. This conception is not unlike the conception of phonological organization in Halle and Vergnaud (1980), where they view different planes of phonological structure intersecting on the axis of the skeletal tier (as in a ring-bound notebook). As a background for our analysis, I outline below the relevant aspects of this conception of linguistic representation.

3.2

Take the English sentence *Who was examined by John?* Along the lines suggested in Chomsky (1992:10), the s-structure representation of this sentence will be as given in (9) or a variant:

(9)

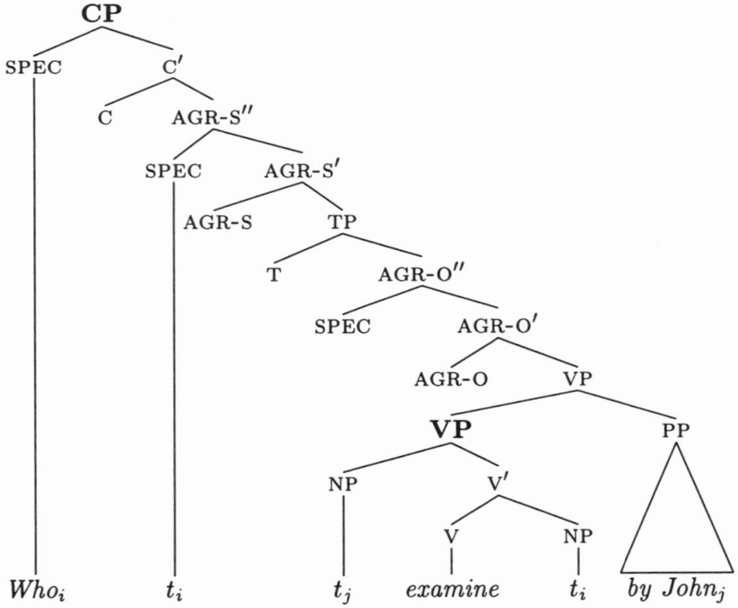

This representation contains three *layers* of structure. The innermost layer is that of the VP in bold face. The second layer lies between this VP and AGR-S″. The outermost layer is above the AGR-S″.

The first layer of structure encodes information about "logical subject" (highest NP in the innermost layer) and "logical object" (direct sister of the verb). Thus, from the VP internal traces in (9), we can tell that *John* is the logical subject of the clause, because it is coindexed with the trace that is the highest node in the innermost layer. We also know that *who* is the logical object, because it is coindexed with the trace of the closest sister of the verb).[5] I will refer to this type of information as *argument structure* (ARG STR).

The next layer of structure contains labels like AGR-S and AGR-O. The SPEC of AGR-S is the grammatical subject of the clause, and the SPEC of AGR-O is the grammatical object. We know that *who* is the grammatical subject of the clause because it is coindexed with a trace in the SPEC of AGR-S. I use the term *grammatical function structure* (GF STR) to refer to this type of information.

Labels like SPEC of C in the third layer generally indicate that the element in question is the topic or focus of the sentence. Thus, we know that in (9), *who* is the focus because it is a *wh* phrase that occurs in the SPEC of C position. In some proposals, information about focus and topic are represented separately in terms of focus phrase and topic phrase. I use the term *discourse structure* (DIS STR) to refer to information of this kind.

3.3

As the above discussion reveals, the different layers of structure in (9) represent different kinds of syntactically relevant information. Let us factor apart the three layers into sub-trees with more transparent labels:[6]

(10) a.

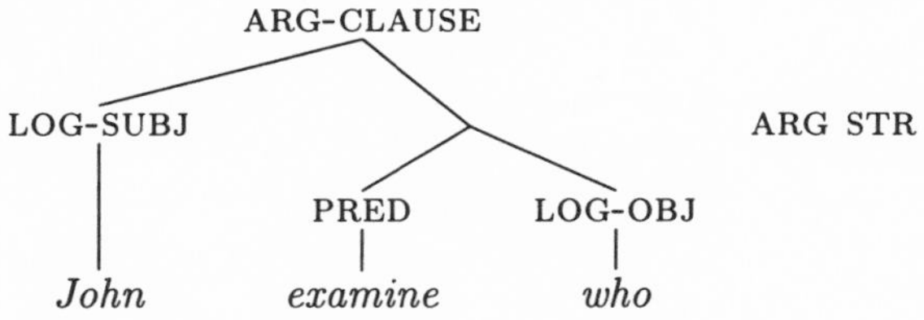

[5]The logical subjecthood of *John* in (9) holds irrespective of whether it is encoded in terms of a co-indexed trace or some other mechanism.

[6]The reader who feels uncomfortable with the labels in (10) may replace them with the more familiar labels in (9). Thus, in (10a), ARG-CLAUSE = VP; LOG-SUBJ = sister to VP; PRED = V; LOG-OBJ = sister to V. In (10b), GF-CLAUSE = AGR-S PHRASE; SUBJ = SPEC of AGR-S, and so on. Whether the coding of the information relies on mother-daughter relations, as in [NP of S] and [NP of VP] for subjecthood and objecthood, or is neutral to mother-daughter relations, as in [−r,−o] and [−r,+o] for subject and object in the Lexical Mapping Theory in LFG, is also not crucial for my purposes.

b.

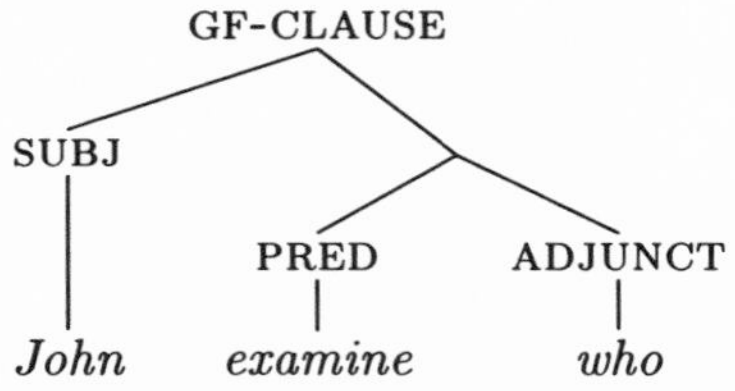

GF STR

c.

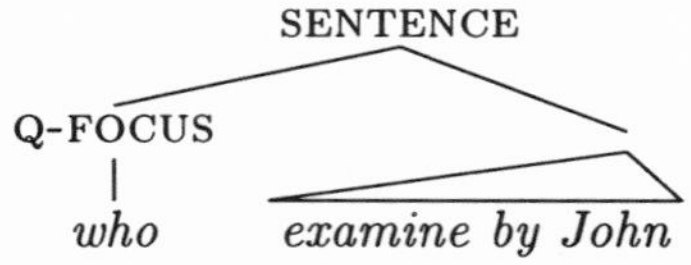

DIS STR

The actual order of words is expressed by the precedence relations of the overt elements. Now, each layer of representation in (9) encodes precedence relations. Suppose we assume that the representations in (10), like the LF trees in GB syntax and the Feature Geometry trees in phonology, do not encode precedence relations, and hence do not signal word order information.[7] We can represent word order separately, in what may be called a word string. A WORD STRING is a string of words, each word being a morpheme string consisting of one or more morphemes:

(10) d. *Who* < *was* < *examined* < *by* < *John* WORD STRING

In transformational frameworks, coindexed traces are a way of associating or linking the different layers of information within the same level or dimension of representation. Instead, one may explore the idea of putting together the different pieces of information as *linked* structures along different *dimensions of representation.* Let us imagine that the different trees in (10a), (10b), and (10c) are drawn along three different planes in a multidimensional space, and that these planes intersect along the axis of the word string in (10d), as given in (11):

[7]That the LF trees do not signal word order information is uncontroversial. Whether or not they are like the feature geometry trees in not encoding precedence relations may be controversial. The way I see it, since LF representations make no claims about the order of words, encoding precedence relations in LF is redundant.

(11)

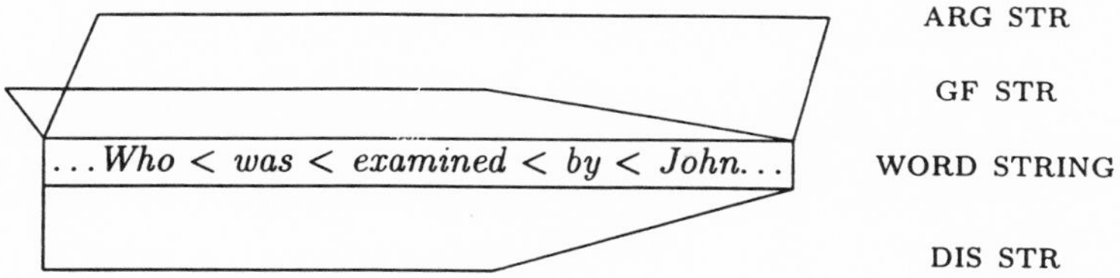

At this point, (10)–(11) may appear to be a notational variant of (9): the coindexed nodes in a structure in a single dimension of representation in (9) are translated as linked nodes in structures along different dimensions in (10)–(11). The difference between these two modes of representing linguistic information will emerge as we go along.

3.4

Following Mohanan and Mohanan (this volume), we will refer to the approach embodied in (9) as the unidimensional approach, as opposed to the multidimensional approach in (11). As an illustration of the difference between these two approaches, take the representation of noun incorporation in Hindi. The example in (12) illustrates the construction:

(12) anil-ne kitaabẽ becĩĩ.
Anil-E(M) book-pl-N(F) sell-PERF.F.PL
(i) Anil sold books.
(ii) Anil did book-selling.

As argued in T. Mohanan (forthcoming) on the basis of the convergence of various syntactic, semantic and phonological properties, the Hindi sentence in (12) has two structures, one being an incorporated structure corresponding to the reading in (12ii). In the incorporated structure, the verb *bec* 'sell' and the preceding noun *kitaabẽ* 'books' form a single compound verb. For the purposes of phenomena that depend upon grammatical categories, such as adjacency, adjectival modification and coordination, we need the representation in (13a). Yet, for the purposes of theta role assignment, agreement, and so on, the noun incorporated into the verb behaves like a regular object. These facts require the representation of grammatical functions in (13b):

(13)

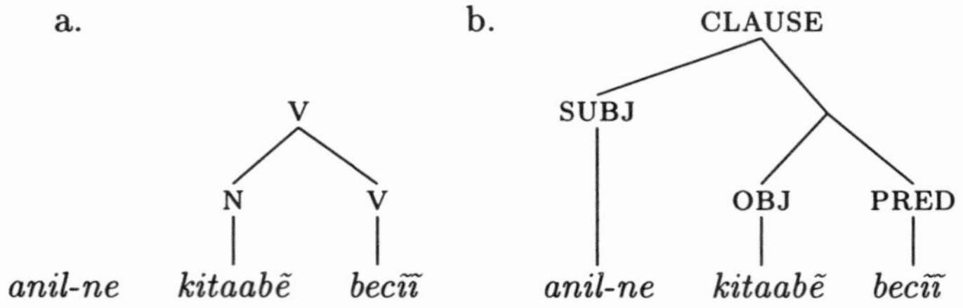

If we represent subjecthood and objecthood in terms of phrase structure configurations (NP of S; NP of VP), then the information in (13a) and (13b) are put together in a *unidimensional representation* with multiple layers as follows, à la Baker (1985):

(14)

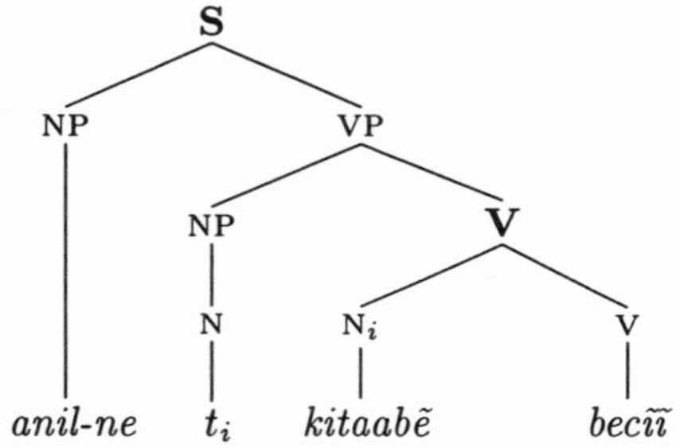

In (14), the inner layer expresses the information in (13a), and the outer layer, that in (13b). A *multidimensional representation* puts the two together as (15), where the structure below the WORD STRING is the dimension of grammatical category information (GC STR), which includes the representation in (13a):

(15)

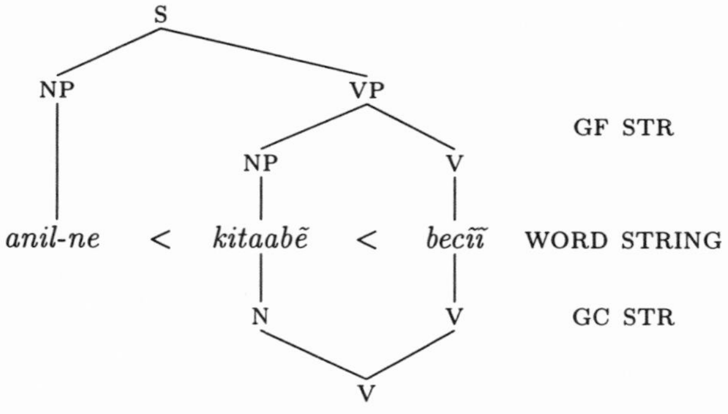

The multidimensionality in (15) is similar to that in the autolexical representations in Sadock (1985, 1991). The crucial difference between (15) and (13) is that the two dimensions in autolexical syntax separate morphology and syntax, while the two dimensions in (15) separate grammatical categories and grammatical functions. In our view, both word internal structure (morphology) and structure across words (syntax) contain representations of grammatical categories and grammatical functions.[8]

3.5

To take yet another example, Pesetsky (1985) argues that for the purposes of morphology, the comparative suffix *-er* in a word like *unhappier* is attached to *happy*, prior to the attachment of the prefix *un-*. This means that the morphological structure of *unhappier* at the level of s-structure is as given in (16):

(16) S-structure

Nevertheless, the semantic interpretation of *unhappier* is: 'in a state of being more unhappy', not 'not in a state of being more happy'. Pesetsky takes this to be evidence for the LF configuration in (17):

(17) LF-structure

Within the framework of unidimensional representations that Pesetsky subscribes to, these two structures are put together in terms of coindexed traces as in (18):

(18)

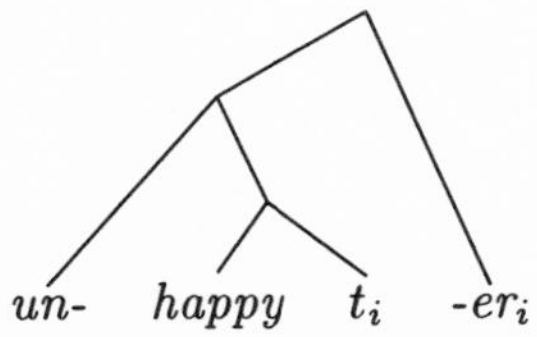

Here, the inner layer provides the morphologically relevant tree structure, while the outer layer provides the semantically relevant tree structure. Within the framework of multidimensional representations, these two structures are put together as (19):

[8]For a detailed discussion of the similarities and differences between Autolexical Syntax and the conception of multidimensionality adopted in this paper, see T. Mohanan (forthcoming).

(19)

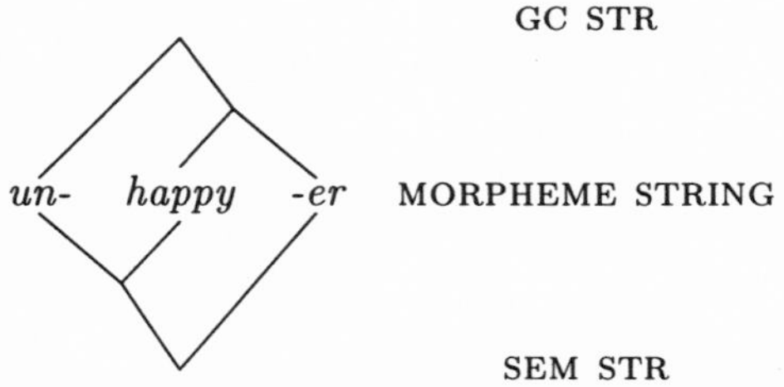

The structure above the string (GC STR) provides the word internal structure in terms of grammatical categories. The structure below (SEM STR) provides the word internal structure in terms of grammatically relevant meanings. To make this aspect clearer, we may spell out some of the details of (19) as (20):

(20)

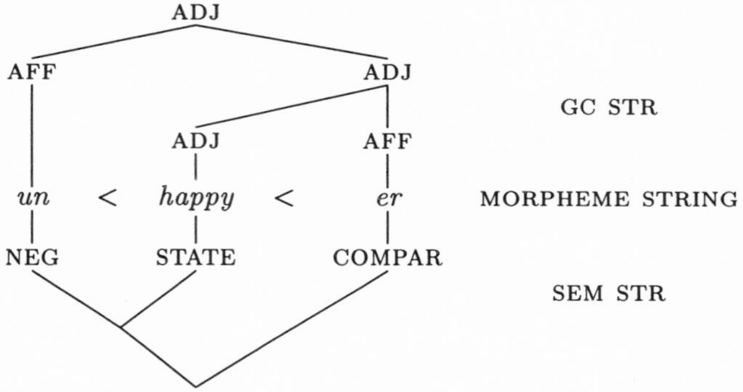

Comparing (20) and (18), it is clear that SEM STR expresses the same intuitions as the LF representation in GB: both LF and SEM STR encode grammatically relevant semantic information word internally and across words. The MORPHEME STRING is the representation of word internal morphemes along with their linear precedence.

In GB frameworks, the semantic information that participates in grammatical structuring is coded in two places. One, as the above example illustates, is the level of LF representation, which expresses notions such as scope and coreference, both within words (e.g., (18)) and across words (e.g., quantifier scope). The other is the level of Lexical Conceptual Structure (LCS), which expresses the structure of the meanings of words relevant for determining the argument structure of verbs. Take, for example, the lexical representation of the verb *give* in Speas (1990), which includes the LCS and the predicate argument structure (PAS):

(21) GIVE:

x cause y to come to be at [possession] z LCS

<1 2 3>

What I call SEM STR is a single dimension of representation that roughly corresponds to the combination of LF and LCS.

3.6

Let me give one last example of multidimensional representation, which comes from the phonology-syntax interface. In an English sentence like *Jack's arriving tomorrow*, the copula is contracted and forms a single syllable with *Jack* ([jæks]), so that the underlying voiced /z/ of the copula undergoes the syllable internal voicing assimilation rule. The phonological representation including SYLLABLE and PHONOLOGICAL WORD (P-WORD) that this expression requires is that in (22):[9]

(22)

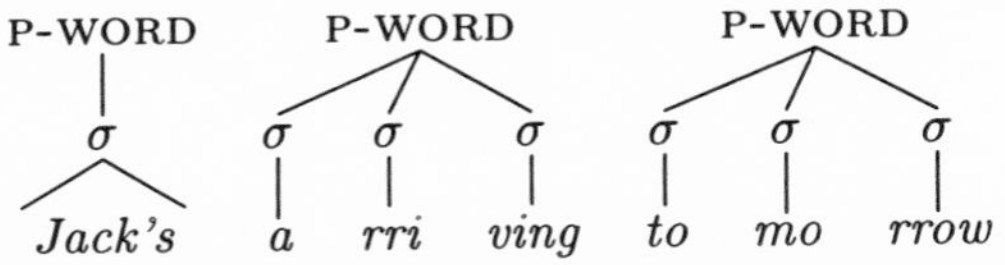

However, the syntactic category structure of the sentence is roughly as in (23).

(23)

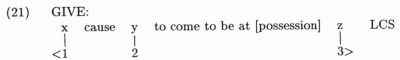

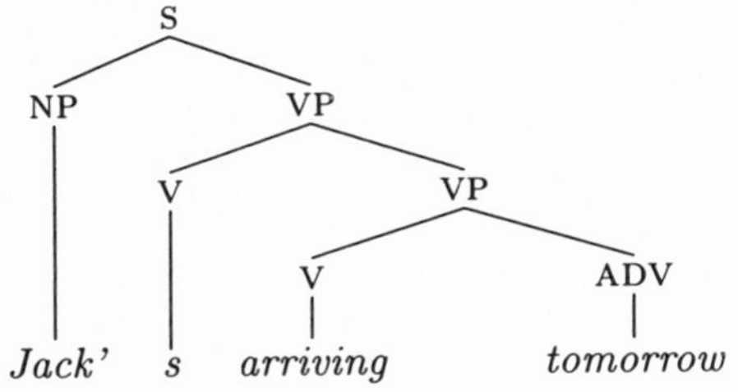

I have not seen any proposals for a unidimensional representation that combines (22) and (23). A multidimension representation of the relevant parts is given in (24):

[9]A P-WORD is a phonological unit that contains a single primary stress and word melody (Liberman and Prince 1977, Selkirk 1984).

(24)

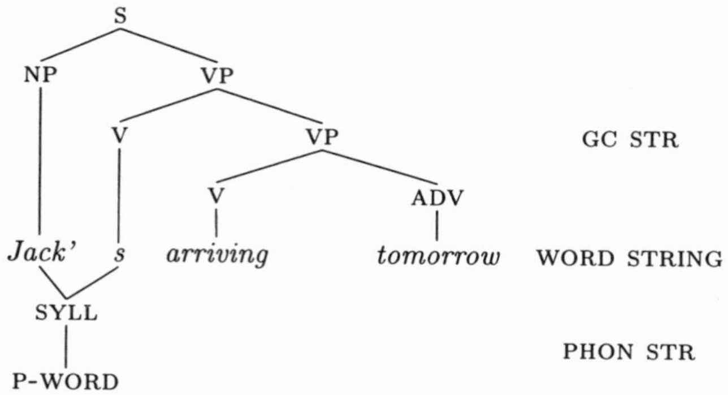

The conception of multidimensional representations underlying (11) is a logical extension of the idea of linked structures along different dimensions implicit in (24). (See also Mohanan and Mohanan, this volume.)

3.7

In this section, I have sketched a way of representing the organization of linguistic information as a multidimensional representation made up of linked structures along different planes that intersect on the axis of the word string. The different planes of linguistic structuring include SEM STR, ARG STR, GF STR, GC STR, DIS STR, and PHON STR. Principles of grammar may make statements about word order in terms of entities on any of the dimensions of representation; these statements are checked in terms of the information contained in the word string. Such checking requires the following general principle:

(25) Given
(i) α and β on some dimension of representation D, and
(ii) word strings s_i and s_j dominated by α and β respectively:
if a principle of the grammar requires α to precede β,
then s_i precedes s_j;
if a principle of the grammar requires α and β to be adjacent,
then s_i and s_j are adjacent.

(25) expresses the intuitive substance of the no-crossing constraint as a condition on the interpretation of the principles of word order (=linear precedence plus adjacency), rather than as a condition on the representations. We can now state word order requirements on entities in dimensions of structure which do not carry precedence relations, and check whether these requirements are obeyed in a structure that does encode word order.

4 A Constraint against Adjacency

The prohibition against nouns with identical case endings illustrated in (2b), (6d), (7e,f) and (8a) is a recurrent pattern in natural languages. An analysis of the facts in (2)–(8), therefore, involves two problems. One is to account for the unacceptability of (2b), (6d), (7e,f) and (8a). The other is to account for the recurrence of the constraint against adjacent identical elements across languages, in terms of a general universal explanation. This section addresses the first problem of analysing the Hindi phenomenon, bearing in mind, however, the problem of arriving at a unifying solution for the recurrence of the pattern across languages.

4.1 A First Formulation: Identity of Case Endings

Let us begin by stating a tentative principle that will account for all the data given so far:

(26) Adjacent nouns with identical case endings are disallowed in Hindi. (not absolute)

In (2b), the nouns with identical case endings *raam-ko* and *baccõ-ko* are adjacent, violating (26).[10] These two nouns are separated by an adjunct in (3), the modifier of the second noun in (4), and a pause in (5); therefore, (3)–(5) do not violate (26).

4.2 Participanthood

Consider the following example

(27) pʰal bʰuucaal-kii **vajah-se** **peḍ-se** girne
fruit-N earthquake-G reason-I tree-from fall-NF
lage.
bestruck-PERF
Fruit started falling from the tree because of the earthquake.

We explained the unacceptability of (2b), (6d), (7e,f) and (8a) as resulting from the violation of (26). Why is (27) exempt from the constraint? An obvious guess is that, in the previous examples, the nouns that are subject to (26) denote entities that are part of the structural meaning of the verb. The specification of the agent and instrument is part of the meaning of 'beat' (6), and the specifications of the locative source

[10]The specification not absolute makes explicit that at least for some speakers, the violation of the constraint does not produce complete unacceptability. Another way of expressing this might be to say that the constraint is optional. But that would only explain why it is completely acceptable to some speakers and completely unacceptable to others. It would not give the effects of a range from partial acceptability to complete unacceptability.

and the instrument are part of the structure of drive out of in (7). In contrast, the specifications of 'reason' is not part of the meaning of fall (27). Suppose we represent the SEM STR of the three verbs as follows:

(28) a. *piiṭ* 'beat': [x act upon y with z]
b. *bʰagaa* 'drive away from':
[x act upon y with z & x cause [y move out of m]]
c. *gir* 'fall': [x move from y]

In (28), x is the agent, y is the undergoer, and z the instrument of beating. Let me use the term PARTICIPANT to refer to the variables that are part of the representation of the structural meaning of the predicate. All syntactic theories acknowledge some of these participants, such as the agent and undergoer, to be associated with syntactically required arguments of the predicate in ARG STR. The argumenthood of some of the other participants is less clear. To this class belong the instrument of beating, the instrument of driving an undergoer away from a locational source, and the source itself.

To repeat, the adjacent nouns with identical case endings in (2), (6), (7), and (8) are PARTICIPANTS in the SEM STR of the verb. In (27), on the other hand, the first *-se* marked noun is not a participant. We may therefore revise (26) as (29):

(29) Adjacent nouns with identical case endings, associated with participants of the same predicate, are disallowed in Hindi. (not absolute)

As with *-se*, not all nouns with *-ko* participate in the constraint. Thus, in (30a,b) below, the *-ko* ending time specification of the event is adjacent to a *-ko* marked participant, but creates no unacceptability, exactly as predicted by (29):

(30) a. **raam-ko raat-ko** ravii milaa.
Ram-D night-at Ravi-N meet-PERF
Ram met Ravi at night.
b. ilaa aaj **šaam-ko ravii-ko** kʰat likʰegii.
Ila-N today evening-at Ravi-A letter-N write-FUT
Ila will write a letter to Ravi this evening.

The specification participants of the same predicate in (29) predicts that if adjacent nouns with identical case endings belong to two different clauses, the result will not be unacceptable. This prediction is borne out by (31a,b):

(31) a. ilaa **raam-ko baccõ-ko** bulaane bʰejegii.
Ila-N Ram-A children-A call-NF send-FUT
Ila will send Ram to call the child.

b.	**ilaa-ko**	**baccõ-ko**	samhaalne	sahelii-ke	g^har
	Ilaa-D	children-A	look after-NF	friend-G	house-N
	jaanaa	hai.			
	go-NF	be-PR			

Ilaa has to go to her friend's house to look after the children.

In (31a), for instance, *raam-ko* is a participant of the verb *b^hej* 'send', while *baccõ-ko* is a participant of the embedded verb *bulaa* 'call'. Hence, (29) is not violated.

4.3 Case Feature, Case Morpheme, and Case Formative

In (2b), the two adjacent nouns with identical case endings carry two different case features: the *-ko* marked subject is DAT, while the *-ko* marked object is ACC. Hence the decision to formulate the constraint in terms of case endings, or *formatives*, rather than case features.[11] This predicts that adjacent nouns without case endings will not create a violation of (29) even if they are associated with the same case feature. This prediction is borne out by the acceptable examples in (32).

(32)	a.	**šer**	**aam**	nahĩĩ	k^haataa.
		lion-N	mango-N	not	eat-HAB
		A lion doesn't eat mangoes.			
	b.	**patt^{h}ar**	**botal**	toḍegaa.	
		stone-N	bottle-N	break-FUT	
		The stone will break the bottle.			

NOM case in Hindi has no phonological realization. Hence, the adjacency of two NOM nouns does not violate (29).[12]

Evidence from pronouns shows that (29) cannot be formulated in terms of case morphemes. The morpheme *-ko* in Hindi on pronouns has two different formatives, /-ko/ and /-e/:

(33)	A	B	Gloss
	ham-ko	*ham-e*	'pronoun-1-PL-ACC/DAT'
	tum-ko	*tum-he*	'pronoun-2-ACC/DAT'
	us-ko	*us-e*	'pronoun-3-SG-ACC/DAT'

The formative /-e/, available only on pronouns, is in free variation with the formative /-ko/.

[11] I use the term formative in the sense of Chomsky and Halle (1968). For example, the endings *-en* in *children* and *-z* in *roses* are different formatives associated with the plural.

[12] Given the constraint under discussion, the acceptability of examples in (32) provides evidence against the idea of "zero formatives".

The formulation in (29) predicts that as long as the formatives are different, nouns with identical case morphemes can be adjacent. This prediction is also borne out by the following examples:

(34) a. ??**ham-ko** **bacce-ko** uṭ^{h}aanaa paḍaa.
we-D child-A lift-NF fall-PERF
We had to pick up/carry the child.

b. **hame** **bacce-ko** uṭ^{h}aanaa paḍaa.
we-D child-A lift-NF fall-PERF
We had to pick up/carry the child.

(35) a. ??**raam-ko** **ham-ko** uṭ^{h}aanaa paḍaa.
Ram-D we-A lift-NF fall-PERF
Ram had to pick up/carry us.

b. **raam-ko** **hame** uṭ^{h}aanaa paḍaa.
Ram-D we-A lift-NF fall-PERF
Ram had to pick up/carry us.

(34a) and (35a) are unacceptable because adjacent nouns carry the same formative /-ko/. In (34b) and (35b), on the other hand, one of the formatives is /-ko/, while the other is /-e/. These sentences are acceptable. If both nouns bear /-e/, as in (36b), the result is again unacceptable, as predicted by (29):

(36) a. ??**ham-ko** **us-ko** uṭ^{h}aanaa paḍaa.
we-D (s)he-A lift-NF fall-PERF
We had to pick up/carry him/her.

b. ??**hame** **use** uṭ^{h}aanaa paḍaa.
we-D (s)he-A lift-NF fall-PERF
We had to pick up/carry him/her.

c. **hame** **us-ko** uṭ^{h}aanaa paḍaa.
we-D (s)he-A lift-NF fall-PERF
We had to pick up/carry him/her.

d. **ham-ko** **use** uṭ^{h}aanaa paḍaa.
we-D (s)he-A lift-NF fall-PERF
We had to pick up/carry him/her.

4.4 Phonological Wordhood

The formulation of the constraint faces two problems. The first problem relates to the need to access phonological information. The crucial difference between the unacceptable sentence in (2b) and its acceptable version in (5) is that the nouns in (5) are separated by a pause. As formulated in (29), our constraint is insensitive to pauses, and incorrectly predicts that (5) is unacceptable.

The second problem relates to the syntactic relation between the case formatives and nouns. On the basis of the fact that case endings exhibit phrasal scope, and can be attached to a coordinate NP, and that a pause may occur between a noun and the case ending, I have argued elsewhere that a case formative in Hindi is attached to a phrasal category, not to the noun that precedes the formative (T. Mohanan 1990:79–80). Thus, in (4), repeated below for easy reference, the second *-ko* is attached to *apnii bahin-ke baccõ* 'self's sister's children':

(4)	**raam-ko**	apnii	bahin-ke	**baccõ-ko**	samhaalnaa	paḍaa.
	Ram-D	self's	sister-G	children-A	take care-NF	fall-PERF

Ram had to take care of his sister's children.

I assume that the grammatical category representation of *apnii bahin-ke baccõ-ko* is that in (37a), not (37b):[13]

(37) a.

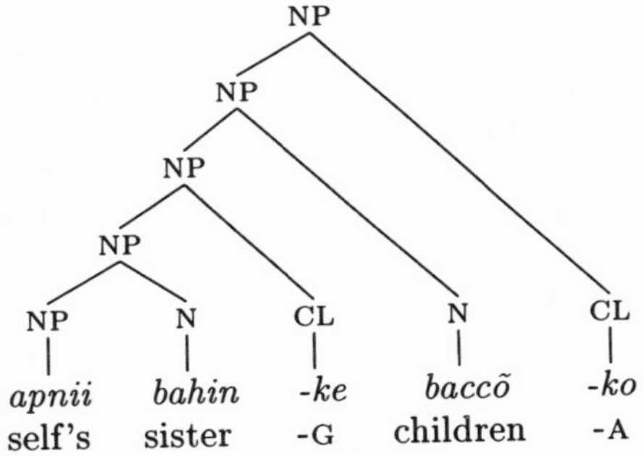

b.

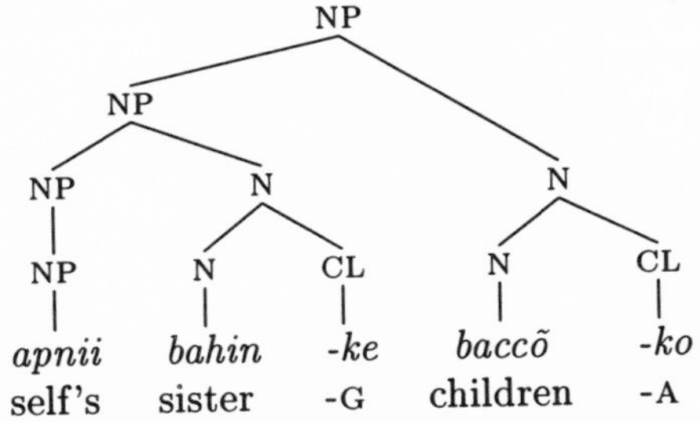

Given that case formatives are attached to NPs, the sequence noun+case formative does not form a single GC STR unit. Therefore, nouns with identical case endings in (29) is not a legitimate specification.

I suggest that the two problems raised above, namely, insensitivity to pauses and the use of an illegitimate specification, can be resolved by assuming that the relevant unit that participates in the constraint

[13]Systematic differences between the formatives /-ko/ and /-e/ with respect to pauses and coordination show that while /-ko/ is attached to the NP as in (37a), /-e/ is lexically attached to the pronoun as in (37b).

against adjacency is the phonological word, not the syntactic category noun (see the representation in (24)). The revised principle is given as (38):

(38) STRINGS which contain *identical* CASE FORMATIVES and are associated with *adjacent* PHONOLOGICAL WORDS and with PARTICIPANTS OF THE SAME PREDICATE are *disallowed* in Hindi. (not absolute)

(39) is a translation of (38) in terms of the entities of representation assumed in Section 3:

(39) The following configuration is disallowed in Hindi (not absolute):

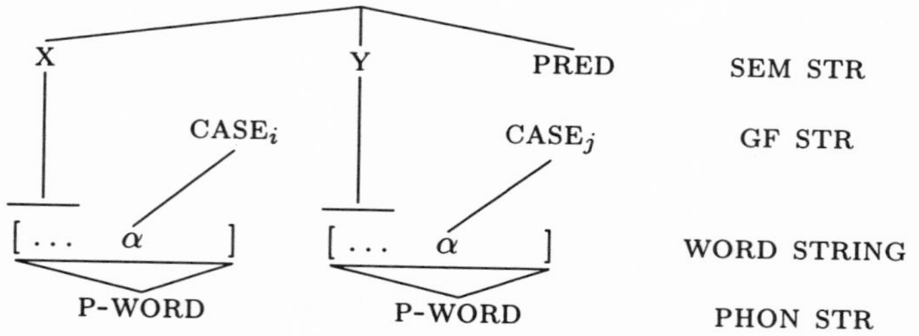

The representation of (2b), repeated for easy reference as (40a), gives an illustration of the multidimensional representations on which (38) holds. The representation includes four dimensions, namely, GC STR ((40b)), GF STR ((40c)), SEM STR ((40d)), and PHON(ological) STR ((40e)). The various dimensions, as we said earlier, intersect at the axis of the word string:

(40) a. ??**raam-ko** **baccõ-ko** samhaalnaa padaa.
Ram-D children-A take care of-NF fall-PERF
Ram had to take care of the children.

b.

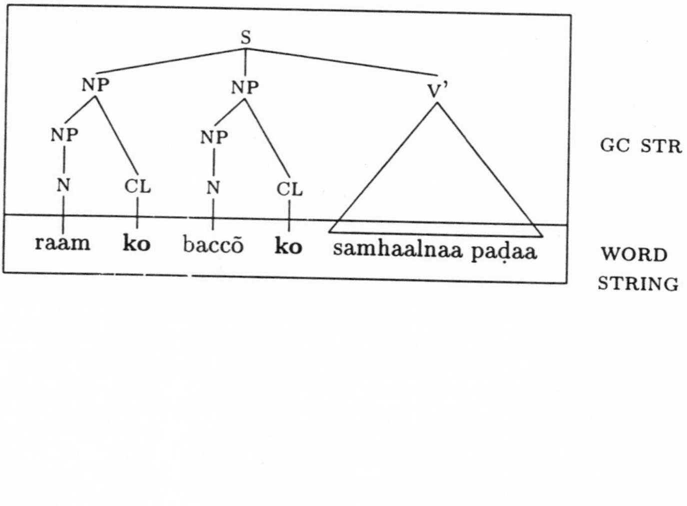

c.

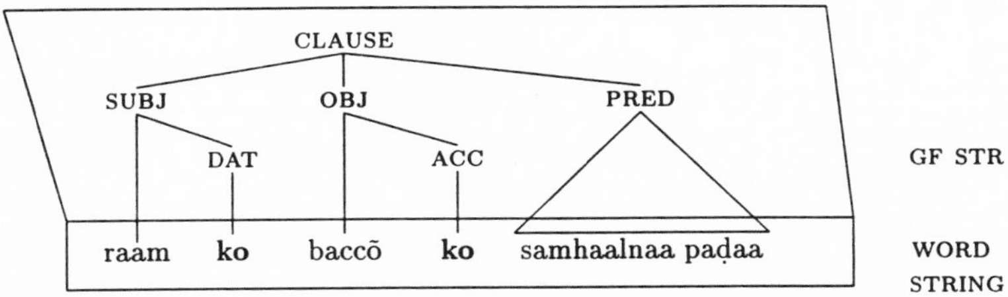

d.

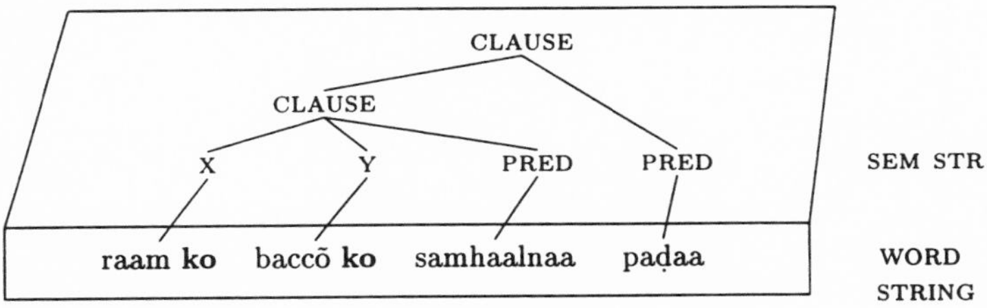

e.

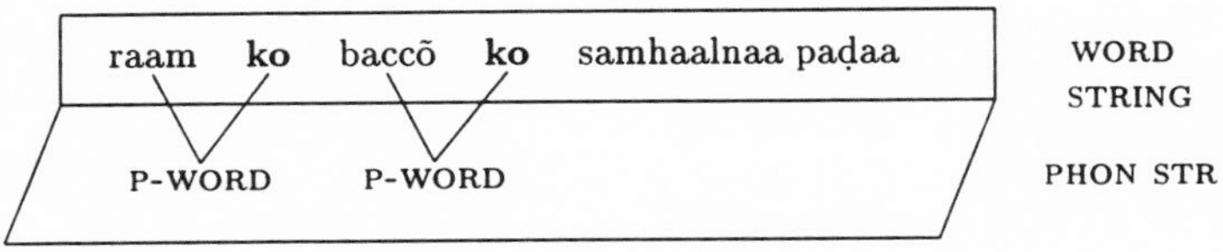

The adjacency relation relevant for (39) is checked at PHON STR, while the checking of the identity of the string requires simultaneous scanning of the the PHON STR, SEM STR and GF STR. A pause between two nouns does not make them non-adjacent at GC STR. However, a pause between two phonological words renders them non-adjacent at PHON STR. Hence, (39) correctly predicts the contrast between (2b) and (5).

4.5 Further Confirmation

The formulation in (39) predicts that prosodic structure (stress and word melody) can play a role in the observed effects of the constraint, independently of morphological and syntactic structure. Evidence from five different constructions confirms this prediction: the behaviour of the emphatic particle *hii* 'only', co-compounding, the noun incorporation construction, the effect of intervening adjuncts, and finally, quantifier float.

4.5.1

Hindi has a particle *hii* which can mean either 'only' or emphatic 'oneself'. Consider the effect of *hii* attachment on (39):

(41) a. ??**raam ko** hii **baccõ-ko** samhaalnaa paḍaa.
Ram-D EMPH children-A take care-NF fall-PERF
Only Ram/Ram himself had to take care of the children.

b. **raam ko** HII **baccõ-ko** samhaalnaa paḍaa.
Ram-D EMPH children-A take care-NF fall-PERF
Ram had to take care of the children.

In (41a), *raam-ko* and *hii* form a single phonological word, and *baccõ-ko* is another phonological word adjacent to it, thus violating (39). In (41b), the particle *hii* is emphasized, and is therefore a separate phonological word. Since the two phonological words containing *-ko* (*raam-ko* and *baccõ-ko*) are no longer adjacent, there is no violation of (39).

4.5.2

The second construction that demonstrates the relevance of phonological structure to the constraint under study is co-compounding. In Hindi, as in other South Asian languages, each stem in a co-(ordinate) compound (*dwandwa* compound) is an independent phonological word (T. Mohanan 1990:146–147). Given the phonological structure of co-compounds, (39) correctly predicts that when the second *-ko* bearing nominal in a sequence is a co-compound, the result will not be unacceptable:

(42) a. aaj-kal roz savere purohit baccõ-ko
these days everyday morning priest-N children-A
prasaad detaa hai.
blessed food-N give-HAB be-PR
These days, the priest gives blessed food to the children every morning.

b. ??aaj-kal roz savere **purohit-ko baccõ-ko**
thesedays everyday morning priest-D children-A
prasaad denaa paḍtaa hai.
blessedfood-N give-HAB fall-HAB be-PR
These days, the priest has to give blessed food to the children every morning.

c. aaj-kal roz savere **purohit-ko**
these days everyday morning priest-D
patii-patniyõ-ko prasaad denaa paḍtaa
husband-wife-PL-A blessed food-N give-HAB fall-HAB
hai.
be-PR
These days, the priest has to give blessed food to the couples every morning.

In (49b), *purohit-ko* and *baccõ-ko* are adjacent phonological words, and hence the sentence is unacceptable. In (49c), however, this sequence is broken by another phonological word *patii*, which exempts the sentence from (39).

4.5.3

The third construction relevant for our predictions is that of a noun incorporated structure ((12)–(15)) inside a *-vaalaa* compound, as in *sabzii-becne-vaalii* 'vegetable seller' (*sabzii* 'vegetable', *becnaa* 'to sell', *-vaalii* 'agentive marker'). Unlike the co-compound, the NI+*vaalaa* construction is a single phonological word (T. Mohanan, forthcoming). As predicted, sentence (43) is unacceptable, since *sabzii-becne-vaalii-ko* is a single phonological word.

(43) ??**raam-ko** **sabzii-becne-vaalii-ko** paise dene
Ram-D vegetable-sell-agentive-A money-N give-NF
hãĩ.
be-PR
Ram has to give money to the vegetable vendor.
(=has to pay her)

4.5.4

Given the relevance of SEM STR to the formulation of (39), we derive a very striking result. A noun associated with the time specification of an event is not a participant, and therefore should not be subject to (39). Such a noun in Hindi can be marked with the case clitic *-ko* (for example, *raat-ko* 'at night' in (30a)). Now, anything that intervenes between two phonological words associated with strings containing identical case formatives and associated with participants of the same predicate makes the phonological words nonadjacent for the purposes of (39). It follows, therefore, that if we put a word that is a time specification bearing *-ko* between two *-ko* marked arguments in a sentence such as (2b), the result should be acceptable. That is, a sequence of three *-ko* marked words, the middle one of which is not a participant, will not violate (39). In short, an unacceptable sequence of two *-ko* marked words must become acceptable if a third *-ko* marked word intervenes between them. This somewhat unusual and apparently implausible prediction turns out to be correct. Consider the contrast between (44a)/(2b) and (44b):

(44) a. ??**raam-ko** **baccõ-ko** samhaalnaa paḍaa.
Ram-D children-A take care-NF fall-PERF
Ram had to take care of the children.

b. **raam-ko** *raat-ko* **baccõ-ko** samhaalnaa paḍaa.
Ram-D night-at children-A take care-NF fall-PERF
Ram had to take care of the children at night.

Whereas (44a) is unacceptable, (44b) is perfectly acceptable.

4.5.5

Finally, yet another striking prediction made by (39) is that when two phonological words containing *-ko* are part of the same argument, as in the quantifier float construction, there will be no effects of the non-adjacency constraint. This prediction is borne out by (45):

(45) **raam-ko** raat-ko **baccõ-ko** *sab-ko* samhaalnaa
Ram-D night-at children-A all-A takecare-NF
paḍaa.
fall-PERF
Ram has to take care of all the children at night.

In (45), the quantifier *sab* 'all' occurs in the postnominal position as a separate NP, and hence it copies the case morpheme of its functional head. Even though *baccõ-ko* and *sab-ko* are two different NP's at the level of GC STR, they constitute a single participant at the level of SEM STR. Therefore, as predicted by (39), the result is acceptable.

Before going further, I must point out that the constraint against adjacency under investigation cannot be the result of a stylistic prohibition such as 'avoid ambiguous structures'.[14] First, if it were the result of a such a principle of the use of language, separating two identically case marked nouns with a modifier of the second noun should not make a difference, since non-adjacency does not eliminate ambiguity. Since identical case formatives are allowed under non-adjacency ((3), (4)), the principle cannot be one of the avoidance of ambiguity. Second, ambiguity is not eliminated by changing the formative ((34b), (35b), (36c, d)); yet the effect of the constraint disappears when the formatives are distinct even when the case morpheme remains the same. Finally, the occurrence of the double nominative (as in (32a,b)) creates ambiguity, and yet NOM case does not participate in the constraint, because it

[14] I am grateful to Alice Davison for bringing up this issue.

does not have a case formative. We must therefore conclude that the phenomenon is a principle of Hindi grammar, not one of pragmatics or stylistics.

5 The Dative Subject Construction

Before we proceed to the question of the relation between (39) and UG, it is necessary to make a small digression. All the examples that I have discussed so far involve constructions which allow identical case endings on two nominals, as long as they are not adjacent. Now, there is a construction which does not allow identical case marked nominals at all, whether adjacent or non-adjacent. It might be useful for the reader not to mistake the properties of this construction for the effects of the non-adjacency constraint.

The construction in question is the dative subject or psych-verb construction which takes a dative subject and a nominative object, as illustrated in (46a,b):[15]

(46) a. ilaa-ko anuu-kii ciṭṭʰii milii.
Ila-D Anu-G letter-N receive-PERF
Ila received Anu's letter.

b. raam-ko anuu dikʰii.
Ram-D Anu-N be visible-PERF
Ram saw Anu. (Lit.: To Ram Anu became visible.)

Inanimate objects in Hindi are typically in NOM case, and animate objects bear ACC case. If we assume that animate NPs that bear the grammatical function OBJ are assigned ACC case, and that the animate theme argument in (46b) is an OBJ, then we incorrectly predict that (46c) below should be acceptable:

(46) c. *raam-ko anuu-ko dikʰii.
Ram-D Anu-A be visible-PERF
Ram saw Anu. (Lit.: To Ram Anu became visible.)

One might conjecture that the unacceptability of (46c), and NOM case on the OBJ in (46b), are consequences of the constraint in (39). That this is not so is demonstrated by (46d), which is ungrammatical even though the two nominals are not adjacent:

(46) d. *raam-ko kal šaam anuu-ko dikʰii.
Ram-D yesterday evening Anu-A be visible-PERF
Ram saw Anu yesterday evening.
(Lit.: To Ram Anu became visible.)

As shown in Section 4.3., the identity prohibited by (39) is that of for-

[15] I am grateful to Tej Bhatia for raising this question.

matives, not case morphemes or case features. In contrast, the dative subject construction is not sensitive to differences in formatives. Thus, (46e) is ungrammatical even though one of the case endings is /-ko/ and the other is /-e/:

(46) e. *hame kal šaam anuu-ko dik^{h}ii.
We-D yesterday evening Anu-A be visible-PERF
We saw Anu yesterday evening.
(Lit.: To us, Anu became visible.)

The unacceptability of (46c–e) is simply an effect of case assignment (see T. Mohanan 1990:126–128 for a discussion). It cannot be deduced from (39), and is orthogonal to the issue at hand.

6 The Obligatory Contour Principle

The constraint in (39) is formulated as a stipulation in the grammar of Hindi. Such a formulation sheds light on the specific details that must be formally expressed in the constraint. However, an explanatory account of the phenomenon must also express the intuition that (39) is a manifestation of a pattern repeatedly found in languages. For instance, English exhibits a prohibition against sequences of the formative /-z/ on the same noun, as shown by the contrast between *children's* and **boys's* [bɔiziz]: if a form is plural and possessive, the two features are realized in a single formative (*boys'* [bɔiz]). In Malayalam, the formative /-um/ may be either the universal quantifier or the coordinating conjunction. Syntactic structures which require the universal quantifier as well as the coordinating conjunction are realised with a single /-um/ (K.P. Mohanan 1989). Another instance is the Mandarin *le* haplology. In a sentence with the perfective verbal suffix *le* and the sentence final change-of-state particle *le*, if the two *le*'s are adjacent, only one is realized.[16] A variant of this pattern is found in Malayalam where, in a sequence of the verb forming /-ikk/ and the causative /-ikk/, the structure is repaired by replacing the first /-ikk/ with /-ipp/.

One strategy of accounting for the recurrence of a pattern is to assume that it stems from UG. Adopting this practice, I assume the constraint against adjacent identical elements to be part of UG. In the examples of the prohibition against identity given above, the recurrent pattern is the following:

(47) Adjacent identical formatives are disallowed. (not absolute)

(47) must be part of UG, because it is repeatedly found in natural languages. However, it is not inviolable: there are speakers of English

[16] I thank Moira Yip for bringing this to my attention.

who accept [bɔiziz] as the possessive plural form of *boy*. Hence we must assume that (47) is an unmarked or nonabsolute universal.

In phonology, the constraint against adjacent identical elements is formulated as the Obligatory Contour Principle (henceforth OCP). The OCP was originally proposed as a morpheme structure constraint that prohibits sequences of identical tones (Leben 1973, Goldsmith 1976), and was extended to hold on segmental representations (McCarthy 1981, 1986, Yip 1988).[17] Since its original conception, the OCP has grown in phonology to the status of "an omnipresent well-formedness filter" (Yip 1988:98) that constrains morpheme structure as well as the form and mode of operation of rules, blocks rule applications that create violations of the OCP, and triggers rule applications that repair such violations.

In short, the earliest formulation of the OCP was: Adjacent identical tones are disallowed. The recognition of similar patterns in segmental phonology led to a revision of OCP as: Adjacent identical melodic units are disallowed. The striking resemblance between the phonological OCP and the morphological constraint in (47) forces us to put them together as an even more general condition:

---

[17]For an example of the effect of the OCP, consider the fact that English disallows adjacent segments with identical manner and primary place of articulation within a syllable. Take the examples in (i)–(iii):

(i) æ**kt** ke**pt**

(ii) li**st** be**lt**

(iii) *li**tt** *li**dd** *ke**pp** *li**ss** *li**zz** *ke**sz** *be**nn**

Adjacent segments may have identical manner, as in (i), or identical primary place, as in (ii). However, adjacent segments identical in both manner and primary place, as in (iii), are impossible syllable internally. Now, the concatenation of two morphemes can create the impossible sequences in (iii), as in (iv)–(v):

(iv) rowz + -z ⟶ row**zəz** *row**zz**

(v) bɔnd + -d ⟶ bɔn**dəd** *bɔndd

When the plural morpheme *-z* is attached to the word *rose* in (iv), or the past tense morpheme *-d* to the verb *bond* in (v), the adjacent identical segments make the result illformed. These forms are repaired by the insertion of schwa between the identical segments, to yield [rowzəz] and [bɔndəd]. Yip (1988:86–88) argues that the schwa epenthesis in these forms is simply a result of the general requirement of the OCP.

(48) **The Generalized OCP: Universal**
Adjacent identical elements (melodic units/formatives) are disallowed. (not absolute)

Stated this way, it is clear that the language particular constraint in (39) is a manifestation of the universal constraint in (48). There is, however, one crucial difference. The ban against the identity of case formatives in Hindi holds across two different words: morphologically, the two formatives are not adjacent in the sense in which the English plural and possessive formatives are adjacent in *boyss*. One way of bringing (39) under the rubric of generalized OCP is to revise (48) as (49):

(49) **The Generalized OCP: Universal (revised)**
Identical elements (melodic units/formatives) are disallowed in adjacent units. (not absolute)

What (49) does is to separate the unit relevant for identity from the unit relevant for adjacency. Given (49), the language particular formulation in (39) can be derived by selecting the language particular values of (49) as (50):

(50) **Hindi: Case OCP**

Identical element	:	case formative
Adjacent unit	:	phonological word
Environment	:	participants of the same predicate

The reader must be warned that the claim that (49) is a universal is not to be interpreted as the claim that it is a constraint that holds exceptionlessly in all human languages. First, OCP, like markedness universals in phonology, is a recurrent pattern, not an exceptionless pattern.[18] Second, what is given in (49) is not a constraint, but the form of a constraint which is fleshed out by filling in the language particular substance such as in (50). The claim that I am making is that there is a non-accidental relationship between a language specific phonological constraint which says that adjacent syllables with identical tones are prohibited, and a morphological constraint which says that adjacent nouns with idential case morphemes are prohibited.

[18]One of the reviewers objects to the idea of formulating recurrent patterns as part of UG. (S)he claims that all that (49) is saying is that languages may nor may not restrict relevantly similar things from occurring adjacent to one another in some constructions. If we take this view, we will have to say similar things about markedness statements such as "[+nasal] segments are [+voiced]," and "[−back] segments are [−round]".

7 Conclusion

To summarise, we observed that sentences such as (2b) are either completely or partially unacceptable for many speakers of Hindi. The reason for this unacceptability is the presence of two adjacent (phonological) words with identical case formatives. The unacceptability disappears if (a) the two words are separated by either a word or a pause; (b) if one of the words is not an argument of a predicate; (c) if the words are not arguments of the same predicate.

This phenomenon was analysed at two different stages. First, I showed that all the relevant facts discussed in the paper follow from the language particular constraint in (39) which forbids identical case formatives in a configuration involving adjacent phonological words and semantic participants of the same predicate. Second, I argued that this language particular constraint expressed a recurrent crosslinguistic pattern, which can be stated in UG as the Generalized OCP which unifies the restriction against adjacent formatives with that against adjacent units of phonological melody. Given the universal statement in (49), (39) can be derived by specifying in Hindi grammar a small number of language particular values for the parameters in the Generalized OCP. The advantage of thus generalizing the OCP is that statements in individual grammars can be simplified by abstracting away the universal pattern in (49) from the language specific details such as in (50). The conception underlying the treatment of Case OCP in Hindi as a combination of (49) and (50) offers a way of understanding invariance and variability across languages in terms of universal archetypes and specific manifestations.

In order to state the constraint that makes the correct predictions, whether as (39), or as the combination of (49) and (50), we found it necessary to assume that linguistically relevant phonological, syntactic, and semantic information is organized along several dimensions of representation which converge on the axis of the word string. Word order requirements are stated in terms of entities at any of these dimensions. The word order constraint in (39) forbids the adjacency of certain elements that are simultaneously associated with entities on the phonological, syntactic, and semantic dimensions. To the extent that this analysis is correct, then, it supports the need for multidimensional representations.

A central claim of a multidimensional conception of linguistic organization is that the various dimensions are available in parallel to principles of the grammar. In contrast, the unidimensional conception of representations assumes that principles of the grammar, except those that map one level of representation on to another, cannot access information contained in two different levels. Thus, although it is acknowledged that the representation of the Argument Structure is governed by the Lexical Conceptual Structure, and that Argument Structure is projected into VP internal structure, most work in GB assumes that the Lexical Conceptual Structure itself is not accessible to principles of syntax. Similarly, implicit in the T-model of GB is the assumption that there are no linguistic regularities which require simultaneous reference to the information at the levels of PF and LF. Thus, the information belonging to two different levels of representation are "encapsulated", prohibiting interaction between different levels.

When a principle of the grammar requires information from two different levels of representation, the strategy has been to copy the required information from one level to the other. For instance, argument structure information in GB is copied from d-structure to s-structure in terms of traces (see (9)). Likewise, information about argument structure, grammatical functions, and discourse functions is copied from s-structure to LF. The effect of such copying has been to represent different types of interacting information as a single multilayered representation.

If our analysis of the Hindi facts in this paper is correct, then it conflicts with the current assumptions about information interaction. To see this clearly, let us translate the analysis into GB. Since the adjacency requirement holds on phonological words, the constraint must hold at the level of PF. Since it also refers to semantic participanthood, the relevant LCS information must also be available at PF. Given this, if PF information and lcs information are not part of the same level of representation, then the hypothesis of encapsulation is incorrect. On the other hand, if a mechanism is devised to copy LCS information into PF representations, but not into s-structure representations, then the hypothesis of encapsulation is empirically vacuous.

Acknowledgements

I thank the SALA XIV audience for helpful comments and questions. Reactions, comments and suggestions from Joan Bresnan, Miriam Butt, Bruce Hayes, Jonni Kanerva, K.P. Mohanan, N.S. Prabhu, Moira Yip, and five anonymous reviewers have contributed to substantial improvement of the paper. I am grateful to my informants, particularly Akhil Gupta, Purnima Mankekar, and Alka Warrier for their patience, and for the confidence they have given me in my own intuitions. Work on this paper was supported in part by the Center for the Study of Language and Information, Stanford, California.

References

Baker, M. 1985. *Incorporation: A Theory of Grammatical Function Changing*. Doctoral dissertation, MIT.

Chomsky, N. 1992. A Minimalist Program of Linguistic Theory. *MIT Occasional Papers in Linguistics* 1.

Chomsky, N., and M. Halle. 1968. *The Sound Pattern of English*. New York: Harper and Row.

Goldsmith, J. 1976. *Autosegmental Phonology*. Doctoral dissertation, MIT. Published 1979, New York: Garland Press.

Halle, M. and J-R. Vergnaud. 1980. Three Dimensional Phonology. *Journal of Linguistic Research* 1:87–105.

Jackendoff, R. 1986. *Semantics and Cognition*. Cambridge, MA: The MIT Press.

Leben, W. 1973. *Suprasegmental Phonology*. Indiana University Linguistics Club.

Liberman, M., and A. Prince. 1977. On Stress and Linguistic Rhythm. *Linguistic Inquiry* 8:373–418.

McCarthy, J. 1981. A Prosodic Theory of Nonconcatenative Morphology. *Linguistic Inquiry* 12:207–263.

McCarthy, J. 1986. OCP Effects: Gemination and Antigemination. *Linguistic Inquiry* 17:207–263.

Mohanan, K. P. 1989. Universal Attractors in Phonological Theory. Paper presented at the Berkeley Workshop on Rules and Constraints in Phonology.

Mohanan, K.P., and T. Mohanan. 1993. Issues in Word Order in South Asian Languages: Enriched Phrase Structure or Multidimensionality? In M. Butt, T. H. King, and G. Ramchand (Eds.), *Theoretical Perspectives on Word Order Issues in South Asian Languages*. Stanford, CA: CSLI.

Mohanan, T. 1990. *Arguments in Hindi*. Doctoral Disseration, Stanford University.

Mohanan, T. Forthcoming. Wordhood and Lexicality: Noun Incorporation in Hindi. *Natural Language and Linguistic Theory*.

Pesetsky, D. 1985. Morphology and Logical Form. *Linguistic Inquiry* 16:193–246.

Sadock, J. 1985. Autolexical Syntax: A Proposal for the Treatment of Noun Incorporation and Similar Phenomena. *Natural Language and Linguistic Theory* 3:379–440.

Sadock, J.M. 1991. *Autolexical Syntax: A Theory of Parallel Grammatical Representations*. Chicago: The University of Chicago Press.

Selkirk, E.O. 1984. *Phonology and Syntax: The Relation between Sound and Structure*. Cambridge, MA: The MIT Press.

Speas, M. 1990. *Phrase Structure in Natural Language.* Dordrecht: Kluwer.

Yip, M. 1988. The Obligatory Contour Principle and Phonological Rules: A Loss of Identity. *Linguistic Inquiry* 19:65–100.

9

Thematic Roles, Word Order, and Definiteness

MONA SINGH

1 Introduction

It is traditionally believed that bare Noun Phrases in article-less languages may arbitrarily be definite or indefinite, or even ambiguous between the two readings (Heim 1982:229). This view might seem justified in light of the apparent lack, in such languages, of systematic rules that predict whether a given NP is definite or indefinite. Bare NPs occur extremely frequently in normal conversation in article-less languages. Therefore, the claim of ambiguity is unsatisfactory: for how could the speakers of article-less languages, more than half the world's population, get by with such ambiguity in their everyday utterances? The other possibility, namely, pure arbitrariness, is more reasonable. But, as I hope to show, it too is false.

In this paper, I present rules that unambiguously determine the definiteness of bare NPs in the article-less language, Hindi. These rules involve the thematic roles and the syntactic positions of the relevant NPs. While these rules are designed for Hindi, I believe that my core conceptual claims are true in general, i.e., also for Slavic languages, Japanese, Chinese, and Persian. These claims are that

- Bare NPs are not ambiguous in a given context; and
- Definiteness of NPs depends on both thematic *and* word order information.

Hindi is an SOV language. Since it has a rich case system, it is not particularly sensitive to word order. Word order is not entirely free: it turns out to have some impact on the definiteness of NPs. It is possible to have NPs with determiners, demonstratives, or with a possessive

Theoretical Perspectives on Word Order in South Asian Languages
Miriam Butt, Tracy Holloway King, Gillian Ramchand (Eds.)

marking: the definiteness of such NPs can be easily determined. I shall focus, therefore, on bare NPs.

The distribution of bare NPs is quite subtle. A bare NP may be indefinite if it has not been part of the discourse and, therefore, introduces a discourse referent. In (1a), a bare NP, *kitaab*, has an indefinite interpretation — (1a) could, for instance, be a reply to the question *What was Ram doing this morning?* Note that *kitaab* can be given a definite interpretation in (1a), if it occurs at a point in a discourse where a particular book is salient. That would be the case, for instance, in a reply to the question *When was Ram reading the book?* In sentence (1b), *kitaab* has only a definite interpretation, since this sentence presupposes that a particular book is being referred to. The referent may be determined from the discourse context. A bare NP can be said to be looking for an *anchor*, i.e., an entity in the discourse to which it may refer. If it finds one, it is definite, otherwise it introduces a new anchor.

(1) a. raam aaj savere kitaab paRh rahaa thaa
Ram today morning-OBL book read PROG was
Ram was reading *a* book this morning.

b. kitaab premcand kii likhii thii
book Premchand by written was
The book was written by Premchand.

Let sentences (1a) and (1b) describe a simple discourse. It is easy to see from these examples that the interpretation of an NP as definite or indefinite depends on where it occurs in the discourse. However, much remains to be said for the cases where no particular salient referent is available. These cases are of primary interest in this paper. The analysis that I present in later sections involves a semantic classification of the verbal predicates, the syntactic positions of the relevant NPs, as well as the thematic relations they participate in.

An interesting phenomenon in most article-less languages is the adaptation of the word for 'one' as an indefiniteness marker. Sentences (2a) and (2b) exemplify such a use of *ek* ('one' in Hindi).

(2) a. ek aurat ke-pas ek kuttaa$_1$ hæ
one lady POSS one dog is
A lady has a dog$_1$.

b. *ek kutte$_1$/kutte$_1$ ka naam moti hæ
a dog/dog-OBL POSS name Moti is
The dog's name is Moti.

These sentences indicate that the NP *ek kuttaa* introduces a discourse referent and hence is indefinite, whereas the NP *kutte* presupposes its referent and hence is definite. Using *ek* in the second sentence would introduce a new referent, distinct from the dog introduced in the preceding discourse. The presence of *ek* immediately identifies a given NP as indefinite. It can thus be used as a reliable marker of indefiniteness. The syntax and semantics of *ek* are formalized in Section 4. Just as the marker *ek* unambiguously identifies a noun as indefinite, demonstratives can be used in Hindi to unambiguously identify a noun as definite.

The rest of this paper is organized as follows. Sections 2 and 3 present the relationship between thematic roles and definiteness. Section 3.4 describes the effect of word order on the determination of definiteness. The formal framework used for representing thematic relations, word order and definiteness is discussed in Section 4. The interpretation of all example sentences is based on the assumption that they occur discourse initially.

2 Thematic Roles

In this section, I discuss the relationship of the definiteness of a bare NP with its thematic role. Traditionally, thematic roles include AGENT, PATIENT, EXPERIENCER, INSTRUMENT, GOAL, and SOURCE (Fillmore 1971). But rather than deal with these roles directly, I find it useful to consider the metaconcepts of *prototypical agent* and *prototypical patient*. Not only does this simplify the theory that results, as we shall see, it also accounts for INSTRUMENTS better than otherwise possible.

Dowty (1991) defines thematic relations in terms of proto-agent and proto-patient entailments. The proto-agent properties proposed by Dowty include volition, sentience, causing an event, having independent existence, and movement relative to the position of another participant. The properties of patienthood include undergoing a change of state, being an incremental theme, being causally affected by another participant, being stationary relative to the movement of another participant, and not having independent existence.

Of the traditional roles, AGENTS and EXPERIENCERS have more proto-agent properties than proto-patient properties. PATIENTS, GOALS, and SOURCES have more proto-patients than proto-agent properties. INSTRUMENTS can be in either category depending on their sentience, though they are proto-patients by default.

Briefly, I show that arguments with more proto-agent properties are definite irrespective of their syntactic position. Whereas arguments with more proto-patient properties can be definite or indefinite. Their definiteness depends on factors such as word order, whether a given sentence is discourse initial or not, and, for PATIENTS, the structure of the verbal form used. The behavior of PATIENTS is by far the most complex and, therefore, is discussed separately in Section 3.

2.1 Agent

Bare nouns with more proto-agent entailments are *always* definite. For example see sentences (3) and (4), which involve a different word order, and sentence (5), which involves passivization. The indefiniteness of an agent has to be explicitly specified by the indefiniteness marker, *ek*, or some such qualifier, as in sentence (6).

(3)	laRke-ne	ciTThii	likhii	
	boy-ERG	letter	write-PERF	
	The boy wrote a letter.			
(4)	ciTThii	laRke-ne	likhii	
	letter	boy-ERG	write-PERF	
	The boy wrote the letter.			
(5)	ciTThii	laRke-dwaaraa	likhii	gayii
	letter	boy-by	write	PASS
	The letter was written by the boy.			
(6)	kisii	laRke-ne	ciTThii	likhii
	some	boy-ERG	letter	write-PERF
	Some boy wrote a letter.			

Even when the agent is inanimate, as in sentence (7), we get a definite interpretation. This is consistent with this analysis, since an inanimate bare NP has more agent properties than patient properties, even though it lacks the property of sentience.

(7)	bijlii-ne	ghar	jalaa	diyaa
	lightening-ERG	house	burn	give-PERF
	The lightening burned the house.			

2.2 Experiencer

In sentence (8) below, *laRke-ko* is an EXPERIENCER. I call it a proto-agent, since it has more agent properties (namely, *sentience* and *independent existence*) than patient properties (namely, *being causally affected*). An EXPERIENCER NP is always definite; *ek* must be used, as in sentence (9), to explicitly specify it as being indefinite.

(8)	laRke-ko	bijlii-se	Dar	lagtaa	hæ
	boy-DAT	lightening-INS	fear	feel-HAB	is
	The boy is scared of lightening.				

(9) ek laRke-ko bijlii-se Dar lagtaa hæ
one boy-DAT lightening-from fear feel-HAB is
A boy is scared of lightening.

2.3 Goal and Source

The cases of SOURCES and GOALS are fairly straightforward. In sentence (10), *imaarat* is the SOURCE and *dukaan* is the GOAL. Both occur in their canonical positions and are indefinite. In Section 3.4, I describe the effects of scrambling on the definiteness of these roles.

(10) sitaa imaarat-se nikal kar dukaan-mẽ gayii
Sita building-from exit SEQ shop-in go-PERF
Sita left a building and entered a store.

2.4 Instrument

INSTRUMENTS are more complex than the thematic relations GOAL and SOURCE. They have the proto-agent property of MOVEMENT, and the proto-patient property of being *causally affected*. An INSTRUMENT may or may not be *sentient*. In cases where an INSTRUMENT has the property of *sentience* and thereby has more proto-agent properties than proto-patient properties we get a definite reading as in sentence (12). However, if it does not have the property of *sentience*, the interpretation is indefinite as in sentence (11). It is interesting that INSTRUMENTS behave like proto-patients, even though they have equal number of agent and patient properties. Clearly, a bare NP must be definite or indefinite and instruments are indefinite by default.

(11) raam-ne caakuu-se ciTThii kholi
Ram-ERG knife-with letter open-PERF
Ram opened the letter with a knife.

(12) raam-ne Dakiye-se ciTThii khulvayi
Ram-ERG postman-by letters open-CAU-PERF
Ram had the postman open the letter.

It is important to note that proto-agents cannot be distinguished from proto-patients only on the basis of sentience. This is because there are other significant distinctions between them. In the case of INSTRUMENTS, however, sentience turns out to be the property that breaks the tie. Recall that in the case of AGENTS, sentience did not affect definiteness because AGENTS have no proto-patient properties. For a detailed discussion of INSTRUMENTS in Hindi, especially animate ones, see Singh (1992).

3 Patient

The case of determining the definiteness of PATIENTS is quite subtle. Even in their canonical syntactic position, their definiteness depends on the semantic nature of the verb with which they occur, on whether the associated verb is compound or simple, and on whether they are given an accusative marking. I consider each of these phenomena in the following subsections.

3.1 A Semantic Classification of Verbs

While verbs have been classified in various ways, the following classification proves particularly useful for determining the definiteness of their bare NP PATIENTS. This classification is based on an analysis of over one hundred simple verbs. The classification of verbs in this section help determine the default value of bare object NPs. I refer to this as the default interpretation of the object, without any overt marking or determiner.

3.1.1 Verbs that Totally Affect Their Patients

A crucial property in determining the definiteness of PATIENTS is whether the given verb totally affects its patient. For example, the PATIENT in *eat a cake* is completely affected by the action, while the PATIENT in *buy a cake* is not. It turns out that there is no distinction between verbs that only partially affect their PATIENTS and those that do not affect them at all.

Verbs with totally affected patients occur in predicates such as *draw a picture, eat an apple, dye a shirt, break a glass* and *smoke a cigarette.* Bare NP PATIENTS in these predicates are interpreted as indefinite in their canonical syntactic position (e.g., sentence (13)). Verbs whose patients are not totally affected occur in predicates such as *hang a shirt, hide a book, buy a book, cut a cake* and *hear a story.* Bare NP PATIENTS in these predicates have a definite interpretation in Hindi (e.g., sentence (14)).

(13) us-ne aaj subah kek khaayaa
he-ERG today morning cake eat-PERF
He ate a cake in the morning.

(14) us-ne aaj subah kek kaaTTaa
he-ERG today morning cake cut-PERF
He cut the cake this morning.

Note that the verb by itself cannot determine whether its PATIENT is definite or not. For example, consider the difference in the interpretation of the PATIENTS in *paint a picture* and *paint the door.* The

Verbal predicate	Example PATIENTS	Definite
PEEL	orange	+
WIN	race	+
PAINT	door	+
LIKE	song	+
HATE	song	+
KNOW	song	+
RECOLLECT	story	+
PUT	book	+
ENTER	room	+
CROSS	road	+
LOSE	key	+
OPEN	door	+
CLOSE	door	+
HEAR	story	+
LOAD	hay	+
COVER	wall	+
EAT	apple	−
WRITE	letter	−
READ	book	−
WEAR	sweater	−
PAINT	painting	−
WASH	shirt	−
MAKE	house	−
SMOKE	cigarette	−
BREAK	glass	−
BRING	book	−
ASK	question	−
FIX	program	−
BURN	stick	−

FIGURE 1 Definiteness of Patients

former is indefinite, whereas the latter is definite. The difference lies in the fact that, while painting a door merely affects the surface of the door (hence, it is not totally affected), painting a picture *creates* a new picture (hence, it is totally affected). This shows that the entire predicate is relevant in determining the definiteness of the PATIENT, not just the verb.

3.1.2 Verbs of Possession

The bare PATIENTS of Verbs of possession or ownership are indefinite. The verbs *own* and *have* belong to this class. The verb *wear* can also be considered as belonging to the same class. In fact, many languages employ the verb *have* to connote *wear*. For example, *an.haben* in German and *to have on* in English both mean *to wear*.

(15) raam-ne laal kamiiz pæhnii hæ
Ram-ERG red shirt wear is
Ram is wearing a red shirt.

(16) siitaa-ke-pas saikal hæ
Sita-POSS cycle is
Sita has a cycle.

3.1.3 Non-Possessive Stative Verbs

Stative verbs other than verbs of possession, e.g., *know*, *like*, and *hate*, have definite PATIENTS even when they are not overtly marked as being so. The definiteness interpretation holds only for *patients* of these verbs, as in sentence (17) and not for *patients* in a subordinate clause as in sentence (18).

(17) raam šlok jaantaa hæ
Ram hymn know-HAB is
Ram knows the Hymn.

(18) sitaa jaantii hæ ki raam-ne laal kamiiz pæhnii hæ
Sita know-PRES is that Ram-ERG red shirt wear is
Sita knows that Ram is wearing a red shirt.

3.1.4 Speech Act Verbs

Consider the verbal predicates *ask a question* and *answer the question*. In the case of the verb *ask*, the bare NP is indefinite, whereas in the case of the verb *answer*, the bare NP is definite. A plausible explanation for this phenomenon is the following. When a question is asked, there is no salient question and, therefore, the interpretation is indefinite. However, the asking of a question introduces it into the discourse. Therefore, the bare NP of the predicate *answer the question* (which in

Hindi takes the form *give the answer*) is definite. This is exemplified by the brief discourse in sentence (19).

(19) a. šikšak-ne vidyarthii-se prašn puucha
teacher-ERG student-source question ask-PERF
The teacher asked a student a question.

b. vidyarthii-ne jawaab diyaa
student-ERG answer give-PERF
The student gave the answer.

Furthermore, if sentence (19b) occurs by itself, it is still interpreted as having a definite interpretation; i.e., it presupposes a salient question to which the answer is given by the student. This phenomenon is more clearly exhibited by sentence (20) below, where an issued command is indefinite, but when it is responded to, it is definite.

(20) a. raaja-ne mantrii-ko nirdeš diyaa
king-ERG minister-ACC order give-PERF
The king gave an order to the minister.

b. mantrii-ne nirdeš maanaa
minister-ERG order obey-PERF
The minister obeyed the order.

3.1.5 Sensory Verbs

The verbs of this class correspond to the five senses. Verbs of sensation do not exhibit a single pattern with respect to the definiteness interpretation of their patients. The verbs *see, hear, smell*, and *feel* always have their bare NP patients as indefinite. The verb *taste*, on the other hand, always marks its patient as definite. This reflects the perception of Hindi speakers that one can intentionally taste only something specific. This also explains why the verb *taste* cannot be used with the adverbial *accidentally.*

(21) raam-ne awaaz sunii
Ram-ERG sound hear
Ram heard a sound.

(22) raam-ne seb cakhaa
Ram-ERG apple taste-PERF
Ram tasted the apple.

3.1.6 Verbs of Giving

This class of verbs, discussed in Pinker (1989:213–214), denote a giver having some object and then causing it to enter the possession of a recipient. Verbs belonging to this class mark their PATIENTS as indefinite. This class includes the verbs *give, pass, sell, lend, feed* and *serve.* Although verbs of giving are usually ditransitive, that does not affect the analysis, because the status of the patients does not change. Indirect objects are not considered in this paper because they are always definite.

3.2 Accusative Marking and Definiteness

In Hindi, animate direct objects are marked with a postposition, *ko*. Traditionally, the use of *ko* is said to be optional. As observed by Keenan (1987), however, this marker is absent if the NP is indefinite and present if the NP is definite. Accusative marking is thus yet another way in which NPs can be marked for definiteness in Hindi and another way in which ambiguity can be avoided. The definite NP *murgii* in (23) would be definite if it had a *ko* marking, as in (24). Consider the following sentences taken from Keenan (1987, Ch. 5):

(23) Raam-ne murgii maarii
ram-ERG chicken kill-PERF
Ram killed a chicken.

(24) raam-ne murgii-ko maaraa
Ram-ERG chicken-ACC kill-PERF
Ram killed the chicken.

In some dialects of Hindi, the accusative marking may also be used with inanimate objects. In these dialects, sentence (25) is acceptable.

(25) laRke-ne phuul-ko dekhaa
boy-ERG flower-ACC see-PERF
The boy saw the flower.

This can be accounted for as an analogical extension of the definition of *ko* of the rule that marks only inanimate PATIENTS as definite. The rule for the generalized definition of *ko* applies to all patient NPs and yields definite patient NPs. It is formalized in Section 4.2.

An interesting observation is that while the indefiniteness marker *ek* can be used with animate patients marked with *ko* to indicate indefiniteness, it cannot be used with inanimate patients marked with *ko*. This distinction is accounted for formally in Section 4 by the fact that the morpheme *ko* marks all PATIENTS as definite and *ek* applies to all nouns and marks them as indefinite. The only restriction here is the obvious one requiring that case markings apply before determiners. Consequently, *ek* and *ko* can go together without resulting in a semantic conflict. The ungrammaticality of (27) is best explained on the basis of Grice's maxims. The maxim of manner requires that the speaker be perspicuous. In the case of sentence (27) the indefiniteness of the PATIENT can be conveyed to the speaker by the use of a bare NP PATIENT *phuul*. The NP *phuul-ko* would be used if the PATIENT was definite. Using the determiner *ek* in this case to indicate indefiniteness would merely be redundant.

(26) laRke-ne aaj subah ek laRkii-ko dekhaa
boy-ERG today morning one girl-ACC see-PERF
The boy saw a girl this morning.

(27) *laRke-ne aaj ek phuul-ko dekhaa
boy-ERG today one flower-ACC see-PERF
The boy saw a flower this morning.

3.3 Compound Verbs and Definiteness

The distinction between definites and indefinites is also crucial in the study of events and aspect. Recent work by Krifka (1991) provides a well-motivated analysis of the connection between the reference type of NPs and the temporal constitution of verbal predicates. There are two main types of events: *telic* and *atelic* (Vendler 1967). Telic events are those that have a natural endpoint, e.g., *eat an apple*, and *win a race*. Telic events have two major categories, *accomplishments* and *achievements*. Accomplishments are telic events like *eat an apple* that are gradual; achievements are telic events like *win a race* that are instantaneous. Atelic events do not have a natural endpoint, e.g., *run, eat apples*.

Quantized NPs like *an apple* correspond to telic event types, since both have natural limits. Similarly, cumulative NPs like *wine* correspond to atelic event types, since neither has any predetermined limits. Krifka notes that quantized arguments yield a telic verbal predicate and cumulative arguments yield atelic verbal predicates. He cites the example of Slavic languages which, like Hindi, mark the perfective aspect, but not the definiteness of NPs. In Czech, for example, *vino* can mean 'wine' or 'the wine'; *hruska* can mean 'a pear' or 'the pear'. In their definite readings, these nouns are quantized; in their indefinite readings, they are cumulative. Furthermore, in their definite interpretations these nouns are compatible only with the perfective aspect; in their indefinite interpretation they are compatible only with the imperfective aspect.

In Hindi, the situation is a little more complicated, since it does not have any imperfective marker. The aspectual system of Hindi includes the perfective aspect and the non-perfective aspect. The non-perfective aspect has two subclasses, namely, the progressive and the habitual. Hindi lacks an imperfective marker that is present in many articleless languages like Czech and Russian. However, Hindi has a more complex verb structure. Hindi and other Indo-Aryan languages have verbal constructions called "Compound Verbs" (CVs). These verbs have aspectual as well as non-aspectual content (Hacker 1961, Singh 1990). In general, CVs refer to constellations of verbs of the form [Verb1 + Verb2], in which Verb2 loses its independent meaning to a large extent. When a verb is used by itself (I call this a "Simple Verb" or SV), inflections for agreement are applied to it. In a CV, Verb1 appears in its stem form and all inflections are applied only to Verb2. The speaker usually has a choice of what verb to use as Verb2. Sentence (28) is used, if the agent is the beneficiary; (29), if someone else is.

(28) us-ne kitaab paRh lii
he-ERG book read take-PERF
He read the book (for himself).

(29) us-ne kitaab paRh dii
he-ERG book read give-PERF
He read the book (to/for someone else).

CVs play a role in determining the definiteness of some of the NPs in a sentence. However, this function is restricted to achievements and accomplishments. Consider the achievements in sentences (30) and (31). In this class of events, the distinction between the CV and the SV form is precisely the distinction between definiteness and indefiniteness.

(30) us-ne aaj subah billii dekhii
he-ERG today morning cat see-PERF
He saw a cat this morning.

(31) us-ne aaj subah billii dekh lii
he-ERG today morning cat see take-PERF
He saw the cat this morning.

In accomplishments, e.g., sentences (32)–(36), CVs imply that the NP referring to the (affected or consumed) PATIENT refers to *all* of it; SVs imply that the NP refers to some unspecified *part* of the PATIENTS (Singh 1991). In addition to specifying the completion of the event, CVs also imply the definiteness of the PATIENT.

(32) us-ne aaj kek khaayaa (par puura nahĩĩ khaayaa)
he-ERG today cake eat-PERF (but all NEG eat-PERF)
He ate a cake today (but not all of it).

(33) us-ne aaj kek khaa liyaa
he-ERG today cake eat take-PERF
He ate the cake today (all of it).

In the case of activities, i.e., in the case of cumulative PATIENTS, a CV transforms the predicate to an accomplishment, as in (35).

(34) us-ne aaj waain pii
he-ERG today wine drink-PERF
He drank wine today.

(35) us-ne aaj waain pii lii
he-ERG today wine drink take-PERF
He drank the wine today.

This phenomenon can be explained by the fact that Hindi lacks the imperfective aspect, it uses the perfective form in sentences like (33). Sentence (32) does not imply that all of the cake was eaten, as the case would be in languages like Czech. Since the NP is neither given a definite interpretation nor quantized, the speaker has to resort to using the verb (here the CV) as a means of distinguishing between 'a book' or 'a part of a book' from 'the book' (all of it).

3.4 Word Order as a Marker of Definiteness

We have seen that most bare proto-patient NPs are indefinite in their canonical position. In this section I describe one of the mechanisms that may be used to specify a proto-patient as definite. Consider the following sentences, which are word order variations of sentences cited earlier in this paper.

(36) aam siitaa-ne aaj subah khaayaa
mango Sita-ERG today morning eat-PERF
Sita ate the mango this morning.

(37) imaarat-se nikal kar Sitaa dukaan-mẽ gayii
building-from exit SEQ Sita shop-in go-PERF
Sita left the building and entered a store.

(38) dukaan-mẽ Sitaa imaarat-se nikal kar gayii
shop-in Sita building-from exit SEQ go-PERF
Sita entered the store after leaving a building.

Sentences (36)–(38) illustrate the phenomenon of *scrambling*. In all these cases, the result is a definite reading of the proto-patient. I do not concern myself here with a discussion of whether this phenomenon should be analyzed as *topicalization*, *focus*, or something else. I concentrate here on the effect of *scrambling* on definiteness. The word order variations of transitive sentences that are possible in Hindi are

- AGENT PATIENT VERB
- PATIENT AGENT VERB
- PATIENT VERB AGENT
- VERB PATIENT AGENT
- VERB AGENT PATIENT

- AGENT VERB PATIENT

In all these variations the AGENT is definite unless it is explicitly marked as indefinite by the marker *ek*. A PATIENT is definite in all scrambled positions, i.e., in all cases where it does not immediately precede the verb. In cases where there is more than one PATIENT, scrambling out of the canonical position for every PATIENT yields a definite reading. The relationship between word order and definiteness in Hindi has been explained by Mahajan (1990) terms of syntactic case assignment.

It has been pointed out by Clark (1978) that there is a strong tendency for indefinite nominals to occur in the non-initial position. Similarly, I think that definites have a very strong tendency to occur in the sentence-initial position. The sentence-initial position is marked for PATIENTS, its function is to move the emphasis away from the AGENT to the PATIENT, which is the new information. Interestingly, in Finnish, which is an article-less language, a PATIENT in the sentence initial position is invariably definite as well (Chesterman 1991). An example of this is the sentence in (39).

(39) Arvostelun kirjoitti toimittaja
review wrote editor-NOM
The review was written by the editor.

Therefore, we can conclude that a proto-patient, though it may be indefinite in its canonical position, is definite in a *scrambled* position. Also a proto-agent is definite in any position. Every movement rule must therefore add at least the information about scrambling in the syntactic representation. A scrambled PATIENT NP that was indefinite in its canonical position may be moved to, say, the sentence initial position. This will result in its being specified as NP[PAT,+SCRAM]. If an NP has been scrambled then the default rules that apply at the end of a derivation will be those that are specific to scrambled NPs. We do not need a new rule for a scrambled AGENT because the default rule presented in Section 4 will work just as well. However, a new rule is required for PATIENTS. This rule is presented in Section 4. It is important to mention that the rules for scrambled NPs apply before the default rules. This is because if the default rules apply first a scrambled NP will default to [−DEF]. An example derivation of a sentence with a scrambled NP is given in Figure 3.

4 The Formalism

I assume a Montague style categorial framework for syntactic representation. This, however, is not essential to the main claims of this paper: one could, in principle, just as well have used something like

HPSG. In the adopted framework, every lexical entry contains syntactic information and semantics. For example, the lexical entry for the verb *khaanaa* 'eat' is represented in (40). The lexical entry specifies the number of arguments and the thematic relations that hold between the verb and its arguments. AG and PAT are used as a shorthand for *proto-agent* and *proto-patient*, respectively.

4.1 Lexical Entries for Verbs

For each verb, I postulate a basic lexical entry that gives its syntax and some components of its semantics. This entry describes its thematic roles and the event predicate associated with the verb. The definiteness of PATIENTS is not determined from this entry, but rather from another mechanism, which is described in Section 4.6. The entry in (40) means that the verb *khaanaa* takes an NP AGENT and an NP PATIENT and returns a sentence.

(40) khaanaa; S/NP[AG],NP[PAT]; λe[khaanaa(e)]

(41) kholnaa; S/NP[AG],NP[PAT]; λe[kholnaa(e)]

The comma notation used here is due to Krifka (1990). It is a generalization of the usual categorial notation that is especially perspicuous when one's framework is based on thematic roles. The comma emphasizes the irrelevance of word order. The arguments to the rule, i.e., the entities to the right of '/' can be supplied in any order, since the syntactic information is encoded in their thematic roles.

4.2 Lexical Entry for *ko*

The accusative marker, *ko*, which was described in Section 3.2, applies to an N PATIENT and yields a definite N. It is important to set the result to be an N because the application of *ko* can be followed by the application of *ek*.

(42) **ko;** N/N; N[PAT, +DEF]/N[PAT]

4.3 Lexical Entry for *ek*

The indefiniteness marker, *ek*, was discussed in Section 1. It takes a noun and yields an NP that is necessarily indefinite. The *ek* applies after the *ko*, and overrides the effect of *ko* by forcing the resulting NP to be indefinite. This was exhibited in sentence (26).

The syntax and semantics of *ek* can be formalized as in (43): it combines with a noun (in any position) to yield an indefinite NP.

(43)
- **ek;** NP[−DEF]/N; $\lambda P'\lambda P\lambda e\exists x[P(e) \wedge AG(e,x), P'(x)]$
- **ek;** NP[−DEF]/N; $\lambda P'\lambda P\lambda e\exists x[P(e) \wedge PAT(e,x), P'(x)]$

4.4 Lexical Entry for the Null Category

We use a null category to convert a noun into an NP. This is required in the absence of an *ek*, or any other determiner, e.g., a possessive. As mentioned above, the null category is required even in the presence of *ko* to convert a N into an NP. The theory of thematic relations requires that the null category be defined for both Agents and Patients. This may seem redundant but is essential given the bigger picture, namely the recognition of the fact that Agents and Patients have separate roles in the interpretation of any given sentence.

(44)
- $\emptyset$; NP[AG]/N; $\lambda P'\lambda P\lambda e\exists x[P(e) \wedge AG(e,x), P'(x)]$
- $\emptyset$; NP[PAT]/N; $\lambda P'\lambda P\lambda e\exists x[P(e) \wedge PAT(e,x), P'(x)]$

4.5 Lambda Application

ek; NP[−DEF]/N; $\lambda P'\lambda P\lambda e\exists x[P(e) \wedge AG(e,x) \wedge P'(x)]$

laRkii-ne; N; *girl*

ek laRii-ne; NP[−DEF]; $\lambda P\lambda e\exists x[P(e) \wedge AG(e,x) \wedge girl(x)]$

$\emptyset$; NP[PAT]/N; $\lambda P'\lambda P\lambda e\exists y[P(e) \wedge PAT(e,y) \wedge P'(y)]$

murgii; N; *chicken*

murgii; NP[PAT]; $\lambda P\lambda e\exists y[P(e) \wedge PAT(e,y) \wedge chicken(y)]$

maarii; S/NP[AG], NP[PAT]; $\lambda e[kill(e)]$

murgii maarii; S/NP[AG]; $\lambda e\exists y[kill(e) \wedge PAT(e,y) \wedge chicken(y)]$

ek laRkii-ne murgii maarii; S[AG[−DEF]]; $\lambda e\exists x\exists y[kill(e) \wedge PAT(e,y) \wedge chicken(y) \wedge AG(e,x) \wedge girl(x)]$

FIGURE 2 An Example of *ek* as a Marker of Indefiniteness

Lambda application operates on the lexical entries for the different syntactic categories. An example derivation is given in Figure 2. Notice that, at the end of this series of applications, we may not have any information about the definiteness of the relevant NPs. This happens when bare NPs occur without any *ko* markers. At this point, the default rules, which are described next, may apply (these rules do not apply in Figure 2). These rules would force the maximal marking of [±DEF] on the bare nouns.

4.6 Default Rules

Next, I propose that default rules apply to NPs and VPs that fill in the information about definiteness. I propose three ordered default rules. These rules apply only when no contradiction would result from their application, given the previous lambda applications and default rules. The first default rule is the one involving scrambling. As discussed in Section 3.4, Hindi admits several word orders, but only AGENT PATIENT VERB is canonical. The present theory relies on information about whether different NPs have undergone scrambling, i.e., it requires scrambled NPs to be marked as +SCRAM. Rather than give a categorial rule for each possible order, I prefer to state only one rule and allow it to be applied on different word orders with the proviso that when it is applied in a noncanonical word order, the proto-patient NPs involved are marked as +SCRAM. For proto-patients (P-PAT), the rule described in (45) applies, and marks it as being definite. No such rule is required for proto-agents, since they are definite anyway.

(45) NP[P-PAT,+SCRAM] → [+DEF]

The second kind of default rules are those related to verbs that mark their PATIENTS as [+DEF]. These default rules are ordered after the default scrambling rule, because scrambling marks *all* PATIENTS as [+DEF].

(46) kholnaa; S/NP[AG],NP[PAT] ⟶ S/NP[AG]NP[PAT, +DEF]

The third kind of default rules are related to the proto-agent and proto-patient properties of the NPs. If an NP has not been marked as definite or indefinite up to this point, then these rules plug in the default values. Proto-agents always default to [+DEF] and proto-patients always default to [−DEF]. These rules are formalized in (47).

(47)
- NP[AG] → [+DEF]
- NP[PAT] → [−DEF]

In Figure 3, I give the derivation of sentence (48). This derivation explicates the application of default rules.

(48) murgii ram-ne maarii
chicken Ram-ERG kill-PERF
Ram killed the chicken.

$\emptyset$; NP[PAT]/N; $\lambda P' \lambda P \lambda e[P(e) \wedge PAT(e,x) \wedge P'(x)]$

murgii; N; *chicken*

murgii; NP; $\lambda P \lambda e \exists x[P(e) \wedge PAT(e,x) \wedge chicken(x)]$

maarii; S/NP[AG], NP[PAT]; $\lambda e[kill(e)]$

murgii maarii; S/NP[AG]; $\lambda e[kill(e) \wedge PAT(e,x) \wedge chicken(x)]$

Ram-ne; NP; $\lambda P \lambda e[P(e) \wedge AG(e, ram)]$

murgii Ram-ne maarii; S; $\lambda e[kill(e) \wedge PAT(e,x) \wedge chicken(x) \wedge AG(e, ram)]$

Default rule for scrambling, since murgii is +SCRAM

$\lambda e[kill(e) \wedge PAT(e,x) \wedge chicken(x) \wedge AG(e, ram) \wedge DEF(x) \wedge AG(e, ram)]$

Default rule for proto-agents

$\lambda e[kill(e) \wedge PAT(e,x) \wedge chicken(x) \wedge AG(e, ram) \wedge DEF(x)$
$\wedge AG(e, ram) DEF(ram)]$

FIGURE 3 An Example of a Scrambled Patient

5 Conclusions

I have considered the principles and mechanisms that Hindi and related languages use to distinguish between definite and indefinite readings of bare Noun Phrases. While the specific details would probably vary from language to language, I expect that the general conclusions will apply to almost all article-less languages. Even though Hindi uses the *ek* as a marker of indefiniteness in some cases, this cannot properly be considered an article, since its main function seems to be that of a reliable marker of indefiniteness (i.e., to exclude the definite reading), in cases where its absence might admit indefiniteness. I have shown that bare NPs cannot be ambiguous in Hindi in a given context. Another important result is that the definiteness or indefiniteness of an NP depends on the semantic properties of the verbal predicate. The semantic properties of an NP interact with its syntactic position in determining its definiteness. Also, I have shown that CVs mark all PATIENTS as definite irrespective of animacy and sentience.

Acknowledgements

I would like to thank Manfred Krifka, Paul Portner, and the anonymous reviewers for comments.

References

Chesterman, A. 1991. *On Definiteness.* Cambridge Studies in Linguistics. Cambridge UK: Cambridge University Press.

Clark, E. 1978. Locationals: Existential, locative and possessive constructions. In J. Greenberg (Ed.), *Universals of Human Language*, Volume 4. Stanford, CA: Stanford University Press.

Dowty, D. 1991. Thematic Proto-Roles and Argument Selection. *Language* 67(3):547–619.

Fillmore, C. 1971. Some problems for case grammar. In *Georgetown Roundtable on Linguistics*, Georgetown University.

Hacker, P. 1961. On the problem of a method for treating the compound and conjunct verb in Hindi. *Bulletin of the School of Oriental and African Studies* 24:484–516.

Heim, I. 1982. *The Semantics of Definite and Indefinite Noun Phrases.* PhD dissertation, University of Massachusetts, Amherst.

Keenan, E. 1987. *Universal Grammar: 15 Essays.* Bristol, UK: Croom Helm.

Krifka, M. 1991. Thematic relations as links between nominal reference and temporal constitution. In I. Sag and A. Szabolcsi (Eds.), *Lexical Matters.* Chicago: Chicago University Press.

Mahajan, A. 1990. *The A/A-bar Distinction and Movement Theory.* PhD dissertation, Massachusetts Institute of Technology.

Mohanan, T. 1990. *Arguments in Hindi.* PhD dissertation, Stanford University.

Pinker, S. 1989. *Learnability and Cognition: The Acquisistion of Argument Structure.* Cambridge, MA: MIT Press.

Singh, M. 1990. The aspectual content of compound verbs. In *Proceedings of the Seventh Eastern States Conference on Linguistics*, 260–271.

Singh, M. 1991. The perfective paradox: How to eat your cake and have it too. In *Proceedings of the 17th Annual Meeting of the Berkeley Linguistic Society.*

Singh, M. 1992. An event based analysis of causatives. In *Papers from 28th Regional Meeting of the Chicago Linguistic Society*, 515–529.

Vendler, Z. 1967. *Linguistics in Philosophy.* Ithaca, NY: Cornell University Press.

10

Binding Facts in Hindi and the Scrambling Phenomenon

VENEETA SRIVASTAV DAYAL

1 Introduction

Gambhir (1981), in the first systematic analysis of word order in Hindi, discusses paradigms like the following:

(1)	a.	raam-ne	mohan-ko	kitaab	dii	[*S IO DO V*]
		Ram-ERG	Mohan-DAT	book	gave	
		'Ram gave Mohan a book.'				
	b.	kitaab raam-ne mohan-ko dii				[*DO S IO V*]
	c.	mohan-ko kitaab raam-ne dii				[*IO DO S V*]
	d.	kitaab mohan-ko raam-ne dii				[*DO IO S V*]
	e.	mohan-ko raam-ne kitaab dii				[*IO S DO V*]
	f.	raam-ne kitaab mohan-ko dii				[*S DO IO V*]

She notes that though (1a)–(1f) express the same proposition, (1a) can be considered basic since it is neutral with respect to preceding discourse. (1b)–(1f), on the other hand, signal shifts in emphasis that require context for full interpretation.

That the correspondence between an English sentence and its Hindi counterparts is one-to-many can be can be described by the statement, standard in typological literature, that English is a "fixed word order" language while Hindi is a "free word order" language. From the point of view of generative linguistics, however, this is not enough. Since language is held to be a system of rules, an investigation into what accounts for the freedom of word order is required in order to arrive at a more explanatory account of the phenomenon. The current assumption within the Government and Binding framework is that all languages

Theoretical Perspectives on Word Order in South Asian Languages
Miriam Butt, Tracy Holloway King, Gillian Ramchand (Eds.)

have a fixed word order at base.[1] "Free word order languages" differ from "fixed word order" languages in allowing an instance of move alpha, namely scrambling. In the case of the Hindi examples above, one can say that at D-structure all of them have the order of arguments S IO DO V, with the variations in surface order seen in (1b)–(1f) resulting from leftward movement of arguments.

Such an analysis begs the question of whether scrambling is an instance of A-movement or A′-movement, the two types of movement noted in the literature. Passive or raising constructions are instances of A-movement, involving movement of an NP from a theta marked position into a non-theta argument position in order to receive Case. Wh-movement or quantifier raising are instances of A′-movement, involving movement of an NP from a Case and theta marked position into a non-argument position in order for interpretation to take place. The claim that scrambling involves movement, therefore, entails that it should display the properties of A-movement or the properties of A′-movement. If it does not, it raises doubts about the adequacy of the standard binary classification of movement types. These issues have generated considerable theoretical interest in recent years.

In a study of scrambling in Japanese, Saito (1985) argues that scrambling is an instance of A′-movement by showing that the empirical behavior of scrambling is similar to that of wh-movement and quantifier raising. In particular, he analyzes scrambling as adjunction of NP's at the sentential level. Under this view a sentence like (1b), for example, would have an S-structure representation like the following with the DO adjoined to IP:

(2)	a.	[$_{IP}$ kitaab$_i$	[$_{IP}$ raam-ne	mohan-ko	t_i	dii]]
		book	Ram-ERG	Mohan-DAT		gave
				[DO$_i$ [S IO t_i V]]		

Gurtu (1985) also analyses Hindi scrambling as an adjunction operation, thereby conflating it with A′-movement. Webelhuth (1989, 1992), however, draws attention to the fact that scrambling in German has, in addition to the properties associated with A′-movement, some properties of A-movement. He thus concludes that though scrambling involves adjunction as in (2a), the adjoined position is both an A and an A′ position. Déprez (1989) and Mahajan (1990) add further support to Webelhuth's stand that scrambling has properties associated with A-movement. Abstracting away from differences between their particular proposals, they both claim that two types of scrambling exist. One has

[1] See Hale (1983), however, for an alternative view in which languages may differ with respect to configurationality and word order at D-structure.

properties of A′-movement and involves adjunction to maximal projections. The other has properties of A-movement and involves movement into argument positions that are empty at D-structure. This latter option is made possible by the conception of phrase structure proposed by Pollock (1989) and Chomsky (1989). Under this view, the verbal complex is actually made up of several functional projections such as Agreement Phrase, Negation Phrase, Tense Phrase etc. which dominate VP. The specifier positions of these functional projections count as argument positions which may be generated empty. In languages that allow scrambling, NP's are generated VP internally and move into these empty Spec positions. Thus, (1b) is analysed along the lines of (2b), where XP and YP stand for functional projections:

(2) b. [$_{YP}$ kitaab$_i$ [$_{XP}$ raam-ne$_j$ [$_{VP}$ t_j mohan-ko t_i
book Ram-ERG Mohan-DAT
dii]]]
gave
[DO$_i$ [S$_j$ [t$_j$ IO t$_i$ V]]]

From this brief summary of the literature on scrambling, it is obvious that there is a fairly complex interaction between empirical and theoretical considerations. The primary thrust of this paper is to reexamine the empirical motivation behind the view that scrambling is an instance of A-movement. In particular, it focuses on the claim made by Mahajan (1990) that scrambled NP's in Hindi can serve as antecedents for reflexives. Since Binding Theory (BT) refers to antecedents in argument positions only, he uses this fact to argue that the landing site of scrambling must be an argument position. While I agree with Mahajan that BT is an effective diagnostic for distinguishing types of movement, I take issue with his application of the diagnostic. Using a general strategy of articulating a version of BT that covers the core binding facts in Hindi before investigating the impact of scrambling on binding possibilities, I come to a different conclusion from him about the type of movement involved in scrambling.

I begin by discussing scrambling to presubject position and establish that the resulting binding possibilities are incompatible with a view of such scrambling as movement to an A-position. I then turn to intermediate scrambling and show that there is no evidence from BT to argue for movement to A-position there either. The conclusion, clearly, is that as far as BT goes, scrambling is an instance of A′-movement only, not A-movement. I then consider those properties that distinguish scrambling from other instances of A′-movement. I follow the lead of several other researchers in drawing the conclusion that the present typology of movement types is too coarse-grained to account for the observed distinctions.

2 Presubject Scrambling as A′-movement

In this section, I will be concerned with scrambling to a presubject position, i.e., I will be considering examples like (1b)–(1e). To keep the discussion simple, I will use an ordinary transitive verb but the conclusions carry over, without any modification, to the ditransitive structures in (1). (3b) is an instance of presubject scrambling:

(3) a. raam-ne mohan-ko maaraa
Ram-ERG Mohan-ACC beat
'Ram beat Mohan.' [*S O V*]

b. mohan-ko$_i$ raam-ne t_i maaraa
[*O S V*]

In order to see what BT can tell us about the nature of scrambling in (3b) let us establish first how it applies to basic transitive structures like (3a). Towards this end, consider the following paradigm:

(4) a. raam-ne$_i$ apne-aap-ko$_{i/*j}$/us-ko$_{*i/j}$ maaraa
Ram-ERG self-ACC/him-ACC beat
'Ram beat self/him.' [*S O V*]

b. raam-ne$_i$ [apne$_{i/*j}$/uske$_{*i/j}$ bhaii-ko] maaraa
Ram-ERG self's/his brother-ACC beat
'Ram beat self's/his brother.' [*S O V*]

c. raam-ne$_i$ raam-ko$_{*i}$ maaraa
Ram-ERG Ram-ACC beat
'Ram beat Ram.' [*S O V*]

As we can see, there is nothing particularly exotic about the binding possibilities of Hindi. The one thing to note is that when a pronoun is in Spec of NP, as in (4b), it cannot be coreferential with the subject, while a reflexive in the same position must be. This contrasts with English, where both the pronoun and the reciprocal is possible in that position. Hindi is similar in this respect to Latin, Russian, and Danish etc.. We may safely adopt for the basic cases considered in (4), then, a fairly standard version of BT:[2]

[2]In this paper I will not be concerned with how BT applies to elements inside embedded clauses. See Gurtu (1985), Harbert and Srivastav (1988) and Mohanan (1990) for discussion.

(5) a. Principle A: An anaphor must be bound in its governing category.
b. Principle B: A pronoun must be free in its governing category.
c. Principle C: An R-expression must be free (everywhere).

Governing Category is defined as the minimal domain containing the expression, its governor and an accessible subject/SUBJECT. *Bound* and *Free* refer to coindexing of an element with a c-commanding argument.

We are now in a position to evaluate the impact of scrambling on binding possibilities. Consider what happens when the the DO of (4a)–(4b) is scrambled to a presubject position:

(6) a. apne-aap-ko$_{i/*j}$/us-ko$_{*i/j}$ raam-ne$_i$ maaraa
self-ACC/him-ACC Ram-ERG beat
'Ram beat self/him.' [*O S V*]
b. [apne$_{i/*j}$/uske$_{*i/j}$ bhaii-ko] raam-ne$_i$ maaraa
self's/his brother-ACC Ram-ERG beat
'Ram beat self's/his brother.' [*O S V*]

We see that scrambling makes absolutely no difference to the binding possibilities, BT applies as if the DO were in its base position. This is parallel to the case of wh-movement seen below:

(7) [Which picture of himself]$_i$ did John$_i$ see t_i ?

The grammaticality of (7) suggests that Principle A of BT applies as if the moved wh-phrase were in its base position and, under standard assumptions, this is done by reconstruction.[3] Transferring this to the case of scrambling in (6a)-(6b), the implication is that the scrambled DO is in an A′-position and hence subject to reconstruction.

This finding, of course, is not incompatible with Mahajan's account, which allows for the presubject position to be an A′ as well as an A position, though not simultaneously. Let us see whether there are binding facts that would support the view that the scrambled object is in A-position. If the scrambled position can be an A-position, the prediction is that it will be able to bind a reflexive. Example (8a) shows that this is not possible:

[3]In the case of raising structures, on the other hand, BT is sensitive to the configuration at S-structure, as shown by (i):

(i) [John$_i$ appeared to himself [t_i to be winning the race]]

If reconstruction were to happen, Principles A and C would be violated. It follows that there is no reconstruction in cases of A-movement.

(8) a. *mohan-ko$_i$ apne-aap-ne$_i$ maaraa
Mohan-ACC self-ERG beat
'Self beat Mohan.' [*O S V*]

Here we have a reflexive in subject position and an antecedent in the presubject scrambled position. The ungramaticality of the sentence provides clear evidence that the presubject position is not an argument position, and hence the movement involved in scrambling is not A-movement. The ungrammaticality of (8a) is expected if scrambling is A′-movement. Once the DO is reconstructed, Principles A and C are both violated.

The conclusion we have drawn from (8a) directly contradicts Mahajan's claim that reflexive binding is possible in such a construction. Mahajan's claim is based on examples like (8b), which differs from (8a) in that the reflexive is in Spec of DO:[4]

(8) b. *mohan-ko$_i$ [apne$_i$ baccoN-ne] maaraa
Mohan-ACC self's children-ERG beat
'Self's children beat Mohan.' [*O S V*]

It is worth emphasizing that Mahajan himself considers such examples marginal. In my own judgement, and most of the speakers I have consulted, it is unacceptable. Now, the point to note is that there is no explanation for the ungrammaticality, or even the alleged marginality, of (8b) under the view that scrambling can be to an A position. Since the reflexive would have a c-commanding antecedent, Principle A should be satisfied. If, however, scrambling is only A′-movement, as I am suggesting, the DO would be reconstructed and the resulting violation of Principle A would account for its ungrammaticality.[5]

On the basis of (8a) and (8b), then, we can conclude that the evidence from reflexive binding shows presubject scrambling to be an instance of A′-movement only. I will now discuss cases of pronominal binding and show that the facts are compatible with the view that presubject scrambling is unambiguously A′-movement. Let us consider the pronominal counterparts of (8):

(9) a. *mohan-ko$_i$ us-ne$_i$ maaraa
Mohan-ACC he-ERG beat
'He beat Mohan.' [*O S V*]

---

[4] Mahajan's example (40) on page 33 also has an adverbial in it. The simplification here does not affect the point of the discussion.

[5] At the end of Section 3, I discuss a dialect in which anaphors may not be subject to Principle A. That may bear on the difference between Mahahan's judgement of (8b) and mine.

b. mohan-ko$_i$ [uske$_i$ baccoN-ne] maaraa
Mohan-ACC his children-ERG beat
'His children beat Mohan.' [*O S V*]

These facts follow straightforwardly on the view that presubject scrambling is an instance of A′-movement. Once reconstruction takes place, the relevant structures will be as follows:

(10) a. [$_{IP}$ us-ne$_i$ [$_{VP}$ mohan-ko$_i$ maaraa]]
he-ERG mohan-ACC beat

b. [$_{IP}$ [$_{NP}$ uske$_i$ baccoN-ne] [$_{VP}$ mohan-ko$_i$ maaraa]]
his children-ERG Mohan-ACC beat

In (10a), the DO is bound by the subject in violation of Principle C, hence the ungrammaticality. In (10b), the pronoun, which is in Spec of NP, and the DO do not c-command each other. There is no violation of BT, hence the grammaticality.[6]

To sum up this section, we looked at the core cases of binding in transitive structures like (4), and decided upon the version of BT articulated in (5). We then considered cases where the DO is scrambled to presubject position and saw that reflexive binding facts shows this to be unambiguously an instance of A′-movement, a conclusion that is also compatible with the pronominal binding facts.

3 Binding in Ditransitive Structures

Let us turn now to the case of intermediate scrambling, i.e, to structures like (1f). Recall that the canonical order of arguments in Hindi is S IO DO V. In (1f) the DO moves to a position between the subject and IO and the question we are interested in investigating is whether this is an A or an A′ position. In order to see what BT tells us about this position, I will once again articulate a version of BT that works for the core cases before applying it to scrambled structures.

The binding relationship between subject and object in Hindi, we saw in Section 2, was pretty straightforward in the case of simple transitive sentences. Thus the version of BT that we used as a diagnostic in analysing the scrambled sentences was the standard one. When we turn to ditransitive structures, however, the binding relationship is

[6] I am grateful to an anonymous reviewer for pointing out that (9) does not provide evidence against Mahajan's claim that scrambling can be A or A′-movement. The ungrammaticality of (9a), for example, is predicted. If the DO is in argument position, Principle B is violated; if it is in A′ position, Principle C is violated after reconstruction. The grammaticality of (9b) is also predicted. The DO cannot be in argument position since there will be a violation of Principle B. However, if it is in A′ position, reconstruction will take place and there will be no violation of BT, as shown in (10b).

fairly complex even in the basic cases. It is therefore even more important that we make our assumptions about BT explicit before using it as a diagnostic.

It is a well-documented fact that the Hindi reflexive is subject oriented. Analogous to this is the fact that the Hindi pronoun is anti-subject oriented (Mohanan 1990). In (11), for example, the reflexive in the DO cannot corefer with the IO, but must corefer with the subject. Similarly, the pronoun in DO must be disjoint in reference with the subject but may corefer with the IO:

(11) a. raam-ne$_i$ mohan-ko$_j$ [apnii$_{i/*j}$/uskii$_{*i/j/k}$
Ram-ERG Mohan-DAT self's/his
kitaab] dii
book gave
'Ram gave Mohan self's/his book.' [*S IO DO V*]

b. raam-ne$_i$ mohan-ko$_j$ apne$_{i/*j}$/uske$_{*i/j/k}$
Ram-ERG Mohan-DAT self/his
baare-meN bataayaa
about told
'Ram told Mohan about self/him.'

It is immediately obvious from the data here that the version of BT we had adopted earlier does not work, or rather seems to work selectively. Principles A and B do seem to be in effect but only in relation to the subject; they do not seem to apply to IO. The problem is to find a way to capture this generalization in structural terms. It is obvious that the subject is hierarchically superior to the other arguments, but not so clear what the structural relationship between IO and DO is. I will consider two current ideas about binding in ditransitive structures that can be used to explain the (anti) subject orientation in Hindi.

An analysis of ditransitive structures in English that has proved quite influential was given by Larson (1988), and can be illustrated by (12):

(12)

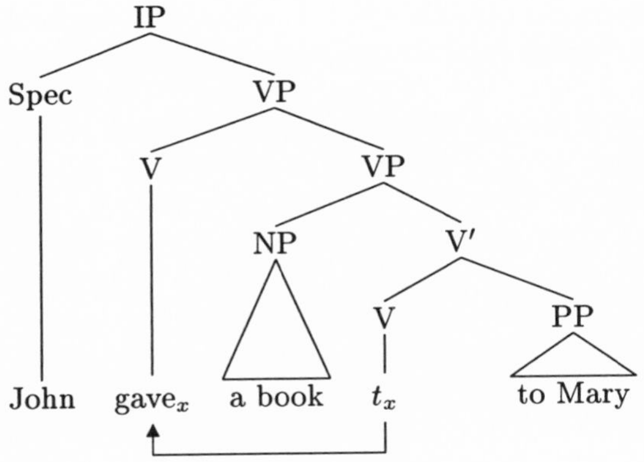

The basic idea is that the VP consists of an empty V taking a VP complement whose Spec is the DO, whose head is the verb and whose complement is the IO. The surface order is a result of the verb raising to the empty V position. Note that in this structure, the DO asymmetrically c-commands the IO so that it is predicted that DO can bind IO, but IO cannot bind DO. In fact, it is the asymmetric binding possibilities that is the primary motivation for Larson's analysis of such verbs in English.

Translating Larson's proposal to Hindi, we get the following representation for (11a):

(13) *S IO DO V*

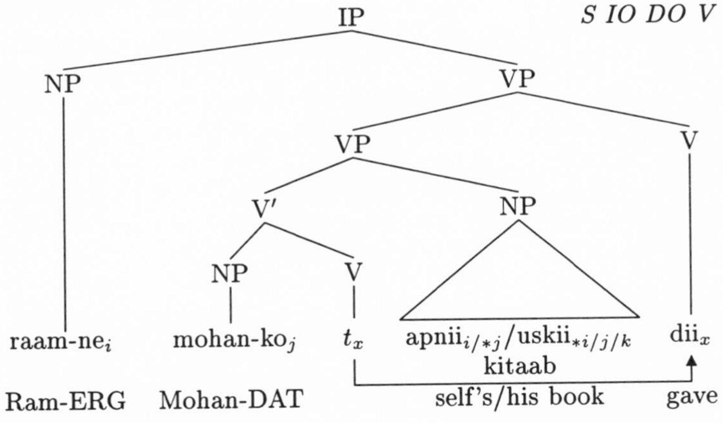

This analysis, we can see, accounts correctly for the binding possibilities shown here. Since the IO does not c-command the DO, Principles A and B ensure that the reflexive or the pronoun inside DO is bound or free with respect to the subject only. Larson's account, however, cannot be accepted as it stands because it makes an incorrect prediction about binding of elements in IO by DO. Since the DO c-commands IO, it should be possible for it to bind reflexives inside IO. This fact does not hold in Hindi, as shown by the following:

(14) raam-ne$_i$ [apnii$_{i/*j}$ maaN-ko] bacca$_j$ thamaayaa
Ram-ERG self's mother-DAT child handed
'Ram handed self's mother the child.' [*S IO DO V*]

One way of reconciling the facts of Hindi while preserving Larson's insight is to incorporate linear order in addition to hierarchical structure in the definition of binding, as was proposed by Barss and Lasnik (1986). BT would then refer to antecedents that c-command and precede, and there would be a simple explanation for the range of facts considered here. In (13), for example, the IO neither c-commands nor precedes DO and therefore does not count as an antecedent for the reflexive/pronoun in it. In (14) the DO c-commands but does not precede the IO, and therefore cannot bind the reflexive inside IO. In Hindi ditransitive structures, then, the only position which precedes and c-commands the NP's inside the VP is the subject, giving rise to the (anti) subject orientation effect.

The core facts of binding in Hindi ditransitives, then, can be accounted for with a minimal modification to the Larsonian analysis of such structures. Let us now turn to another proposal in the literature that can account for the facts we are considering. It has been suggested that subject orientation of anaphors is due to LF raising of the anaphor to INFL (Lebeaux 1983, Chomsky 1986, Pica 1987, among others). If Principle A applies after such raising, the subject is the only c-commanding argument that can bind anaphors inside VP. Recently, this account has been extended to cover anti-subject orientation of Scandinavian pronouns by Hestvik (1992). He argues that pronouns in Scandinavian also raise to INFL at LF. When Principle B applies, the subject is the only c-commanding argument, and therefore it enforces disjointness only with the subject. According to this approach, the LF structure of (11a) would be as in (15), where BT applies to elements in INFL enforcing binding or disjointness with the subject:

(15) [$_{IP}$ raam-ne$_i$ [$_{INFL}$ apnii$_{i/*j}$/uskii$_{*i/j}$ [$_{VP}$ mohan-ko
Ram-ERG self's/his Mohan-DAT
[*t* kitaab] dii]]]
book gave

Note that in this approach, the relationship between the DO and IO at D-structure is not relevant for purposes of binding and the VP could have a flat structure or a structure in which the DO or the IO asymmetrically c-commands the other or a structure in which they are generated in either order, as suggested for Bangla by Bayer (1990).[7]

In this section I have outlined two ways in which binding possibilities in Hindi ditransitive structures can be accounted for. One uses the structure of ditransitives proposed by Larson in conjuction with a version of BT that refers to antecedents that precede and c-command. The other posits raising of anaphors and pronouns to INFL at LF where the only c-commanding NP is the subject. The choice between the two approaches is not critical for purposes of this paper. The important thing, rather, is to make explicit the core binding facts since they are not standard, and show how BT can deal with them. I believe that the discussion here, though by no means exhaustive, provides a basis for testing the type of movement involved in scrambling out of such structures.

Before concluding this section, I would like to note a difference in dialects that is of relevance in the discussion of scrambling to follow. The account I have given is based on the dialect of those speakers who do not find coreference between a reflexive in DO and IO acceptable. There are some speakers, however, for whom the anaphor is not strictly subject oriented (Gurtu 1985, Mahajan 1990). For them the binding possibilities are as follows:

(16) a. raam-ne$_i$ mohan-ko$_j$ [apnii$_{i/j/*k}$/uskii$_{*i/j/k}$
Ram-ERG Mohan-DAT self's/his
kitaab] dii
book gave
'Ram gave Mohan self's/his book.' [*S IO DO V*]

Focusing exclusively on the possibility of the IO binding the reflexive in the dialect under discussion, Gurtu (1985), Mahajan (1990) and Déprez (1989) take the IO in Hindi to asymmetrically c-command the DO, yielding representations like the following for (16a):

[7]LF movement is generally assumed to be unbounded, thereby accounting for the fact that subject oriented anaphors in Italian, Chinese etc. can be bound long distance. The Hindi anaphor, however, must be bound in the domain of the finite clause (Gurtu 1985, Mohanan 1990) but this does not invalidate the view that there is INFL raising of the anaphor in Hindi. Hindi does not allow unbounded wh-movement out of tensed clauses at LF. We might assume that long distance movement of the Hindi anaphor is blocked in the same way that wh-movement is blocked (Srivastav 1991).

(16) b. *S IO DO V*

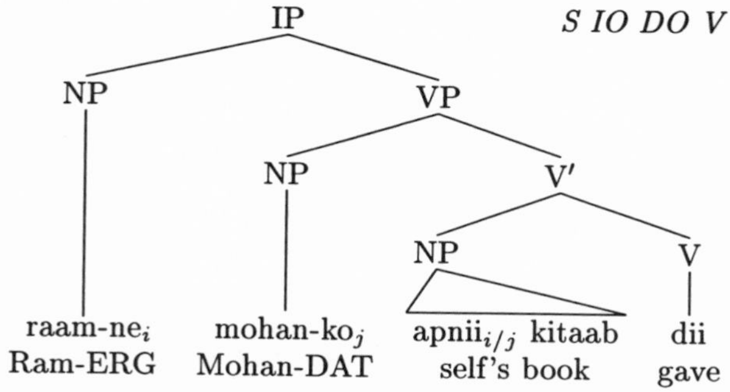

If the IO counts as an antecedent for the reflexive in DO, however, it is predicted that Principle B will enforce disjointness between IO and a pronoun in DO. This, as we know, is not the case. A pronoun is perfect for that reading. Note also that even in this dialect reflexives and pronouns are in complementary distribution with respect to coreference with the subject. Thus it is not clear what assumptions about Principle B would be needed to make this analysis work. It seems to me that failure to address this issue is a serious omission in any account that hopes to use reflexive binding as a diagnostic for movement involving these positions.

I have already provided an account of binding possibilities for the majority dialect and will now attempt to reconcile it with the binding possibilities in the dialect where reflexives are not subject oriented. There are a few things worth noting about this dialect. As mentioned above, even though the reflexive can corefer with the IO, a pronoun is strongly preferred over the reflexive for this reading. That is, this dialect does not disagree with the majority dialect in the anti-subject orientation of pronouns. A second significant fact is that coreference of the reflexive with the subject is far more robust than coreference with IO.[8] It seems to me that there are two separate phenomena at work which are amenable to separate explanations. I suggest that in all dialects of Hindi BT is as outlined above, which accounts for the subject orientation of reflexives and anti-subject orientation of pronouns. In addition, there is a dialect in which reflexives that are not bound in the sense of BT, may still be acceptable as long as there is a possible antecedent preceding it.[9] This would explain not only the possibility of the reflexive coreferring with the IO for some speakers, but also their

[8] I thank Gurpreet Bains for confirming this fact, as well as for other judgements that lead me to make my claims about binding possibilities in this dialect sharper.

[9] I hesitate from calling this a logophoric reading since I do not think a referent in the discourse licenses reflexives.

bias towards subject orientation and their preference for a pronoun for coreference with IO. I therefore assume that there is no dialect difference with respect to BT in Hindi, but that there is one with respect to the acceptability of reflexives which are not bound. And from here on I will use the symbol '?' to reflect the intuition that even for speakers who accept it, coreference of the reflexive in DO with IO is neither as robust as coreference with the subject nor as robust as coreference between a pronoun in that position and IO.

Let me go back at this point to an unsolved mystery with respect to judgements discussed in connection with presubject scrambling. In the dialect of most speakers (8b), repeated below, is ungrammatical, while it is marginal in the dialect Mahajan reports on.

(8) b. *?mohan-ko$_i$ [apne$_i$ baccoN-ne] maaraa
Mohan-ACC self's children-ERG beat
'Self's children beat Mohan.' [*O S V*]

Recall that on his theory (8b) should be fully grammatical since the presubject position can be an A-position. Mahajan (1990) notes in a footnote (#17, p. 33) that such structures are odd because a pronoun is possible, and therefore preferred in place of a reflexive, though he admits that there is no clear answer to why that should be the case.

In the present approach, on the other hand, the scrambled DO is not in argument position, and there is consequently a violation of Principle A for all speakers. For those who accept non-bound reflexives, however, it is possible that the scrambled DO marginally licenses the reflexive in (8b). Note that (8a), repeated below, is still predicted to be ungrammatical because of a violation of Principle A and C after reconstruction:

(8) a. *mohan-ko$_i$ apne aap-ne$_i$ maaraa
Mohan-ACC self-ERG beat
'Self beat Mohan.' [*O S V*]

In this section I have listed the core binding facts in Hindi ditransitive structures, and shown how a principled account can be given for them. I have also tried to reconcile the judgements provided in Mahajan with those of the majority dialect. Let us turn now to intermediate scrambling and see what BT tells us about the type of movement involved.

4 Intermediate Scrambling as A′-movement

Mahajan argues that scrambling to intermediate positions is exclusively to A-positions. There are two pieces of evidence he gives in support of this. One, he claims that such scrambling creates new antecedents for reflexives. In (17a), for example, the NP's are in their canonical positions and the reflexive inside IO cannot be bound by the DO. In (17b), the DO is fronted and, according to Mahajan, the reflexive can now be bound by it:

(17)	a.	raam-ne$_i$	[apne$_{i/*j}$	baccoN-ko]	sher$_j$	dikhaayaa
		Raam-ERG	self's	children-DAT	lion	showed
						[*S IO DO V*]
	b.	raam-ne$_i$	sher$_j$	[apne$_{i/*?j}$	baccoN-ko]	dikhaayaa
		Ram-ERG	lion	self's	children	showed

'Ram showed self's children the lion.' [*S DO IO V*]
(Mahajan = apne$_{i/j}$)

Mahajan's judgements, however, are not accepted by most speakers, and I indicate in the examples above my interpretation of the judgements, noting Mahajan's judgements in parentheses where there is a difference. In the majority dialect, the reflexive in (17b) can only be bound by the subject. In the dialect where coreference with DO is possible, it is marginal in the sense discussed in the previous section. That is, subject coreference is salient, and furthermore, the preferred way to get coreference with the scrambled DO is via a pronoun. The right generalization clearly is along the lines suggested for (7b). As far as BT goes, the scrambled DO does not count as an antecedent, accounting for the possibility of pronominal coreference for all speakers and the impossibility of reflexive binding for most. The speakers who accept reflexives coindexed with the scrambled DO are those for whom non-bound reflexives can be licensed by any preceding NP. The scrambled DO provides such a licensor. It is clear from an examination of the full range of binding possibilities, then, that (17b) shows intermediate scrambling to be to A′-position, not to A-position.

The second piece of data that Mahajan provides in support of the view that intermediate scrambling is exclusively A-movement, as opposed to presubject scrambling, which may be either A or A′-movement, is based on examples like (18b), derived from (18a). Again, I indicate where my findings deviate from Mahajan's:

(18)	a.	raam-ne$_i$	mohan-ko$_j$	[apnii$_{i/*?j}$	kitaab]	dii
		Ram-ERG	Mohan-DAT	self's	book	gave

'Ram gave self's book to Mohan.' [*S IO DO V*]
(Mahajan = apnii$_{i/j}$)

	b.	[apnii$_{i/*j}$	kitaab]	raam-ne$_i$	mohan-ko$_j$	dii
		self's	book	Ram-ERG	Mohan-DAT	gave

'Ram gave self's book to Mohan.' [*DO S IO V*]

According to Mahajan, the reflexive in DO can refer to either the subject or the IO when it is in its base position. When it is fronted to the presubject position, via the intermediate position, it can only refer to the subject. Mahajan gives the following derivation for (18b):

(19) a. [apnii$_{i/*j}$ kitaab]$_k$ raam-ne$_i$ t'_k mohan-ko$_j$
self's book Ram-ERG Mohan-DAT
t_k dii
gave

The presubject position can be an A′-position and allows reconstruction to t'_k, which makes binding by the subject possible. The missing reading, the one where the reflexive is bound by IO, is evidence that reconstruction stops at the intermediate position t'_k. The IO does not c-command this position and binding of the reflexive is ruled out. Since reconstruction to the base position where the IO would c-command it is not possible, he concludes that movement from the base position t_k to the intermediate position t'_k is A-movement.

In the approach I am advocating, it is not crucial whether scrambling is directly from base position to presubject position, or proceeds via intermediate scrambling. If scrambling is first to intermediate position and then to presubject position, both are instances of A′-movement and reconstruction takes place to the base position:

(19) b. [apnii$_{i/*j}$ kitaab]$_k$ raam-ne$_i$ (t'_k) mohan-ko$_j$
self's book Ram-ERG Mohan-DAT
t_k dii
gave

The presubject position being an A′-position, reconstruction is expected, accounting for the binding of the reflexive by the subject, as in Mahajan's account. The question that remains is why the marginal reading in which the reflexive corefers with the IO is lost. Given my basic claim that coreference with IO in (18a) is not due to BT, but is made available for some speakers due to the presence of a preceding NP, the answer to this is obvious. This reading is unavailable because the licensing of a non-bound anaphor is done at S-structure, where the IO does not precede the scrambled DO and cannot license the reflexive.

We see, then, that upon closer examination, the arguments Mahajan gives from reflexive binding do not warrant treating intermediate scrambling as an instance of A-movement. There is, however, an argument from reciprocal binding that needs to be discussed before I can claim that intermediate scrambling is an instance of A′-movement.

Jones (1993, forthcoming) reports that Hindi speakers that he has consulted agree with my judgements, and not Mahajan's with respect to reflexive binding. However, his informants do marginally allow for reciprocal binding in certain cases, and my own intuitions accord with his findings. Two of the relevant cases are given in (20). (20a) is a basic ditransitive structure and (20b) is an ordinary transitive with DO scrambled to presubject position:

(20) a. laRkiyoN-ne laRkoN-ko$_j$ [ek duusre-kii$_{?j}$ kitaabeN] diiN
girls-ERG boys-DAT each other's books gave
'The girls gave the boys each other's books.' [*S IO DO V*]

b. ?jaun aur meri-ko$_i$ ek duusre-ne$_i$ dekhaa
John and Mary-ACC each other-ERG saw
'John and Mary saw each other.' [*O S V*]

Note that in (20a) even though the reciprocal is better than a reflexive when coreference with IO is intended, it is not perfect. The pronoun is still the preferred option. It seems to me, therefore, that this is not in fact a Principle A effect, and may be amenable to a functional explanation. Turning to (20b), Jones notes that the acceptability of this structure is somewhat improved if the context of discourse makes John and Mary salient. This suggests again that the phenomenon in question is not, strictly speaking grammatical, and one is lead to speculate that the Hindi reciprocal may not be a true anaphor. A piece of supporting evidence for this comes from the following:

(21) laRke aur laRkiyoN-ne$_i$ dekhaa ki [unkii$_i$/apnii$_{*i}$/ek duusre kii$_{?i}$ tasviireN] bik rahii thiiN
boys and girls-ERG saw that their/self's/each other's pictures were selling
'The boys and girls saw that their pictures were on sale.'

It is clear from reflexive and pronominal binding that the finite complement in (21) constitutes a binding domain. That the reciprocal is marginally possible in this position shows that the explanation must lie outside of BT. I will suggest here that since the reciprocal gives more specific information than the pronoun it is more informative, in a Gricean sense. And a cooperative listener may accept it for that reason in positions where BT allows a pronoun not an anaphor. What seems quite clear to me even from this brief look at the Hindi reciprocal is that it cannot be used as a sound diagnostic for A-movement in scrambling structures, since its distribution does not seem to be constrained by Principle A.[10]

To sum up so far, I have reviewed the evidence from anaphor binding that has been presented in support of the view that intermediate scrambling must be to A-positions, and shown that BT has not been applied correctly. Once the subtle but real differences in judgements are taken into account, the anaphor binding facts turn out to be better accounted for in terms of intermediate scrambling as A′-movement. I have also emphasized that the possibility of pronominal coreference in these structures provides an important control since there is no dialect difference at work with regard to coreference possibilities for pronouns. The absence of Principle B effects with intermediate scrambling are therefore additional support that scrambled objects do not count as antecedents. Before concluding this section, however, I would like to bring in one final piece of data that appears, at first glance, to be problematic for the view that intermediate scrambling is an instance of A′-movement.

Consider the contrast in the following examples with respect to the possibility of coreference between a pronoun in DO and IO:

(22)	a.	raam-ne	mohan-ko$_j$	[uskii$_j$	kitaab]	lautaaii
		Ram-ERG	Mohan-DAT	his	book	returned
		'Ram returned Mohan his book.' [*S IO DO V*]				
	b.	raam-ne	[uskii$_{*j}$	kitaab]	mohan-ko$_j$	lautaaii
		Ram-ERG	his	book	Mohan-DAT	returned
		'Ram returned his book to Mohan.' [*S DO IO V*]				

As discussed in Section 3, a pronoun in DO can corefer with IO in the basic ditransitive structure of (22a) but when the DO is scrambled to the left of IO, as in (22b), this reading is lost. But if scrambling is A′-movement, it should allow reconstruction to the base position, thereby making the intended coreference available. That it does not, therefore, appears problematic for this analysis. Note, however, that (22b) is also problematic for the view that the scrambled DO is in A-position. Since the pronoun is in Spec of NP, it does not c-command IO, and there should be no Principle C violation and coreference should be possible.

In order to explain the data, let us step back a minute and consider a consequence of the modified Larsonian approach that we have adopted. Recall that in the basic (unscrambled) ditransitive structure, the IO

[10]Reciprocal binding by scrambled arguments have been noted for German (Webelhuth 1989, Frank et al (1992) and Bangla (Sengupta 1990), but I have not seen reflexive binding mentioned except for Hindi by Mahajan. I don't know, at this point, whether the approach I am taking to Hindi reciprocals would appply to these languages.

precedes but does not c-command the DO, and the DO c-commands but does not precede the IO. Thus neither counts as an antecedent for the other. This suggests that the distribution of pronouns and R-expressions will be unrestricted for these NP's. (23a) and (23b) show that this is not the case:

(23)	a.	raam-ne	mohan-ko$_j$	[uskii$_j$	kitaab]	dii
		Ram-ERG	Mohan-DAT	his	book	gave

'Ram gave Mohan his book.' [*S IO DO V*]

	b.	raam-ne	us-ko$_j$	[Mohan-kii$_{*j}$	kitaab]	dii
		Ram-ERG	he-DAT	Mohan's	book	gave

'Ram gave him Mohan's book.' [*S IO DO V*]

The fact that a pronoun in DO can corefer with an R-expression in IO, as in (23a) is expected, as just mentioned. What is unexpected is the fact that a pronoun in IO cannot corefer to an R-expression in DO, as shown in (23b). Since neither is an antecedent of the other, Principles B and C should not be violated. That there is no such violation of BT is further shown by (23c), where two R-expressions in those positions may seem somewhat repetitive, but do not give rise to ungramamticality:

(23)	c.	raam-ne	mohan-ko$_j$	[mohan-kii$_j$	kitaab]	dii
		Ram-ERG	Mohan-DAT	Mohan's	book	gave

'Ram gave him Mohan's book.' [*S IO DO V*]

Given the range of facts considered here, I conclude that the unacceptability of (23b) cannot be due to a BT violation, but due to a constraint against R-expressions following pronouns.[11]

Turning back to the scrambling cases in (22), then, we can give a parallel explanation for the contrast. Since the constraint I am alluding to is based on linearity, it is not implausible to assume that it applies at S-structure. Scrambling of DO in (22) alters the base order, and coreference is now possible only if the position of pronoun and R-expression is switched, as in (24):

(24) raam-ne	[mohan-kii$_j$	kitaab]	us-ko$_j$	lautaa dii
Ram-ERG	Mohan's	book	him-DAT	returned

'Ram returned Mohan's book to him.' [*S DO IO V*]

[11]The claim that backward pronominalization is impossible in Hindi is discussed in Kachru (1980) and Subbarao (1984). To take a stand on the status of backward pronominalization in Hindi is beyond the scope of the present paper. I will settle for making the weaker claim that for arguments inside VP at least, pronominals must follow the R-expressions with which they are coindexed and not the other way around.

Further proof that it is linear order at S-structure that is critical here, comes from sentences in which the DO and IO are both scrambled to presubject position:

(25) a. [uskii$_{*i/*j}$ kitaab] mohan-ko$_j$ raam-ne$_i$ lautaaii
his book Mohan-DAT Ram-ERG returned
[*DO IO S V*]

b. mohan-ko$_j$ [uskii$_{*i/j}$ kitaab] raam-ne$_i$ lautaaii
Mohan-DAT his book Ram-ERG returned
'Ram returned his book to Mohan.' [*IO DO S V*]

The two presubject positions are A′-positions under the present account and require reconstruction. As expected, the pronoun must be disjoint with the subject, regardless of the relative ordering of scrambled elements. But whether it can corefer with the IO is decided on the basis of surface linear order alone. It is thus ruled out in (25a), but acceptable in (25b).

In this section, I have examined binding possibilities with intermediate scrambling, and shown that intermediate scrambling cannot be an instance of A-movement since it predicts that anaphor binding from this position should be perfect, and pronominal coreference ruled out. Both predictions are incorrect. Anaphor binding is, at best, weak and pronominal coreference perfect. Putting together the conclusions for presubject and intermediate scrambling, we can safely say that BT, when applied carefully, shows that scrambling is not an instance of A-movement.

5 Scrambling as Atypical A′-movement

As far as the binding facts go, it is amply clear that scrambling is not an instance of A-movement, but rather an instance of A′-movement. In this section, I will review evidence that shows that scrambling does not have all the properties that are typically associated with A′-movement. I will conclude that a binary classification of movement types is insufficient to accommodate the types of movements under discussion.

In Section 2 it was noted that sentences like (9b), repeated below, are perfectly wellformed in Hindi:

(9) b. mohan-ko$_i$ [uske$_i$ baccoN-ne] t_i maaraa
Mohan-ACC his children-ERG beat
'His children beat Mohan.' [*O S V*]

It was pointed out that this poses no problems as far as BT is concerned. Since the scrambled object is in A′-position, it will be reconstructed. The two NP's not being in a c-command relationship, Principles B and C will not be violated, accounting for its grammaticality.

Note, however, that the possibility of reconstruction implies that the trace left behind by scrambling must be a variable. Coindexation of a variable with a pronoun to its left should result in a weak crossover violation. The following contrast, noted by Gurtu (1985), shows the atypical behavior of scrambling:

(26) a. *uskii$_i$ maaN kis-ko$_i$ pasand kartii hai
his mother whom likes
[*S O V*]

b. kis-ko$_i$ uskii$_i$ maaN t_i pasand kartii hai
whom his mother likes
'Who is such that his mother like him?' [*O S V*]

In (26a) there is a *wh-in-situ*, which is assumed to raise at LF into Spec position, leaving behind a variable trace. Coindexation with a pronoun to its left is consequently bad. In (26b), however, the *wh* has been scrambled, and coindexation of the trace and the pronoun is possible. If there are only two types of movements possible, and one leaves variable traces, the other NP traces, the conclusion must be that the trace in (26b) is an NP trace.

The absence of weak crossover effects with scrambling is a robust phenomenon, and is attested in every language that has scrambling. As such, it constitutes the best evidence for the view that scrambling has properties of A-movement. This conclusion, of course, rests on the premise that weak crossover violations are symptomatic of all and only A′-movements. Examples (27a)–(27b) certainly seem to suggest this:

(27) a. *Who$_i$ did his$_i$ brother beat t_i?
b. Everyone$_i$ appears to his$_i$ mother t_i to be intelligent.

However, as pointed out to me by an anonymous reviewer, topicalization does not give rise to such violations even though its standard analysis is in terms of A′-movement (Baltin 1985):

(27) John$_i$, his$_i$ brother beat t_i.

Saito (1992) argues that if a particular instance of A′-movement is semantically vacuous, it will not create operator-variable chains. Since weak crossover violations are manifested only in operator-variable dependencies, the absence of weak crossover effects in scrambling is to be expected if scrambling is semantically vacuous.[12] Further arguments in support of the view that scrambling is semantically vacuous A′-movement is given in Frank et al. (1992). We see then that weak crossover facts can be incorporated within a view of scrambling as

[12] Saito (1992), however, takes English topicalization to be non-vacuous and tries to show that it does display weak crossover effects.

A′-movement if one departs from a binary classification of movement types.

Another interesting observation that bears on the nature of scrambling is provided by Déprez (1989). She points to the fact that Hindi has long-distance scrambling (LDS) in addition to sentence-internal srambling (SIS) that we have been discussing. One property that distinguishes them is the fact that LDS displays weak crossover effects. Compare (26b) above with (29):

(29)	*kis-ko$_i$	uskii$_i$	maaN	soctii hai	ki	anu	t_i
	whom	his	mother	thinks	that	Anu	

pasand kartii hai
likes
'Who is such that his mother thinks that Anu likes him?'

Déprez then notes a further property that distinguishes the two. SIS allows floating quantifiers in any of the positions to which NP's can be scrambled:

(30) a.	raam-ne	mohan-ko	[saarii	kitaabeN]	lautaa diiN
	Ram-ERG	Mohan-DAT	all	books	returned

'Ram returned all the books to Mohan.' [*S IO DO V*]

b. raam-ne kitaabeN$_i$ mohan-ko [saarii t_i] lautaa diiN [*S DO IO V*]

c. kitaabeN$_i$ raam-ne mohan-ko [saarii t_i] lautaa diiN [*DO S IO V*]

d. kitaabeN$_i$ raam-ne [saarii t'_i] mohan-ko t_i lautaa diiN [*DO S IO V*]

She follows Sportiche (1988) in analysing the quantifier as being generated inside the NP with subsequent movement of the head leaving the quantifier stranded.[13] The data in (30) shows that the quantifier may travel with the head and be stranded at any position to which the NP scrambles.

The point she establishes is that stranding of quantifiers is not a property of A′-movement but of A-movement, as demonstrated by the following English examples:[14]

(31) a. *The children, who$_i$ I will have [all t_i] met before the end of this week, ...

b. The boys$_i$ appear [all t_i to have left].

In (31a), the relevant movement is that of the relative *wh* which leaves

---

[13]See Guilfoyle et al. (1992), however, for a different view of floating quantifiers.

[14]As noted by Sportiche (1988) and Déprez (1989), however, a quantifier cannot be stranded in its base position: *The boys$_i$ were defeated [all t_i]

the quantifier *all* stranded. Since the movement involved is uncontroversially A′-movement, it can be assumed that quantifier stranding is not licensed by A′-movement. In contrast, (31b) shows that quantifier stranding is possible with raising.

Déprez admits, however, that the evidence from Hindi supporting the idea that quantifier stranding is not a property of A′-movement is not very clear. But if LDS is an instance of A′-movement, as shown by (29), she argues that it should not allow quantifier float. Example (32) shows this to be true:[15]

(32) a. [raam samajhtaa hai ki [phal$_i$ anu jaantii hai
Ram believes that fruit Anu knows
[ki [saare t_i] mohan khaa gayaa]]]
that all Mohan ate
'Ram believes that Anu knows that Mohan ate all the fruit.'

b. [phal$_i$ raam samajhtaa hai ki [t'_i anu jaantii hai
[ki [saare t_i] mohan khaa gayaa]]]

*[phal$_i$ raam samajhtaa hai ki [[saare t'_i]$_i$ anu jaantii hai
[ki t_i mohan khaa gayaa]]]

In (32a) *saare phal* 'all fruit' moves to presubject position as an instance of SIS. From there *phal* 'fruit' moves as an instance of LDS leaving *saare* 'all' stranded in the lower clause. In (32b) it moves further up and the sentence is still fine. In (32c) the whole NP moves via LDS first to the presubject position in the intermediate clause. When the head moves further up, leaving the quantifier in the intermediate position, the result is ungrammatical. This shows that positions that are involved in SIS are different from positions that are involved in LDS. According to Déprez, LDS necessarily involves adjunction to IP, while SIS can be movement into Spec of functional projections. The conclusion she draws is that movement to Spec of functional projections has something in common with movements like raising. In this, her proposal is similar to Mahajan's but there is an important respect in which the two proposals differ. Mahajan allows for only two types of landing sites, L-related or non L-related (A and A′, loosely speaking), but Déprez argues for a ternary partition of positions. Typical instances of A′-movement are to [−H(ead)R(elated), −Case] positions and typical instances of A-movement to [+HR, +Case]. Turning to scrambling, she argues that LDS is movement of the first kind. SIS, on the other hand, she suggests can be movement of the second type or of a third type, namely movement to [+HR, −Case] positions, whose

[15](32) is diffferent from the examples in Déprez. I think that (32) makes her point more clearly than her examples (26) on p. 136.

properties are ambiguous. In this her position is not very different from Webelhuth (1989). Note that once a mixed position is allowed, scrambling does not have to be treated as A-movement just because it does not display all the properties of standard instances of A′-movement.

In this section we have looked at two properties that distinguish scrambling from A′-movements like wh-movement. We also noted that there seems to be a growing consensus that a binary classification of movement types may be too coarse-grained to account for the phenomenon of scrambling. The precise characterization of this third type remains, I think, an open question but to discuss the various proposals lies outside the scope of this paper.

6 Conclusion

In conclusion, let us take stock of the empirical data relevant in determining the type of movement involved in scrambling. It turns out on close scrutiny that there are two phenomena differentiating sentence-internal scrambling from standard types of A′-movement, namely the absence of weak crossover effects and the ability to strand quantifiers. If there are only two types of movement, A and A′, scrambling would have to be considered A-movement. As we have seen, however, analysing scrambling as A-movement makes the incorrect prediction that scrambled objects will behave like arguments with respect to BT. A third type of movement, one which behaves like A′-movement for binding but not for weak crossover and quantifier float, is clearly needed to describe the phenomenon of scrambling.

Acknowledgements

I am indebted for helpful comments and discussion to Maria Bittner, Viviane Déprez, Jane Grimshaw, Ken Safir, and Kashi Wali. I am also grateful to two anonymous reviewers whose extensive comments led to a substantively improved version of the original paper. All remaining errors and omissions are my own.

References

Baltin, M. 1985. *Toward a Theory of Movement Rules*. New York: Garland Publishing.

Barss, A., and H. Lasnik. 1986. A Note of Anaphora and Double Objects, *Linguistic Inquiry* 17:347–354.

Bayer, J. 1990. *Directionality of Government and Logical Form: A Study of Focusing Particles and WH-Scope*. Habilitation Thesis, University of Konstanz.

Chomsky, N. 1986. *Knowledge of Language*. New York: Praeger.

Chomsky, N. 1989. Some Notes on the Economy of Derivations. In I. Laka and A.K. Mahajan (Eds.), *MIT Working Papers in Linguistics* Vol. 10.

Déprez, V. 1989. *On the Typology of Syntactic Positions and the Nature of Chains: Move Alpha to the Specifier of Functional Projections*. PhD thesis, MIT.

Frank, R., Y.-S. Lee, and O. Rambow. 1992. Scrambling as Non-Operator Movement and the Special Status of Subjects. Ms., University of Pennsylvania.

Gambhir, V. 1981. *Syntactic Restrictions and Discourse Functions of Word Order in Standard Hindi*. PhD thesis, University of Pennsylvania.

Guilfoyle, E., H. Hung, and L. Travis. 1992. SPEC OF IP and SPEC OF VP: Two Subjects in Subjects in Austronesian Languages, *Natural Language and Linguistic Theory* 10:375–414.

Gurtu, M. 1985. *Anaphoric Relations in Hindi and English*. PhD Thesis, CIEFL, Hyderabad.

Hale, K. 1983. Walpiri and the Grammar of Nonconfigurational Languages, *Natural Language and Linguistic Theory* 1:5–47.

Harbert, W. and V. Srivastav. 1988. A Complement/Adjunct Asymmetry in Hindi and Other Languages, *Cornell Working Papers in Linguistics* 8:79–106.

Hestvik, A. 1992. LF Movement of Pronouns and Antisubject Orientation. *Linguistic Inquiry* 23:557–594.

Jones, D. 1993. A-binding and Scrambling in Hindi: Reflexives vs. Reciprocals. Paper presented at The Workshop on Theoretical Issues in Ergative Languages, Rutgers University.

Jones, D. Forthcoming. *Binding as an Interface Condition: An Investigation of Scrambling*, PhD thesis, MIT.

Kachru, Y. 1980. *Aspects of Hindi Grammar*. New Delhi: Manohar Publications.

Larson, R. 1988. On the Double Object Construction, *Linguistic Inquiry* 19:335–391.

Lebeux, D. 1983. A Distributional Difference between Reciprocals and Reflexives, *Linguistic Inquiry* 14:723–730.

Mahajan, A. 1990. *The A/A-Bar Distinction and Movement Theory*. PhD thesis, MIT.

Mohanan, T. 1990. *Arguments in Hindi*. PhD thesis, Stanford University.

Pica, P. 1987. On the Nature of the Reflexivization Cycle, *North Eastern Linguistic Society* 17.

Pollock, J.-Y. 1989. Verb Movement, UG and the Structure of IP, *Linguistic Inquiry* 20:365–424.

Saito, M. 1985. *Some Asymmetries in Japanese and their Theoretical Consequences*. PhD thesis, MIT.

Saito, M. 1992. Scrambling as Semantically Vacuous A′ Movement. In M. Baltin and A. Kroch (Eds.), *Alternative Conceptions of Phrase Structure*. Chicago: University of Chicago Press.

Sengupta, G. 1990. *Binding and Scrambling in Bangla*. PhD Thesis, University of Massachusetts, Amherst.

Sportiche, D. 1988. A Theory of Floating Quantifiers and its Corollaries for Constituent Structure, *Linguistic Inquiry* 19:425–449.

Srivastav, V. 1991. *WH Dependencies in Hindi and the Theory of Grammar*. PhD thesis, Cornell University.

Subbarao, K.V. 1984. *Complementation in Hindi Syntax*. New Delhi: Academic Publications.

Webelhuth, G. 1989. *Syntactic Saturation Phenomena and the Modern Germanic Languages*. PhD thesis, University of Massachusetts, Amherst.

Webelhuth, G. 1992. *Principles and Parameters of Syntactic Saturation*. New York: Oxford University Press.

11

Compound Typology in Tamil

K.G. VIJAYAKRISHNAN

1 Introduction

Two types of Noun Verb sequences in Tamil are examined here and it is argued that both types are compounds which require lexical listing in the sense of Borer (1988). The distinct characteristics of the two types of verb compounds are discussed in 1 and 2 below.

Since these types of compounds are very productive and since they are more frequently used in the colloquial dialects of Tamil, I have consciously limited myself to my dialect of Tamil — the Brahmin dialect spoken in and around Madras. Moreover, many of the processes which help distinguish the two types of compounds are more frequently attested in colloquial dialects than in the literary dialect.

2 Verb Compounds – Type I

The compound status of the Noun Verb (NV) sequences in (1) is argued for in this section. It is shown that these NV sequences have noncompositional semantics, idiosyncratic subcategorization and selectional properties, and that these — their lexical specification in the sense of Borer (1988) — have to be listed in the lexicon.[1]

(1)	i.	edir	paar	ii.	vajar	eri
		opposite	see		stomach	burn
		'expect' [{ S′,NP$_{acc}$ } —]			'be envious' [—]	

[1]Some of the compounds in (1) and (12) in Sections 2 and 3 respectively are also cited in Steever (1979) where all of them are subsumed under a single type of verb compound with the structure given below ((2) in Steever (1979)).

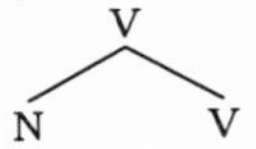

Theoretical Perspectives on Word Order in South Asian Languages
Miriam Butt, Tracy Holloway King, Gillian Ramchand (Eds.)

iii. muukk arɨ
nose cut
'show (someone) up'
[NP_{acc} —]

iv. kaadɨ kuttɨ
ear pierce
'tell a lie'
[NP_{ass} kiṭṭϵ —]

v. aaṭṭã kaaṭṭɨ
play show
'trouble' [NP_{dat} —]

vi. koRaa aḍi
tap beat
'suck up to someone'
[NP_{acc} —]

vii. soop aḍi
soap beat
'suck up to someone'
[NP_{acc} —]

viii. kaakkaa piḍi
crow catch
'suck up to someone'
[NP_{acc} —]

ix. taṇṇi kaaṭṭɨ
water show
'trouble' [NP_{dat} —]

x. naamã pooḍɨ
Vaishnavite mark put
'cheat' [NP_{dat} —]

xi. baJanϵ paṇṇɨ
bhajan do
'do nothing' [—]

xii. kambi niiṭṭɨ
rod straighten
'escape' [—]

xiii. fiḍil vaaci
fiddle play
'scratch' [—]

xiv. kuḷur kaaj
cold dry
'pretend to perform' (sing or recite)
[NP_{ass} ooḍϵ —]

The left element in all the compounds in (1) is a lexical category — a noun. Elements which occur in the specifier position of an NP i.e., determiner, and/or adjectival modifiers are clearly not possible e.g., */orɨ koRaa aḍi/ 'one faucet beat' or */nalla koRaa aḍi/ 'good faucet beat' in the case of (1vi). Only adverbial modification is possible e.g., /nannaa koRaa aḍi/ 'thoroughly suck up to someone'.

As the glosses indicate, the semantics of these NV compounds is completely noncompositional. The subcategorization of these compounds also requires listing since it cannot be attributed to that of the constituent verb in the compound e.g., the verb /kuttɨ/ 'pierce' takes an accusative and an instrumental argument in isolation but in the compound /kaadɨkuttɨ/ 'tell a lie' (1iv), it takes an associative argument. Furthermore, the compounds in (1) do not exhibit any systematicity regarding either argument linking (in the sense of Lieber 1983) or the range of thematic roles which can be associated with the N in the compound, or even a reduction in the valency of the constituent verb, as in the Type I incorporated compounds reported in

Mithun (1984). For instance, in (1iii) /muukk arɨ/ 'show someone up', /muukkɨ/ 'nose' is obviously interpretable as the theme — direct object of the verb /arɨ/ 'cut', yet the compound itself takes an accusative object. It is clear that in the Tamil compounds in (1), unlike the Type I N-incorporated compounds of Mithun (1984), the N does not bear 'a specific semantic relationship to its host V — as patient, location or instrument' (Mithun 1984:856). Finally, the compounds in (1) also have unpredictable selectional restrictions. For instance, (1x) /naamã pooḍɨ/ 'cheat' is used only when some monetary transaction is involved/implied, and (1xi) /baJaneϵ paṇṇɨ/ 'do nothing' requires an animate subject (perhaps an adult) who is expected to behave in a responsible manner.

The compounds in (1) do not permit any change in their word order e.g., */paṇṇɨ baJanϵ/ for /baJanϵ paṇṇɨ/ (1xi). In addition, they do not permit the common element inside pairs of compounds to be factored out e.g., */koRaavũ soopũ aḍi/ for /koRaa aḍi, soop aḍi/ (1vi and vii) is no more grammatical than *'fire and milkman' in English (Allen 1978).[2] The elements of the compound also cannot be moved apart by the process of scrambling.

Conclusive evidence for the lexical status of Type I compounds comes for deverbal affixation involving primary derivation.

(2)	i.	edir paar 'expect'	edir paarppɨ 'expectation'	–ppɨ N
	ii.	muukkarɨ 'show up someone'	muukkarɨppɨ 'the state of being shown up'	–ppɨ N
	iii.	kaadɨ kuttɨ 'tell a lie'	kaadɨkuttal 'lie'	–al N
	iv.	vajar eri 'be envious'	vajattericcal 'envy'	–al N
	v.	aaṭṭã kaattɨ 'trouble'	aaṭṭãkaaṭṭal 'the act of troubling'	–al N

The derived forms in (2) are primary nominals which allow a range of meanings not entirely predictable. For instance, whereas (2iii) refers to the act of someone telling a lie (involving the agent), (2ii) refers to the act of someone being shown up (involving the patient).[3]

I assume that the structure of these compounds is a shown below.

[2]The linear sequencing of elements within compounds may not be disturbed, presumably because it would affect the headedness of the structure of compounds.

[3]In (2iv), it is not clear why the root /vajar/ 'stomach' is replaced by the stem /vajatt/, and why the geminate sequence /cc/ is inserted between the verb /eri/ 'burn' and the nominal /-al/ in this compound.

(3)

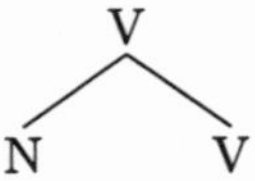

The constituent (inner) V of the verb compound is not accessible in the syntax, and it cannot substitute for the entire compound in response to a yes-no question in discourse.

(4) i. raamã avaḷɛ paakkaraanaa?
Ram-nom. her-acc. see-pr-3sm-q
'Does Ram see her?'

ii. aamãã paakkarãã / illɛ paakkalɛ
yes, see-pr-3sm. no, see-inf.neg.
'Yes, (he) does. No, (he) doesn't.'

(5) i. raamã kimbaḷa edirpaakkaraanaa?
Ram-nom. bribe-acc. expect-pr-3sm-q
'Does Ram expect a bribe?'

ii. aamãã edirpaakkarãã / illɛ edirpaakkalɛ
yes, expect-pr-3sm No, expect-inf.neg.
'Yes, (he) does. *No, (he) doesn't.'

iii. *aamãã paakkarãã / illɛ paakkalɛ
yes see-pr-3sm No, see-inf.neg.
*'Yes (he) does. *No (he) doesn't.'

Having argued that the NV sequences in (1) are lexically concatenated compounds, I would now like to paint out a major difference in behavior between these verb compounds and other compounds in Tamil. A representative sample of the latter type of compounding is presented below in (6).

(6)

i.	N	N	ii.	Adj.	N
	palaa	ppaRã		nalla	paambɨ
	jack fruit	fruit		good	snake
	'jack fruit'			'cobra'	
iii.	V	N	iv.	Adj.	Adj.
	uurgaa			karum	paccɛ
	soak	vegetable		black	green
	'pickle'			'dark green'	
v.	N	Adj.	vi.	V	V
	kiḷippaccɛ			veḷajaadɨ	
	parrot	green		grow	dance
	'parrot green'			'play'	

Type I compounds are different from the compounds in (6) in permitting the infixation of certain affixes in between the constituents of the compound. However, before looking at these affixes in compounds, let us look at the details of the process of affixation in a simple sentence with a non-compounded verb. The question suffix /-aa/, the emphatic suffix /-dãã/, and the reduplicative sequence /-gi.../ are the three affixes considered here in (7), (8) and (9) respectively.

(7) i. raamã siitɛjɛ paakkaraanaa
Ram-nom. Sita-acc. see-pr-3sm-q
'Does Ram see Sita?'

ii. raamanaa siitɛjɛ paakkaraanãã
Ram-nom. q Sita-acc. see-pr-3sm
'Is it Ram who sees Sita?'

iii. raamã siitɛjɛjaa paakkarãã
Ram-nom. Sita-acc.q see-pr-3sm
'Is it Sita that Ram sees?'

iv. raamã siitɛjɛ paakkavaa paakkarãã
Ram-nom. Sita-acc. see-inf. q see-pr-3sm
'Is it (only) sing that Ram does to Sita?'
(Does Ram *see* Sita or does he do something else. . .?)

When the question morpheme occurs at the end of the sentence (7i), the result is simply a yes/no question. However, /-aa/ can take limited scope. Thus, it attaches to NPs, resulting in a question with contrastive focus on that NP, (7ii–iii). This morpheme can also serve to contrastively focus the verb alone. In this case, /-aa/ attaches to a copy of the infinitival form of the verb, i.e., to V, without tense or AGR. In this case of verb focused questioning, /-aa/ appears then to attach to a lexical category (7iv).[4]

Similarly, the emphatic morpheme /-dãã/ can attach to a reduplicated infinitival form of the verb, isolated from the elements in INFL (TNS, AGR). This is shown in (8).[5]

(8) raamã sitɛjɛ paakkadãã paakkarãã
Ram-nom. Sita-acc. see-inf.emp. see-pr-3sm.
'Ram definitely does see Sita (but probably does nothing to her)'.

Considering now reduplicative emphatic sequences, these do not seem to be able to isolate a V from its tense and agreement features.[6]

[4]I assume that the infinitival form of the verb is the citation/stem form of the verb though I am aware that this is a questionable assumption.

[5]Unlike the question suffix and the reduplicative sequence in (9i), the emphatic marker cannot attach to the tensed verb since it is used only to signal contrastive focus.

[6]The constraint seems to be that the reduplicative element must not intervene between a verb and elements in the INFL which need to cliticize onto it. Considering

However, when the verbal element consists of more than one lexical item, such as V+Modal, or V + a 'vector' (auxiliary) verb, it is quite possible to have only the first element reduplicated as in (9ii) below.[7]

(9) i. raamã siitɛjɛ paakkarãã giikkarãã nnɨ
Ram-nom. Sita-acc. see-pr-3sm redup. report.
colladɛ
say-neg.2s
'Don't say that Ram goes about seeing Sita or some such silly thing.'

ii. raamã siitɛjɛ paakka giikka maaṭṭãã
Ram-nom. Sita-acc. see-inf. reduplication won't-3sm
'Ram won't see or do any such silly thing to Sita.'

What this shows is that /-aa/, /-dãã/ and reduplication can appear on lexical items within a verbal complex.

Consider now the affixation of these elements in compounds as in (6) and the NV compounds under discussion in (10i) and (10ii) respectively.[8]

(10) i.

kiḷi paccɛ	jaa q. dãã emp.	*kiḷi	jaa q. dãã emp.	paccɛ

'parrot green'

ii.

edir	aa q dãã emp. gidir redup.	pakkarãã

'expect-q/emp/redup'

That (10ii) can be interpreted only as contrastive focus on the verb is shown in (11).

(11) i. raamã kimbaḷã ediraa paakkarãã
Ram-nom. bribe-acc. expect-q pr-3sm
'Is it expectation that Ram has of a bribe?'
(i.e., leave alone daring to ask)

---

the reduplicative element to be an affix just like the question and the emphatic suffix, the generalization is that elements in INFL cannot cliticize onto affixes.

[7]In (9i) the same VP focus is possible if the entire VP (small caps) is reduplicated.
(i) raamã SIITɛJɛ PAAKKARÃÃ giitɛjɛ paakkarããnnɨ collaadɛ

[8]We cannot attribute this distinction to grammatical category since the verb compound /veḷajɨaaḍɨ/ (6vi) does not permit infixation */veḷajaa aaḍrãã/.

ii. raamã kimbaḷã edir dãã paakkarãã
Ram-nom. bribe-acc. expect-emp. pr. 3sm
'What is definitely expected is a bribe by Ram.'
(though he mightn't SAY it in so many words)

iii. raamã kimbaḷã edir gidir paakkaraanoo
Ram-nom. bribe-acc. expect-redup. pr.3sm.q
ennamoo
what-q
'Maybe Ram has expectation or some such feeling regarding a bribe.'

We now find that these elements appear 'infixed' between the N and the V of the $[NV]_V$ compounds, although they do not appear within the other type of compound in (5). That is, the N of the NV compounds is treated as the relevant 'first' lexical element of the verb compound to achieve contrastive focus on the verb. The verb (small caps) in the compound cannot be reduplicated to create a verbal complex, even though it can in the case of simple verbs, as illustrated by the ungrammaticality of */edir PAAKKAVAA paakkarãã/, */edir PAAKKADÃÃ paakkarãã/, and */edir PAAKKA giikka maaṭṭãã/.

Since the infixing of these affixes is an unpredictable characteristic of Type I compounds, the subcategorization statement regarding the attachment of these affixes to lexical categories must include the infixation requirement in Type I compounds which have a zero level adjoined structure as formulated in (3).

3 Verb Compounds Type II

It is shown in this section that the NV sequences in (12) below also exhibit several traits typical of lexical concatenation like Type I compounds discussed in the previous section. For instance, many of these compounds have noncompositional semantics, unpredictable subcategorization and selectional properties. However, they are distinct from Type I compounds in a number of ways. A detailed investigation of the distinct properties of these compounds — Type II compounds — leads to the postulation of a structure distinct from the one proposed for Type I compounds.

(12) below is a fairly representative sample of this productive type of compounding in Tamil.

(12)

i. kaadal paṇṇɨ
love do
'love' [NP_{acc} —]

ii. eḍaɲJal paṇṇɨ
trouble do
'trouble' [NP_{dat} —]

iii. kuttã piḍi
fault catch
'find fault'
[NP_{acc} —]

iv. mooppã piḍi
scent catch
'discover/find out'
[NP_{acc} —]

v. kaṇ aḍi
eye hit
'wink' [—]

vi. biṭ aḍi
bit (of paper) hit
'copy' [NP_{loc} —]

vii. kuŋguvã kuḍɨ
kumkum give
'offer kumkum'
[NP_{dat} —]

viii. korɛ collɨ
disappointment say
'find fault' [NP_{acc} —]

ix. riil viḍɨ
reel leave
'tell a lie'
[NP_{ass} kittɛ S′ —]

x. kooṭṭɛ viḍɨ
fort leave
'lose something'
[NP_{acc} —]

xi. aalaapanɛ paṇṇɨ
elaborate do
'elaborate (a raga)'
[NP_{acc} —]

xii. karmã paṇṇɨ
duty do
'perform last rites'
[NP_{dat} —]

xiii. puuJɛ paṇṇɨ
puja do
'worship'
[NP_{acc} —]

xiv. sammandã paṇṇɨ
connection do
'establish a relationship through marriage'
[NP_{ass} —]

xv. poṇ paar
girl see
'see bride prospect'
[NP_{acc} —]

xvi. paRi vaaŋgɨ
blame buy
'take revenge'
[NP_{acc} —]

Though many verbs take part in this process, the verb /paṇṇɨ/ 'do' is the one which occurs most frequently. The left element in these compounds, as in the Type I compounds discussed in (1), cannot take a specifier i.e., determiner and/or adjectival modifier e.g., (12viii) /korɛ collɨ/ 'find fault' ~ */orɨ korɛ collɨ/ 'find a fault' ~ */cinna korɛ collɨ/ 'find (a) small fault'. This property, as will become evident as we go along, is crucial for determining the structure of these compounds.

Many of these compounds are not semantically compositional e.g., (12vi, ix, x, xii, and xiv). Take (12vi) /biṭ aḍi/ 'copy' for instance.

It refers to a specific method of copying in an exam — copying from notes written on bits of paper.

As in Type I compounds, the subcategorization properties of these compounds are not predictable. For instance, though (12i and ii), (12v and vi), (12ix and x) and (12xi–xiv)[9] have the same constituent verb, the subcategorization properties of the individual compounds are distinct. Again as in Type I compounds, these compounds cannot be described in terms of argument linking as in Lieber (1983). Consider (12xv) /poṇ paar/ 'see bride prospect'. Though the left element /poṇ/ 'girl' is interpretable as the direct object-theme of the verb /paar/ 'see', the compound takes a theme, direct object in the accusative case.

(13) avaa avalɛ poṇpattaa
they-nom. her-acc. see bride prospect-p.3pl.
'They saw her as a prospective bride (for someone they knew).'

Therefore, any attempt to describe the subcategorization properties of these compounds by way of argument linking is bound to be unsatisfactory. Also, as in Type I compounds of Tamil discussed in Section 1, these compounds do not exhibit any systematic reduction in the valency of the compound unlike the Type I N-incorporated compounds of Mithun (1984). For instance, (12iii and iv) remain transitive like the constituent, inner verb in spite of the presence of the left element. Similarly (12xv and xvi) remain transitive. Therefore it is clear that the subcategorization/argument structure of these compounds needs to be listed in the lexicon.

Let us now examine the selectional properties of these compounds. Example (12iv) /moopã piḍi/ 'discover' takes an inanimate object if the subject is human. Example (12vii) /kuŋguvã kuḍɨ/ 'offer kumkum' requires a human (female) non-widow object. Example (12x) /kooṭṭɛ viḍɨ/ 'lose something' requires an inanimate object. Finally, the selectional properties of (12xiv) /sammandã paṇṇɨ/ 'establish relationship through marriage' and (12xv) /poṇ paar/ 'see bride prospect' are quite interesting. While the former takes a plural object, the object must not refer to a single individual — the subject of the latter need not be only the groom or the groom's family (see (12) above)! The idiosyncratic properties of the sequences in (12) discussed so far are part of their lexical specification which have to be listed.

Apart from these properties which argue for the lexical status of

[9]Some of the Type II compounds like /puuJɛ paṇṇɨ/ 'worship' and /aaraadanɛ paṇṇɛ/ 'worship' have syntactic doublets with distinct properties. In the syntax, both the sequences occur with a dative argument, and the preverbal element is clearly an NP which can take an accusative marker under emphasis.

these compounds, it is found that these compounds are systematically in complementary distribution with related, derived lexical entries. Firstly, derived, deverbal primary nominals never feed this process of compounding, though in principle any abstract noun ought to, e.g., /kaadal paṇṇɨ/ 'love (abstract noun)+do' is possible, but */verɨppɨ paṇṇɨ/ 'hate' (deverbal abstract noun /verɨppɨ/)+do is not. The fact that deverbal abstract nouns are systematically prohibited from feeding compounding can be stated only in the lexicon.

Secondly, within the same dialect, a Type II compound and a related verb are in complementary distribution. The existence of one blocks the formation of the other. For instance, the non-compounded, derived verbs of Sanskrit origin /puuJi/ 'worship' and /aalooJi/ 'consider' do not exist in my dialect but the related compounds /puuJϵ pannɨ/ 'worship' and /aaloocanϵ paṇṇɨ/ 'consider' do, and similarly, the existence of the non-compounded, derived verb /anubavi/ 'experience' (TR) blocks the formation of */anubavã paṇṇɨ/. Surely such instances of blocking are statable only on entries listed in the lexicon. Furthermore, when both exist in the same dialect, they have distinct semantic properties. For instance, in dialects where /kaadal paṇṇɨ/ 'love+do' exists along with /kaadali/ 'love (V)', the former has a specialized, derogatory sense.

Finally, as in the case of Type I compounds discussed in Section 2., the word order of Type II compounds also cannot be disturbed, e.g., */paṇṇɨ kaadal/ for /kaadal paṇṇɨ/, and common elements of pairs of compounds cannot be factored out, e.g., */kaadalũ puuJϵjũ paṇṇɨ/ 'love and worship do'.

So far, I have been focusing on establishing the lexical status of Type II compounds. I now turn to those characteristics of these compounds which distinguish these from Type I compounds. Firstly, unlike Type I compounds, these compounds do not feed primary derivations. Secondly, they permit the constituent verb of the compound to represent the compound in responses to yes-no questions in discourse. Compare (14) below with (4).

(14) i. nii avaḷϵ kaadal paṇrajaa
you-nom. her-acc. love pr.2s.q
'Do you love her?'

ii. aamãã paṇrẽẽ / illϵ paṇṇalϵ
yes do-pr.1s no do-inf.neg.
'Yes, (I) do. No, (I) don't.'

Apart from the fact that the constituent verb is accessible in the syntax, and can substitute for the entire compound, Type II compounds permit certain phrasal sequences to occur in between the elements of the compound in addition to permitting the affixes discussed in (10) to be infixed as in Type I compounds. The phrases which are permitted to occur in between the constituents of the compound are the following: wh-phrases, phrases to which the affixes listed in (9) have been suffixed, and adverbial and other phrases if accompanied by a contrastive focus intonation. Example (15) below illustrates the point concerning phrasal infixation in Type II compounds. The intonation associated with contrastively focused phrases can be impressionistically described as an extra low high melody notated as shown in (15iv and v) below.

(15) i. eḍanJal jaarɨkkɨ paṇrɛ
trouble who-dat. pr.2s
'Who is the person whom you trouble?'
(meaning 'You think you can trouble *me*?')

ii. avaḷɛ kaadal avanaA paṇrãã
her-acc. love he-nom.q pr.3sm
'Is it he that loves her?'

iii. ponnɨ avaḷɛdãã paattãã
see bride her-acc.emp. p.3sm
'It was only her (he) saw as bride prospect.'
(not somebody else)

iv. avaḍɛ kuttã **nanna** piḍiccaa
her-acc. find fault well p.3pl.
'Thoroughly (they) found fault with her.'

v. dasaratanɨkkɨ karmã **catrugnã** paṇṇinãã
Dasaratha-dat. last rites Chatrugna-nom. p.3sm.
'It was Chatrughna who performed the last rites of Dasaratha.'

These are all instances of optional phrasal adjunction under contrastive focus. Horvath (1981, 1986) proposes an analysis of contrastive focus in Hungarian which involves the movement of an X into a preverbal node. The relevant structure she proposes is (16).

(16)
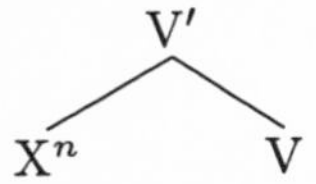

Let us assume a similar, optional process of adjunction of contrastively focused elements to the verb in Tamil. However, I propose a slight modification of the structure proposed by Horvath. I assume that adjunction to a category does not 'add to' the bar level of that category. Thus if we accept that the bar level of the category after adjunction of a focused phrase is V′, as in Horvath, it must be the case that the category to which the focused phrase is adjoined is also a V′. Therefore the relevant structure should be as in (17) below.

(17) Contrastive Focus Adjunction in Tamil

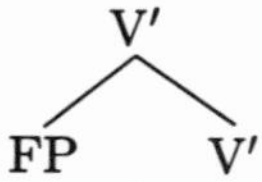

The tacit assumption behind (17) is that phrasal adjunction is only to a nonlexical (V′) category and not to a lexical category (V) as in (16).

Assuming that (17) is the appropriate formulation of the optional process of adjunction of contrastively focused elements to the verb in Tamil, I propose the following structure for Type II compounds in Tamil when the daughter V′ is optionally subject to adjunction under contrastive focus.[10]

(18) Type II Compound

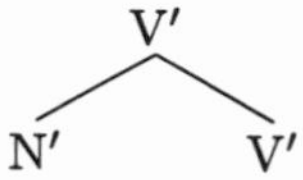

Given. then, that the right element in this compound is a V′, what about the left element? It is clear from the previous discussion that the left element is not a maximal projection of N since specifiers cannot co-occur with the compound. Furthermore, the left element can take neither plural nor case marking. Is it then a zero level category?[11]

[10] That the verb in Type II compounds is not simply a V accords with our earlier observation that these verbs are accessible in the syntax e.g., in discourse (see (14)).

[11] As pointed out by a reviewer, it could be argued that the left element is an NP which does not bear any marker for plural number or case and appears without a determiner because of its genericity. However, generic NPs in the syntax have a range of realizations which are conditioned by the syntactic context. Consider the sequence given below in (i) where the generic NPs take the determiner /orɨ/ 'one' and one of them is in the locative case.

(i)	orɨ	uurɨlɛ	orɨ	raaJaa...
	one	town-loc.	one	king...

'(Once upon a time) there was a king...'

In the case of Type II compounds, if the left element is claimed to be a maximal projection solely dominating a lexical category because of its generic nature, it would merely be a stipulation since it would not derive from any independent property of the nominal constituent of the compound.

Furthermore, it must be pointed out that, in that case, genuine idioms which have

Consider the example of a rare Type II compound given below which throws light on the bar level specification of the left element.

(19) [kaadɨlɛ puu] vej
ear-loc. flower put
'take someone for a ride'

It is plausible to analyze /kaadɨlɛ puu/ as a constituent of a single bar level comprising the complement and its head on the basis of (19).

(20) caamski meelɛ pustahã
Chomsky on book
'Book on Chomsky'

To argue that /kaadɨlɛ puu/ is a constituent, it is necessary to devise independent constituency tests. Going back to the affixes discussed in (10), the phrasal affixation of the question morpheme /-aa/, and the reduplicative morpheme is possible with the VP and its constituents.[12] While the constituenthood of the sequence /kaadɨlɛ puu/ is demonstrated by its reduplicative possibility in (21i) (as in Type I and Type II compounds), the ungrammaticality of reduplicating the sequence /talɛlɛ puu(vɛ)/ 'head-loc. flower-acc. ' which is a part of the VP /siitiɛkkɨpuu(vɛ) veccaa/ 'Sita-dat. head-loc. flower-acc. put' shows that nonconstituents may not be reduplicated.

(21) i. raamã siitɛkkɨ KAADɨLɛPUU giidɨlɛ puu veccaa...
Ram-nom. Sita-dat. take for a ride reduplication-p.if
'If it is taking for a ride that Ram does to Sita...'

ii. *raamã siitɛkkɨ TALɛLɛ PUU(Vɛ) gilɛ puuvɛ
Ram-nom. Sita-dat. head-loc.flower-acc.reduplication
veccaa...
put-p.if...

Secondly, whereas the word order of /kaadɨlɛ puu vej/ cannot be

---

phrasal constituents could not be differentiated from Type II compound. Take the idioms given below, for instance.

i. talajɛ pooḍ
head-acc. put
'die'

ii. paṇattɛ kuḍɨ
money-acc. give
'bribe'

The presence of the accusative marker clearly establishes the maximal status of the left element here. It must be pointed out that these NPs with case markers are also amenable only to a generic interpretation. Therefore I assume that it serves no purpose to claim that the left element of Type II compounds are maximal projections.

[12]The emphatic morpheme cannot attach to the VP, though it can attach to all the constituents of VP (see Fn. 5).

disturbed by scrambling, all the arguments (internal and external) of the verb in (21ii) can be freely reordered.

(22)	puuvɛ	talɛlɛ	siitɛkkɨ	raamã	veccãã
	flower-acc.	head-loc.	Sita-dat.	Ram-nom.	put-p.3sm
	'Ram put flowers in the head for Sita.'				

Thirdly, (23) shows that contrastively focused phrases cannot occur between the complement and the head in /kaadɨlɛ puu/, unlike the sequence /talɛlɛ puu/ which is not a single constituent (see example (24)).

(23) i. *kaadɨlɛ jaarɨkkɨpuu veccãã

ii.	kaadɨlɛ puu	jaarɨkkɨ	veccãã
	take for a ride	who-dat.	p.3sm
	'Who was it that (he) took for a ride?'		

(24)	talɛlɛ	jaarɨkkɨ	puu	veccãã
	head-loc.	who-dat.	flower-acc.	put-p.3sm
	'For whom did (he) put flowers in the head?'			

Thus the constituenthood of the sequence /kaadɨlɛ puu/ can be established beyond doubt.

So far, I have argued that the complement and the head /kaadɨlɛ pul/ make up a single constituent of a single bar level — N′. What remains to be shown is that no other element can occur at this level. The question that comes to mind is: What about modifiers? Generally, modifiers are believed to iterate at the level of N′. However, in Tamil, it is quite clear that modifiers do not occur along with complements under N′.

While (25) is a possible surface sequence in Tamil with a determiner, modifier and head, (26i and ii) illustrate the point that when a complement is present, the obligatory order is complement–{det.,mod.}–head.

(25)	orɨ	nalla	pustahã
	one	good	book
	det.	mod.	head
	'a good book'		

(26)	i.	a.	*orɨcaamski meelɛ pustahã		
		b.	caamski meelɛ	orɨ	pustahã
			Chomsky-on	one	book
			compl.	det.	head
	ii.	a.	*nalla caamski meelɛ pastahã		
		b.	caamski meelɛ	nalla	pustahã
			Chomsky-on	good	book
			compl.	mod.	head

That the modifier is never part of the complement structure under N′ is proved by the scrambling possibilities in (27).

(27)	a.	*orɨ	nalla	caamski meelɛ	pustahã
		one	good	Chomsky-on	book
		det.	mod.	compl.	head
	b.	caamskimeelɛ	orɨ	nalla	pustahã
		Chomsky-on	one	good	book
		Compl.	det.	mod.	head
	c.	orɨ	nalla	pustahã	caamskimeelɛ
		one	good	book	Chomsky-on
		det.	mod.	head	compl.

Though the details of the phrase structure of the Tamil NP are yet to be determined, it is clear that modifiers cannot be grouped with the complement under N′.

Having proved the constituenthood of the sequence /kaadɨlɛ puu/, the following structure is suggested for this type of compound.[13]

(28)

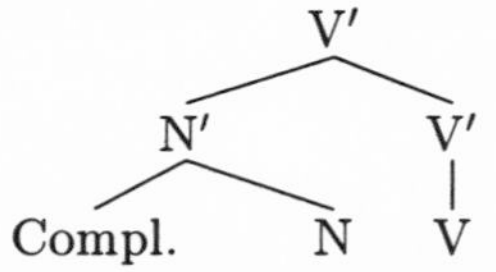

The structure in (28) is interesting when compared to the structure (see (3)) for Type I compounds. The claim is that lexical compounding in Tamil can take place at submaximal levels, between constituent elements of the same level. Recall that we have argued that Type II compounds in general cannot have full phrasal structure like idioms because of subcategorizational properties, among other things. The non-maximality of the N projection /kaadɨlɛ puu/ points in the same direction.

[13]Perhaps the examples given below are also instances of Type II compounds like (19).

i.	vaaRa	ppaRattɨlɛ	uuci	eettɨ
	banana	fruit-loc.	needle	raise
	'make a snide remark' [___]			
ii.	panattaalɛ	kaṣṭa	ppadɨ	
	money-because	trouble	suffer	
	' suffer because of lack of money' [___]			
iii.	karpuurattɨmeelɛ	satjã	pannɨ	
	camphor on	promise	do	
	'make a promise on lighted camphor' [NP_{dat} ___]			

4 Conclusion

The distinct structures proposed for the compounds Type I and II match the clustering of properties associated with the respective types of compounding. Only Type I compounds permit primary nominalization because only lexical categories feed derivation. The constituent verb of a Type I compound is not accessible in the syntax for reference since elements within a lexical category are not accessible in the syntax, unlike the constituent verb of a Type II compound, which has a single bar level specification. Though the proposed structure of Type II compounds concatenated in the lexicon involving single bar level categories is controversial, there is no viable alternative proposal which can take care of the range of facts associated with these compounds. We thus see that verb compounding in Tamil involves non-maximal constituents of the same bar level.

Acknowledgements

I thank R. Amritavalli, K.P. Mohanan, Tara Mohanan and the reviewers who went through the earlier drafts of this paper.

References

Allen, M. 1978. *Morphological Investigations.* Doctoral Dissertation, University of Connecticut.

Borer, H. 1988. Morphological Parallelism between Compounds and Constructs. In Boij and Merle (Eds.), *Yearbook of Morphology,* 45–66. Dordrecht: Foris.

Horvath, J. 1981. *Apects of Hungarian Syntax and the Theory of Grammar.* Doctoral Dissertation, University of California, Los Angeles.

Horvath, J. 1986. Remarks on the Configurationality-Issue: Topic, Focus, and Configurationality. W. Abraham, and M de Sjaak (Eds.). Amsterdam: John Benjamins.

Lieber, R. 1983. Argument Linking and Compounds in English. *Linguistic Inquiry* 14:251–285.

Mithun, M. 1984. The Evolution of Noun Incorporataion. *Language* 60:845–895.

Steever, S. 1979. Noun Incorporation in Tamil, or What's a Noun like you doing in a Verb like this? In *Papers from the 15th Regional Meeting of the Chicago Linguistic Society,* 279–290.